Ways of Growth

Contributors

Sidney M. Jourard
Harold Greenwald
Magda Proskauer
Minor White
Herbert A. Otto
Bernard Gunther
Gerhard Neubeck
Gerard Haigh
Jack R. Gibb
Lorraine M. Gibb
Paul Bindrim
Claudio Naranjo
George Brown
Stephen M. Schoen
Ruth C. Cohn
Renee Nell
Edward W. Maupin
Willis W. Harman
Gayle Privette

WAYS OF GROWTH

Edited by
Herbert Otto and John Mann

New York · The Viking Press

Acknowledgement

This collection of articles by pioneering professionals was first suggested by Dr. Abraham Maslow to Michael Murphy, President of Esalen Institute, Big Sur, California. Michael Murphy and Herbert Otto were the original editors of this volume. Mike's thoughtful contribution in the selection and editing of this collection is gratefully acknowledged.

Contents

INTRODUCTION

In the world today and particularly in the United States, there is a renewal of interest in methods that are designed to foster the personal growth of normal individuals. Such methods are being developed and used by psychotherapists, teachers, artists, social scientists and creative laymen in various settings throughout the country, including adult education, human-relations training, and a variety of more specialized forms. These efforts all share the common goal of seeking to cultivate normal human functioning beyond the level of average performance, and are thus classified as a part of the human potentialities movement.

This book is designed to bring together these efforts for the first time. Heretofore, the methods of developing the human potential have been either buried in the forbidding semantics of professional publications or described inadequately in the laymen's versions. This book is directed both to the enlightened layman interested in extending his intellectual and social/emotional horizons, and to the professional interested in increasing his technical skills in the field of human potentials. The articles are written at various levels of understanding and action; therefore it is necessary to give some guidance as to the use of this book.

Several types of article are presented: the general personal expressions of an individual viewpoint such as in the articles by Jourard, Greenwald and Privette; accounts of new methods requiring professional background and specialized training before they can be appropriately and successfully applied, such as the approaches described by Naranjo, Bindrim, Cohn, Proskauer and Nell; and approaches that the layman can directly apply to his own life for purposes of studying and enhancing his own development. In this latter group we would place the contributions by White, Neubeck, Otto, Maupin, Gunther and Brown.

To some extent, each reader will have to decide for himself which of these avenues of self-exploration seems most promising. Not all of the articles are intended for direct application, although all of them are intended to clarify the methods, models, and interests that are stimulating the human potentialities movement at this time.

The editors do not necessarily subscribe to what the authors have written. Our purpose was not to present our own opinions through the words of others, but to provide a forum for the expression of divergent viewpoints. To choose an extreme example: the inclusion of two articles derived from work with LSD does not imply that we are indirectly urging the reader to have such an experience; what it does imply is that the power of the hallucinogenic drugs, such as LSD, and the implications of the experiences they seem to produce, are too striking to be ignored in any book dealing with "Ways of Growth." We do not feel that fear or repression will ever lead to proper understanding of this or any other borderline area surrounded by public controversy. It is in this spirit of openness and scientific objectivity that we have sought to include a certain amount of controversial material.

Beyond the intellectual stimulation this book may provide, it is *intended essentially as a challenge to each reader's own interest in, and dedication to, his own growth.* The mobilization of one's own potentialities requires an investment of self, the application of personal energies, and disciplined dedication. Personal growth, more often than not, takes place when a person has risked himself and dared to become involved in experimenting with his own life. To take responsibility for self-creation can be both exhilarating and frightening; it is exhilarating because growth is accompanied by joy, frightening because one is approaching new and unknown inner territory. Personal growth can become our most exciting and challenging lifetime adventure. Personal growth is a lifelong adventure reaffirming that man is the shaper of his own boundless possibilities—that man is a continuous act of self-creation.

Herbert A. Otto
John Mann

Ways of Growth

Sidney M. Jourard

Growing Awareness
and the Awareness
of Growth

Everything looks different when I visit the neighborhood where I grew up. The stores and houses look smaller, decayed, less imposing than I remember them to have been. My old school chums are balder, fatter; some look defeated and resigned, and others are smug, more self-satisfied than I knew them to be years ago. Their change appears to me as a kind of fall, a failure to realize many of the dreams which I knew animated them in their younger days. My own change (which I become acutely conscious of at times like these) feels to me like growth. I feel I have grown, while they have just grown older.

What is growth? What is my growth? How does it appear from the outside, from the point of view of another? Do I experience my growing? Or do I only see a difference, say, between old and more recent pictures of myself, and conclude that I have changed? Indeed, I have heard tape recordings of my speech, and have seen moving pictures of myself, made several years ago, and seeing how I looked and sounded makes me almost nauseous. I do not recognize myself as the source of those impressions. I experience myself from the "outside" and cannot recapture the "feel" of the person I was. Yet at times I have undergone some engrossing experience and, in a flash, realize I am changed. I experience myself and the world in new dimensions, as if a veil has suddenly been lifted.

What is the essence of this change? Is it growth? What brings it about? Can I help it along or hinder its occurrence? Can another person bring it on? Prevent it? I am going to speak here of growth from an "inside" point of view, of the growth of experience, and the changed experiencing that is growth. There are many accounts available about growth as it appears on the "outside," as recorded by instruments, or by scientific observers, but few about growing awareness. Since I *am* my awareness, an account of growing, changing awareness must at the same time be an account of my growth.

Growth is the dis-integration of one way of experiencing the world, followed by a re-organization of this experience, a reorganization that includes the new disclosure of the world. The disorganization, or even shattering, of one way to experience the world, is brought on by new disclosures from the changing being of the world, disclosures that were always being transmitted, but were usually ignored.

I

Change is in the world. The being of the world is always changing. My body is in the world, and it changes from instant to instant. Things and other people are in the world, and they metamorphose swiftly, or ever so slowly. I may not be aware of the change that *is* the world. The world-for-me may not appear to change, but rather it may seem congealed, constant, fixed. I may also experience my own being as unchanging.

In fact, people *strive to construct* a stable world, a world they can control and get their bearings in. A view of the world as constant is an achievement, a *praxis*, not a "given." A naive view of the world sees it both as a "buzzing, blooming confusion" and as stable and "structured." We simply cannot navigate in a world that is swiftly changing. And so we "freeze" it by pledging not to notice change until it has reached some critical degree, until it has gone on so far that it can no longer be ignored. Then, we might acknowledge it. If everything changed, during the night, so that you awakened to a new experience of yourself and the world, you might be terrified. But if suddenly the world froze, so that as everything now is, it would remain for eternity, you would be horrified. It would be hell. A hell of perfect predictability and boredom.

The disclosure of change is going on all the time. Change is *experienced,* however, only at moments. The awareness of change is frequently the experience of *surprise;* the unexpected has just been presented to us. The world, and my own bodily being, are not as I had believed them to be. My expectations about being, my concepts and beliefs about the world, have just been disconfirmed. The awareness that things are different is not growth, though it is a necessary condition of growth. A growth *cycle* calls for (a) an acknowledgment that the world has changed, (b) a shattering of the presently experienced "world-structure," and (c) a restructuring, retotalization of the world-structure that encompasses the new disclosure of changed reality.

The retotalization of experience that consummates a growth cycle happens when a person sets goals and projects for himself, when he envisions a possibility and sets about trying to bring it to fruition. In fact, the growth cycle is often tripped off by a *failure* in goal-seeking. As one sets about trying to make or do something, he finds that his initial concepts and beliefs about what and how things *are,* are false. Faced with failure, he must then suspend his present beliefs and let the world disclose itself to him as it *now* is. If he does this, he can revise his concepts and get on with his project.

A growth cycle can also be triggered when goals and projects turn stale, when money can no longer buy anything that the person wants, when the fame that was once the person's glory has turned to ashes, and when the love of that woman long pursued is now experienced as cloying, suffocating possessiveness. The lack of fulfillment when long-sought goals are achieved signifies, however indirectly, that *our personal being* has changed, unnoticed by us. Our *concept of ourselves* as the person who would be fulfilled by this pleasure or made happier by that success, *has gotten out of touch with the reality of our being*. We are in for some surprises. The boredom signifies the imminence of growth. The time is ripe for the experience both of new goals and of new unfoldings of our being. It is time to let the world and ourselves disclose their being to our experience. We may undergo this new experience (if we let it happen) in delight, or in the terrifying realization that we are going out of our minds.

II

The world is full of Being, of many beings—some human, some animal, some inanimate. Being has many forms. Every being in the world can be likened to a kind of broadcasting station, transmitting signals of its being to other beings in the world. This transmission is ceaseless. As people and things and animals exist, they change, and they broadcast the fact of this change into the world. You and I are both beings, but beings of a special kind. We have (or are) awareness. We are embodied consciousness. We experience the transmissions that originate in our bodies, and through our bodies we experience some of the transmissions of being that originate elsewhere.

As human beings, we originate transmissions of our being, and we receive transmissions from other beings. My being discloses itself to me—I experience my own being—and it is disclosed to you through my appearance and behavior. *My* experience of *my* being is different from *your* experience of *my* being. And my experience of the being you disclose to me differs from your experience of your own being.

Man is a *concept-maker*. He forms *concepts* of the being of the world, and of his own self-being. A concept is an abstraction from what *is*. From a phenomenological and existential perspective, *a concept is a commitment to stop noticing the changing disclosures (disclosures of change) incessantly being transmitted by the beings in the world*. When I identify something as a cow, I rubricize it. I let it disclose enough of its being for me to classify it into the category *cow*. Then I stop receiving, though the cow hasn't stopped sending. It is a cow. It is this very cow, Bossie. Bossie is that cow which presents itself to me as black and white, of the kind "Holstein," with a big chip flaked off her left front hoof. I know Bossie. I can anticipate what she will do, on the basis of her past disclosures to me, and my awareness of these disclosures. I can get milk from Bossie. She will kick me if I approach her from the right side. And so on. But Bossie is continually changing, and these changes are continually revealed to the world. So long as I think of Bossie as I always have, I ignore these disclosures. I address Bossie as though she has not changed. Indeed, for the purposes I pursue in my transactions with Bossie, these changes may not make any difference until enough change has occurred that my predictions about Bossie are not borne out and my purposes are thwarted.

I start milking Bossie, and no milk comes. I say, "Something's wrong. Bossie is different. She has changed. She is not the Bossie I knew." Of course she isn't. She never is. No sooner did I form a *concept* of Bossie (stop perceiving her disclosures) than it was out of date. When I say, "Bossie has changed," all I am doing is belatedly acknowledging a change that has been inexorable and continuous. For my purposes (getting milk out of her), she did not change. When my purposes were thwarted, I was forced to expand my awareness of Bossie, to suspend my concept of her being, and let her being address me. My concept of Bossie (which terminated my perception of the multiple disclosures of her changing being) enabled me to fulfill my milking project. When the project was stymied, my concept became perceptibly incongruent, out of date with the actuality of Bossie's being. In fact, if I propose some new projects that involve Bossie, I may find my concept of her being requires revision. I may wish to enter her in a race. I believe she is a fast runner and can win me a prize. I test her—I put her in a situation where she can disclose her running ability. I find her slow. My concept of Bossie's being must now include the assertion, "She is slow."

III

Enough of cows, and enough of Bossie. I am going to contend that when my concepts, of myself, of you, of cars, of cows, trees and refrigerators, are shattered; and when I again face the world with a questioning attitude; when I face the being in question and *let it disclose itself to me* (it always has, but I paid it no attention after I conceptualized it) ; and when I re-form my concept on the basis of this newly received disclosure—then, *I have grown*. I will suspend my concepts when my projects in life (which depend on accurate concepts of reality for their fulfillment) are thwarted, when my predictions about how things will act or react prove wrong. Then, if I adopt the attitude of "Let the world disclose itself to me," I will receive this disclosure and change my concepts, and I will have grown.

My concepts of being can change under more pleasant circumstances than failure. In those rare moments when I have gratified all of my urgent needs—I have done my work, I feel good and fulfilled, and I want nothing out of the world just now—then the world will disclose all kinds of new faces to me. I am letting the world be itself, for itself. I may then notice all kinds of things about my friends, trees, the sky, animals, whatever is there, things that call upon me to enlarge my previous concepts of those same beings. Thus, success and gratification can open up my world for me, and let me experience it in new dimensions.

IV

You may notice that I seem different from the last time you saw me. My behavior and my verbal disclosures will show a change to you. You will say of me, "He has changed, he has grown." You will have to modify your concept of me at that time. *If you do, then you will have grown.* Your action toward me will reflect your changed concept of me, your changed experience of me. And I will then say to you, "You have changed, you have grown." You will feel confirmed in your being. You will feel understood. You will feel that the disclosure of your changed being—in words and actions—has been received and acknowledged by me.

V

I have a certain concept of my being, of myself. This is my *self-concept.* It is my belief about my own being. My being discloses itself to me, in the form of my intentional experience of myself. I experience the feel of my body's existence. I experience my own action from the inside. I form a concept of myself—what I am like, how I react, what I am capable of and what I cannot do, on the basis of this self-experience. You may also tell me what and who you think I am, on the basis of your experience of the outside of my being, and I take your belief into account. We may agree that I am thus and such a kind of person—a man, a psychologist, kind, strong, able to play a fair game of handball, unable to sing in key, etc. Once I have formed this concept of who and what I am, I proceed to behave in the world as if that is all and everything I am or can be. My behavior, my self-disclosure, endlessly confirms my self-concept. It is as if I have taken a pledge to show this and only this as my being.

VI

In fact, my being, like all Being, *is change*. This change discloses itself to me through my experience, and to others through my behavior. But if you and I have formed a concept of my being, neither of us pays attention to the ceaseless transmission of my changing being. It is transmitted, but no receiver is tuned in to acknowledge the change. Things can get more complicated: I may notice the changes and change my concept of myself accordingly. You may not notice the changes. You treat me as if I were the same person. I do not recognize myself as the one you believe I am. I feel you are talking to somebody else, not me.

Or, you may notice the changes before I do and change your concept of me accordingly. Again, I may not recognize the "me" that you seem to be addressing. Your concept of me is disjunctive from my self-concept.

Or, I may display and disclose the newly experienced facets of my being to you. You may say, "I don't recognize you. You are not yourself today. I don't like the person you seem to be. I'll come see you when you have gotten back into your right mind." If you thus disconfirm my newly experienced and tentatively disclosed being, and if I am unsure of myself, I may try to suppress and repress my newly emerged being and seek to appear to you and to me as the person I was. If I do this chronically and successfully, I may become mad.

There is also another way in which I might grow through a relationship with you. I may have a fixed concept of you and hence behave toward you in an habitual, stereotyped way. My action to-

ward you is predictable. I always become aggressive in your presence. I experience you as a source of harm to me, and I attack first,
to protect myself. My concept of you is that you are menacing, that
you harbor ill will toward me. *When I experience you, I may not be
undergoing a perceptual experience, but rather an imaginative experience of your being.* I tune out your disclosed being and replace it
by an imaginative experience. Imagination veils perception. In fact,
much of our experience of the people in our lives, even when they
are face to face with us, is *not* perceptual, but *imaginative*.

The perceptual mode of experiencing entails the readiness to
receive revealing inputs from the other, so that one's awareness of
the other is constantly changing. But the imaginative mode of experiencing tunes out fresh disclosures. My image of you remains fixed,
unchanged by your disclosures, because I do not pay them any
attention. Now, if you can break through my imaginative experience
of you, if you can catch my attention, by a shout, a blow, a scream of
pain or joy, I may, as it were, wake up from my daydreamlike
experience of your being, and undergo a fresh perceptual experience
of you. You will surprise me. If you do this, if you get me "un-hung"
from fixation on one *mode* of experiencing you—the imaginative
mode—so I can now perceive you, I will have grown. My consciousness of you will have expanded. My awareness will have grown, and
where I had previously been aware of you only as an image (though
I didn't know this was an image), now I can experience you percep-
tually. If my consciousness expands, so I can experience you or the
world in many more modes than I could hitherto: imaginatively, per-
ceptually, recollectively, in the mode of fantasy, then I have grown;
I *am* my awareness, and if my awareness expands, *I* have grown.

My world of awareness may not only be fixed in one *mode* of
experiencing, e.g., the abstracting, conceptual mode or the imaginative mode; *my world may also be confined to some one or two
sensory 'channels' of awareness.* For example, I may limit my clear
awareness to only visual and auditory impressions and exclude the
worlds of smelling, tasting, or the feel of my own body. If you can
"turn me on" to my feelings, to smells, to tastes; if you can wake up
my imagination; if you can get me to experience the feel of my body,
you will have expanded my awareness and helped me to grow. You

could back-rub me out of my mind and into my experience of my body.

VII

If I, from time to time, suspend my concept of myself, and "tune in" on my being; if I meditate, or reflect on my experience, then I must re-form my self-concept. I will believe myself to be different. I will act differently. I *am* different. Moments of meditation are the times (rare in our culture) when we try to let the changing flux of our being disclose itself to us. Meditation, if we learn how to do it, or let it happen, can give us the *experience* of transition in our being and can yield transitional experiences. In meditation we also let the world disclose more of its changing being to us, and we may find ourselves experiencing more of the variety in the world.

VIII

But meditation is not the only occasion when our self-concepts are put into question and temporarily suspended. Whenever we are unself-conscious, whenever our attention is fully focused upon some task, some project, our being changes; and our changing experience of our changed being goes on spontaneously. We let our personal being *happen*. We do not try to monitor and control it so it conforms to a concept. Fascinated engagement with *anything* can let change happen and be experienced, such that the next time I reflect upon myself, I find my experience of myself different from how I remember it the last time I reflected. And my concept of myself will have to be changed to encompass the new experiencing I have undergone. Challenge, fascination, total involvement in some task or project such that self-consciousness and self-conceptualizing is *not* the mode of experience, will permit the changed self-being to be experienced.

IX

If I engage in conversation with you, in dialogue; and if you disclose your experience of yourself and of me to me in truth; and if I receive your continuing disclosure; and if I disclose my experience of myself and of your disclosure to you in truth, *then I must be letting change happen and be disclosed to us both.* If I reflect upon my experience of the dialogue, I must notice that I am different from the way I was when we began the dialogue. But if I have (as it were) pledged myself to appear before you and to myself as *this* kind of man and no other, then my intentional disclosures to you will be very selective. Perhaps I will lie to you, to preserve your present concept of me, or at least *my* concept of *your* concept of me. Indeed, if my pledge of sameness is made to myself, then every time my *actually* changed being discloses itself to me, I will feel threatened, and repress it. I will pretend to myself I did not have the experience of hatred, or of anxiety, or of lust. And I will believe my own pretense to myself. Then, I will not grow. My concept of myself will become increasingly estranged from the ongoing change of my being. If my self-concept is too discrepant from actuality, the disclosure to me of my changed being will become more insistent. I will then have to pretend and repress much harder. If the change is too great, the experience of change will no longer be repressible. It will declare itself in my experience, and perhaps in my behavior. I may become terrified, and feel I have "gone out of my mind." Actually, I have, if by "mind" we mean "self-concept." If I still insist on trying to appear to you as the same person I *was,* I may develop neurotic symptoms. Or if I am terrified enough, I may become psychotic.

X

You can help me grow, or you can obstruct my growth. If you have a *fixed* idea of who I am and what my traits are, and what my possibilities of change are, then anything that comes out of me beyond your concept, you will disconfirm. In fact, you may be terrified by any surprises, any changes in my behavior, because these changes may threaten your concept of me; my changes may, if disclosed to you, shatter your concept of me, and challenge you to grow. You may be afraid. In your fear, you may do everything in your power to get me to un-change, and reappear to you as the person you once knew.

But if you suspend any preconceptions you may have of me and my being, and invite me simply to be and to disclose this being to you, you create an ambience, an area of "low pressure" where I can let my being happen and be disclosed, to you and to me simultaneously—to me from the inside, and to you who receive the outside layer of my being.

If your concept of my being is one that encompasses more possibilities in my behavior than I have myself acknowledged; if your concept of my being is more inclusive and indeed more accurate than my concept of my being, and if you let me know how you think of me; if you let me know from moment to moment how you experience me; if you say, "Now I think you dislike me. Now I think you are being ingratiating. Now I think you can succeed at this, if you try"; if you tell me *truly* how you experience me, I can compare this with my experience of myself, and with my own self-concept. You may thus insert the thin edge of doubt into the crust of my self-concept, helping to bring about its collapse, so that I might re-form it. In fact, this is what a loving friend, or a good psychotherapist, does.

XI

There is another way you can help me grow, and that is through challenging me and encouraging me to attempt new projects. We actually construe and conceptualize the world and ourselves in the light of the projects we live for. It is our commitment to these which "structures" our world. The beings in the world, including our own being, reveal different facets of themselves to us, depending upon the projects we are pursuing at the moment. The trees in the forest reveal their timber footage to the lumber merchant, the bugs in their trunks to the insect-collector, their colors to the painter. My muscular strength or weakness reveals itself to me as I try to chop the forest down, and I form a concept of my muscular strength. I may never come to question or doubt this estimate I made. My self-concept gets frozen if my projects are frozen and if I become too skilled at fulfilling them.

Suppose, when I find my existence dull and boring, I decide to try some new project—to write a book, climb a mountain, change jobs. I tell you of this faint resolve. I am afraid to try, because, as I presently think of myself, I don't believe I have the capacity to succeed. If you encourage me to try, and encourage me and support me when the going gets rough, so I stick with the project with more and more single-mindedness, I discover in myself transcendent powers I never experienced before, and never imagined I had. I do not and cannot transcend my *possibilities;* I don't know what these are and won't know until I stop living. I only transcend my *concept* of what my possibilities might be. You can help me transcend my self-concept by challenging and supporting me in new projects that I mount.

Even the decision to *attempt* something new results in a new experience of myself and the world, *before* I actually get going. If I decide to start a new book, I begin to experience friends as interferences in this project; movies and television, formerly very inviting, become dull and boring. The whole world and my experience of myself change with the change in projects. If you help me give up old projects which are no longer satisfying, delightful or fulfilling, and encourage me to dare new ones, you are helping me to grow.

XII

Growing entails going out of our minds and into our raw experience. Our experience is always of the disclosure of the world and of our own embodied being. When we function smoothly, habitually, and effectively in the world, our concepts are confirmed, and we do not receive new disclosure. When we meet impasse and failure in the pursuit of our projects, then our habits and concepts (a habit can be seen as the "outside" of a concept) are challenged. Failure of our projects gives us a whiff of the stink of chaos, and this can be terrifying. Our concepts get cracks in them when we fail. Through these cracks, the encapsulated experience "contained" by the concept might leak or explode; or through the crack there may occur an implosion of more being. When there are no concepts, there is nothing, no-thing, we can grapple with, get leverage on, in order to get on with the projects of living. There is the threat of pure chaos and nothingness. If we experience the pure nothingness, we panic, and seek quickly to shore up the collapsing world, to daub clay into the cracks in our concepts. If we do this, we don't grow. If we let the concepts explode or implode, and do not re-form them veridically, we appear mad, and are mad. If we re-form them, to incorporate new experience, we grow.

XIII

Once again we must consider projects, this time in relation to integration, a vital and crucial phase of growth. When our projects are obstructed because our concepts are out of phase with being, the concepts must explode, or become fractionated, differentiated into parts. We experience chaos. Our commitment to the old projects, or recommitment to new projects, serves as the field of force that organizes the fractionated experience of being into meaningful wholes, concepts, gestalten. Growth is our experience of our concepts and percepts being detotalized and then retotalized into newly meaningful unities.

XIV

I know I am ready to grow when I experience some dissonance between my beliefs, concepts, and expectations of the world, and my perception of the world. I am also ready to grow when I experience boredom, despair, depression, anxiety or guilt. These emotions inform me that my goals and projects have lost meaning for me; that my being has gotten too big, too out of phase with my concepts of my being. I have a choice at such moments, if indeed I can experience the emotions. I may have become so unaccustomed to and maladept at reflection and meditation that I simply don't notice these "all is not well" signals, and continue to pursue my projects and believe my beliefs as if experience were confirming them.

But if I do acknowledge the signals, my choice is: either to meditate, suspend my concept and preconception of self, and let my changed being disclose itself to me even when it hurts (it frequently does); or to affirm the project of being the same (an impossible project, but one that many people try to live). If I decide to try to be the same, then I will repress my experience of change, of the "all is not well" signals. I will have resolved, really, to stop perceiving myself.

Since nothing *definite* is possible, purposeful action is *im*possible.

Yet, if a person can endure this voyage within his own experience, he can emerge from it with a new concept of his being and with new projects; the new concept of being will include more of his being in it. But this new integration will last only so long, and then the entire process must be repeated again. A sentient life is an endless series of getting out of one's mind and concepts, only to re-enter, and depart again.

The experience of surprise is also a sign of one's readiness to grow. Amazement and wonder signify that one's concepts of self and of the world and of other people are "loose," ready to be re-formed. The "know-it-all," the "cool" one, has pledged himself never to be surprised. Everything that the world discloses is no more than an unfolding of what he has expected and predicted, or so he tries to convey to others. But when a man can be dumbfounded and surprised at what comes out of him, or what his friend or spouse is capable of doing and disclosing, he is a growing person.

In fact, if I intentionally adopt the "set" that all of my concepts are tentative and provisional, I invite others, myself, and the world to reveal new facets of their being to me, so that even my daily life can be an unfolding of newness, where simply perceiving the world or the self is a source of endless variety and surprise.

If I am with you, and I have wilfully adopted the set that I do not know and cannot ever fully know all your possibilities, my very presence embodies an invitation to you to surprise me, to show off, to transcend your (and my) previous concepts of your being. I can tell when I am in the presence of a person with a closed mind. I feel constrained to shut off most of my possibilities. But in the presence of a wonderer, I feel an absence of prejudgment, a permissive acceptance, and my terror and self-consciousness about revealing surprises are diminished.

In short, if you and I both retain our capacity for surprise, we aid and confirm one another's growth.

[2]

Harold Greenwald

Play and
Self–Development

Often when I am in trouble about how to start a
piece of writing about a particular subject, I turn to
the dictionary for a definition. Then I can start my
article in a time-honored, if not very original, manner by saying, "Webster's New Collegiate Dictionary
defines *play* as. . . ."

Unfortunately, when I turned to my copy of
Webster's Seventh New Collegiate Dictionary, I
found that the various definitions of *play* took up over
thirty closely-packed lines of fine print. For a while I
contemplated including all the definitions (it seemed
like a good way of padding the article and making it
seem scholarly and imposing) ; then I realized that this
would hardly be a style appropriate to the subject of
play. In addition, many of the definitions would be
misleading and not in the sense I intend.

The word *play*, as I will be using it in this article,
means first of all a pleasurable activity. So if you are
not interested in pleasure and are grimly devoted to
self-development through hard labor, I suggest you
stop reading right now and turn to more serious fare.

In line with this I would like to distinguish between play and games. A game is bound by rules and may often be anything but pleasurable. A fanatic golfer once consulted me because his anxiety about his golf score had become so great that he could not wait for weekends and vacations to end so that he could leave the drudgery of the golf course and return to the relaxed atmosphere of the advertising agency where he earned his living. Similarly, when I see a couple for marital therapy who "play" poker for high stakes, I usually find that the gambling has become a major threat to the security of their marriage. Such games as poker, golf and bowling, when entered into with a driving competitive compulsivity, are obviously neither pleasurable nor play.

If we observe young children or other young animals such as puppies or kittens at play, we can soon see that it is usually a way of venting excess energy while at the same time practicing for life. Perhaps the most important distinction between play and games is that a game is entered into for the purpose of winning. Games are, therefore, by their very essence competitive and aggressive.

Play, on the other hand, is by its very nature creative. One of the few really outstanding teachers I had once defined art as "concentrated play." What a splendid and enjoyable definition of the creative process. Many, if not all, of the most creative writers, artists and performers I have known had about them a playful, humorous attitude to life.

As a beginning therapist I tried to be serious, thoughtful and understanding. Like many beginners I found myself becoming increasingly grim and super-serious. Even worse, I found myself to be going against my own nature, so I found my work exhausting and debilitating. Fortunately, as I began to be more confident of my craft, I started to revert to my more normal state of being and discovered ways of making my naturally playful disposition useful to my patients. While this is not meant to be a learned paper on therapeutic technique, I would like to share with you some of the methods that led one of my students to dub my technique "Play therapy with children over twenty-one."

Often, as I listen to patients talking, lines from plays, song titles or movie titles spring unbidden into my mind. Instead of keeping them to myself, I now frequently share such associations and often find them helpful. Recently a patient was complaining about the difficulty he had preparing for an examination, and I started to sing the first lines of a song made popular by the Beatles:

> *It's been a hard day's night*
> *And I've been working like a dawg.*

Suddenly he burst out laughing and realized he had been pitying himself and that his complaints had been a covert demand for sympathy. He realized that he actually enjoyed studying for the course but was afraid of admitting this to his fellow students for fear of being considered odd; therefore, he had convinced himself that he hated the work and wasted a lot of energy on self-pity and complaints.

Often I have had the impulse to react in what would seem an irrational manner to something that was being said, and found that if I permitted myself to play out the impulse, it led to a considerable reduction in anxiety, and the patient found the experience helpful. A rather serious career woman found it difficult to talk during our sessions, and the less she spoke, the more anxious she became; the greater the anxiety, the less she could speak. Trying to find the causes of this difficulty, I encouraged her to speak about how she had used to talk to her parents; she told me that as a young child she often found the only way she could speak to her father was if she was under the table in their dining room.

"Why don't you get under the desk?" I asked her.

"Oh, I couldn't do that," she answered with a giggle, "Why don't *you?*" she challenged me.

Happily I squeezed under my large desk, and for the rest of the session she spoke with much greater ease. At the next session, when she hesitated I started to get under the desk again, and she stopped me, saying, "OK, OK, I'll talk; just don't go under that dammed desk again." Then she added thoughtfully, "I guess I've been afraid to make a fool of myself by saying something silly or stupid; but since you showed me that you don't mind making a fool of yourself, why should I?"

In a group therapy session a patient once complained to the other members of the group, pointing at me, "As long as I see his ugly puss in front of me, I can't speak about any of the things that bother me.

I can't look at his face and talk." Obligingly I turned my back on the group. Then she declared, "As long as you are in the room I can't talk." This time I got up from my desk and started out of the room. "That won't do any good," she complained. "Then how will you be able to hear me?"

So I went into the closet in my office and sat there for a while until she declared, "Now I realize what I've been doing to everybody I come into contact with. I try to control them. Other people have told me this, but until you started with your crazy tricks I never saw it so clearly. Even my refusal to talk was an attempt to control."

One of the most troublesome types of patient can be the extremely suspicious one. When such patients used to ask me if an innocent electric socket was a concealed microphone for taping their remarks, I explained carefully the real purpose of the socket, and they still remained suspicious. When a suspicious woman recently asked me that question, I told her that not only was it a microphone, but that even as she spoke to me her remarks were being broadcast over a national radio network and millions of housewives were letting their dinners burn on the stoves while they listened to her problems. She laughed and said, "I really believe you are more disturbed than I am, but at last I've realized that my suspicion is really a wish to be the center of attention. When I worry about people talking about me, it is really because I would like everyone to talk about me. What really concerns me is that I am afraid I am so uninteresting that nobody will talk about me."

Robert Burns, for whom the popular cigar was named, was also incidentally an incisive poet, and his lines:

> *Oh wad some power the giftie gie us*
> *To see oursels as ithers see us!*

are a useful reminder to all of us. To the psychotherapist these are extremely important lines, because many of our patients are suffering from precisely this divine oversight in that they have not received the gift of being able to see themselves as others see them. Here one of the most elementary forms of play, mimicry or mirroring, can be used (without malice) to help make up this deficit.

For months I had learned to anticipate Thelma's depressions. Every time she made a step forward professionally or socially she would arrive at the next session sighing, crying, and generally describing her misery, loneliness and hopelessness. Usually she took care to dress for the role. While Thelma had excellent taste, and on a very limited clothes budget could manage to look as though she had just stepped out of *Harper's Bazaar,* when she prepared to play her tragic role she would appear in shapeless, dark, drab costumes.

One day she arrived in her tragic garb and sank down on the couch in my office. With equal despondence I sat and stared at her vacantly. Finally she sighed from the soles of her feet and said, "I feel horrible, just horrible. Tell me, doctor, why should I live?" Needless to say, the word "doctor" was uttered with sarcasm and contempt.

Reluctantly I stirred myself, for now I was beginning to enjoy my silent, withdrawn depression. I, too, sighed and answered hopelessly, "Maybe I could help you, but what's the use—what good would it do?"

She stared at me but continued to describe her misery. I matched her, misery for misery, hopelessness for hopelessness; but each time I made it even more despairing than hers.

At last she broke off in the middle of a sentence of sorrow, faced me, and screamed, "Listen, Dr. Greenwald, when my last therapist didn't feel well, she would cancel her sessions."

I remained hopeless and continued to despair. Thelma became more energetic; she straightened out and started to work on my problems. For once she was not involved with herself but was genuinely concerned about someone else. Suddenly she stopped and yelled at me, "You dirty scoundrel, you have been acting like me. Do I really sound so terrible? Is this the way I behave? How have you been able to put up with me for so long?" Her depression had lifted, and Thelma began to examine how she had gone about shaping her entire life to one paean of pain.

In a group therapy session Mildred seemed incapable of hearing what anyone said to her. Every time another member of the group spoke to her, she would say, "I'm sorry, I was blocked—I just can't hear what you are saying." After this had happened several times, she turned to me and asked, "What's the trouble? Why am I so blocked—why can't I listen to what people say to me?"

"I'm sorry," I replied. "What did you say? I find it difficult to follow you today."

She explained again; again I couldn't follow her. The other members of the group recognized what I was doing; and one of them attacked me for making fun of Mildred, for mocking her in her problem. Mildred sprang to my defense. "Don't you see?" she demanded. "He understands how I feel, and he is showing me he understands, by feeling the same way." For the rest of her stay in the group, Mildred stopped being blocked and was able to follow conversations much better.

With a chronic hypochondriac who was concerned about taking a vacation for fear he would be stricken ill while driving from New York City to Cape Cod, I worked out a marked map showing him where every hospital was en route and suggested that he write each of them and tell them to be ready to receive him in case of an attack. After a while he attacked me for catering to his hypochondria; then finally he informed me that I could go to hell and that he didn't need anyone to treat him this way. Eventually he gave up his hypochondriacal preoccupations and joined me in laughing about the absurdity of his fears.

In addition to these reflective methods, I have often found other play techniques useful. One of these techniques is freely adapted from Moreno's psychodrama. In formal psychodrama, the patient gets up on a stage and with the aid of a director and other members of the audience re-enacts scenes from his life that trouble him. Rather than use the formal stage, I often slip into the role of an individual with whom the patient is having difficulties, so that now the difficulties he has in life are difficulties with me.

An intelligent woman explained that one of her problems was her supersensitivity to her husband's criticism. At a later session I started to criticize her clothes. Instantly she grew furious and attacked me bitterly. I remained quiet and she started to speak of other things. Again I criticized her, this time for her diction; once more she lashed out at me. After several repetitions she suddenly blurted out, "You are just as bad as my husband." Soon, though, she became more thoughtful and began to examine with me the reasons why criticism made her so frantic. Eventually she became desensitized to my criticism as she began to understand the reasons for her own responses; she was even able to say jokingly, "How about a little criticism today? I need a reminder of how crazy nervous I used to be."

In all of these examples, I was using play not only for my patients' direct benefit but also to make it possible for me to deal with their problems without undue suffering. It is not helpful to the sufferer to permit his difficulties to engulf the therapist. One of the reasons many patients cannot be helped is that they arouse such intense emotions in the therapist that he cannot cope with them. Some studies have indicated that psychiatrists tend to hospitalize or give shock therapy to those patients who most anger them. My retention of a playful attitude insulated me from becoming vengeful or punitive to my patients.

As consultant to several industrial and commercial firms, I have noted that often the executives who managed to maintain their humor and to treat work like *play* were more productive, more creative, and generally more efficient than the grim, serious, hard-driven and hard-driving, ulcer-ridden types that one expects to be efficient. It is unfortunate that many employers only recognize the "hard worker," the one who uses an enormous amount of wasted energy, as being effective. Usually I have found it is the man who "works easy" who gets the most done.

But the concept of *play* is more important than a useful tool in therapy or a way of managing men and machines. It is a way of being in the world, a way of coping with the absurdities of the human condition; it is a way of armoring ourselves against "the slings and arrows of outrageous fortune."

To many of us all medicine must be bitter and ill tasting to be effective. Similarly we are imbued with the attitude that work must be taxing and unpleasant to be productive. Too often we look askance at our children when they play, and ask them if they only have *play* on their minds. When properly channeled, play can be one of the most useful and constructive of learning experiences. It is through play that animals and primitive peoples train their young for the tasks of living. Perhaps there is a profound wisdom here that the antipleasure elements in civilized society have made us forget.

Herb Otto, who has given considerable thought to the area of adult play, pointed out in a recent conversation that adult play can take a variety of forms. Otto distinguishes the following:

A. Spontaneous play—relatively rare; the adult, in a completely childlike manner and proceeding from a natural, personal impulse without planning or premeditation, engages in various forms of play. This type of activity is characterized by an abrupt transition from one set of activities to another and is charged with the elements of joy.

B. Play with children—highly creative whether planned or spontaneous as long as the adult *can really get in there with the children* and join with the essence of their being. Herb Otto told of two members of his Los Angeles Human Potentialities Training Group, Emily Coleman and Fran Goodwin, who engaged in spontaneous play with children on their block. They played jump-rope, hopscotch, jacks, and O'Leary-O. Housewives came out of their homes to laugh and watch, then joined, commenting, "I used to be an expert." Soon the whole block was involved in the fun, creating a unique and light-hearted spirit that persisted for a long time after all had returned to their homes.

C. Play with animals—often an animal's invitation to engage in spontaneous play goes unnoticed by the preoccupied adult. Interestingly, Menninger cites a person's playing with his cat (for example, dangling a string in front of the animal) as having considerable therapeutic value. When, however, animal play isolates the adult from finding satisfactions in other forms of play or keeps him from engaging in other forms of play, potential is not developed but usually diminishes.

D. Nature play—the adult feels a high degree of oneness with nature. He rolls in the grass (smelling, touching, tasting flowers, herbs, etc.) and partakes of nature through various forms of bodily contact.

E. Primitive play—closely related to the foregoing are forms of primitive play which can open up the adult to himself. Included here are playing in and with mud, building and shaping sand on the beach, damming a brook, eating like pirates (watermelons with no hands), etc.

F. Thrill play—the element of risk and danger of exultant rushing and "flying" are uppermost here, for example, riding a bike over the top of a steep hill at full speed.

G. Mastery play—this includes acquiring mastery of certain skills and enjoying the play elements contained therein. Sports such as tennis, basketball, golf, and the wide popular range of sports-related activities fall in this category. In much of this mastery play the competitive focus is the tail that wags the dog.

In essence *play is more an attitude than an activity*. It is approaching life's experiences looking for the lighter side. With the buoyancy of a happy, playful spirit, solutions and inspirations can "float in on the tide" of expectancy. Thus, the recreative aspect of play is to have a playful spirit in the process of daily living—in the encounters with people and problems—meeting them with a perspective through which they can be happily resolved.

3

Magda Proskauer

Breathing Therapy

I

My present approach to human growth is the outcome of early childhood experiences. When I was
young, I loved to skate. Once the river in my home
town was solidly frozen, I spent every free minute on
the ice. As my body glided effortlessly, it seemed I was
carving handwriting on the mirrorlike surface. After
I had practiced ardently for hours, all restraint fell
away, and the smooth shift of balance brought with it
a sense of weightlessness. The joy of life that flowed
through me in those days has never been forgotten.
Thinking of it years later evoked the question: what
is it that releases life?

In those early experiences was a first realization of
discipline leading to spontaneity, of effort leading to
effortlessness. In those frosty hours, tireless concentration led to the kind of delicate balance that is a prerequisite for figure skating. Once the will power had
been summoned to provide the skill, the same will
power could be shed; nature took over once more, so
that the genuine movement came through, bringing
the sort of release I was looking for unconsciously.
The spontaneous motion brought with it the
"e-motion" of joy, of being fully alive.

It is a long way from one's own experience to teaching a new sense of awareness to others. The way led me to a degree in physiotherapy from Munich University, through hospital work in Germany, Yugoslavia, New York Medical Center and private practice. In these years I had ample opportunity to explore traditional ways of treatment with the application of breathing therapy to asthma, polio, cerebral palsy and related diseases. Often we witnessed strange and unpredictable results from the breathing exercises that were prescribed for our patients. With one patient the cure seemed miraculous and lasting; with another a quick recovery would reverse itself all too soon into the former misery. One patient would flatly refuse to collaborate, while another one would form an attachment to his therapist that developed into an unhealthy dependence or into a hopeless power struggle. We encountered these irrational responses only during breathing therapy and not in other kinds of treatment, because breathing reaches the unconscious.

Gradually it became clear that cure of symptoms could no longer be expected by predetermined means—fixed sets of exercises and arbitrary manipulations. The whole of the personality had to be taken into account. The question of the *meaning* of the disturbance entered the picture. What unfulfilled needs or underlying conflicts were being expressed by the symptom? The unfolding of the new therapeutic methods came as the development of psychoanalysis shed new light on the psychosomatic character of many disturbances. Orthodox therapy was confronted with challenging questions, and new schools of thought arose. Practical work with some of these schools shaped my techniques to a considerable degree. The strongest influence was the analytical psychology of C. G. Jung.

Experiments had to be created by which the patient became conscious of hindering influences, so that awareness of these obstacles could introduce the desired change. The same principle had to be applied as in psychotherapy, where patient and doctor work together in a common search for the unknown need of the patient. All expectations and former attitudes had to be set aside; each patient had to be met as a new challenge. *Only when subliminal feelings and sense perceptions were allowed to come to the surface could there be a change.*

To achieve this, new methods slowly evolved. Certain breathing techniques were combined with subtle motions to cultivate perception. The breathing function proved valuable because of its intimate connection with the emotions as well as with the two nervous systems: the voluntary, consciously directed one, and the autonomous or vegetative one which works without the mind. Normally, we breathe automatically, but we can also take a breath or hold it for a time. In this respect, respiration is different from other autonomous functions, such as digestion. The stomach and intestines cannot be contracted at will. *The breath thus forms a bridge between the conscious and the unconscious systems.* By watching it, one can observe an unconscious function at work, learn to exclude interferences, and help self-regulating processes set in. One may be able to yawn before becoming overtired, to sigh before feeling overly restricted.

Because of its close relationship to the circulation, breath equals life. At the moment of birth, the first breath is the signal for amazing change to take place. The blood, until then supplied from the maternal source, becomes within seconds the independent, nourishing agent. With the environmental change, inhalation and exhalation begin to compress and dilate inner spaces as blood and lymph rush in and out of ever-changing vessels. The rhythmic filling and emptying acts like a compression wave, regulating the blood pressure and massaging the inner organs with gentle vibrations. At times of heightened sensitivity, some of these sensations can be experienced.

One wonders if this intricate process of birth might not better be named re-birth, since life exists already in the womb. Could it not be compared to the metamorphosis of certain animals and be a first transformation into a different kind of existence? From here on growth means constant change, continuing through a lifetime. It always implies abdication of nourishment by means of past methods in favor of the opening up of new resources. Being ready for the impending changes, like the infant's preparedness for meeting the atmosphere, leads in the direction of life. Resisting or evading the new situation leads to stagnation. Sensitivity and alertness are therefore valuable tools for dealing with the ever-changing demands of life.

Just as we behave, move, act, according to our specific make-up and express ourselves uniquely through gestures, *so does our breathing pattern express our inner situation,* varying in accordance with inner and outer circumstances. The usual arrhythmic respiration goes with our normal diffusion of attention, and changes with emotional states: agitated in anger, stopped momentarily in fear, gasping with amazement, choking with sadness, sighing with relief, et cetera.

With neurotics, we frequently find the so-called reversed breathing pattern, which reduces the breath to a minimum. The abdomen is pulled in; no breath can enter, since there is no exhalation. The bottle is filled with consumed air.

Normally, when at rest one breathes more with the diaphragm, like the abdominal breathing of the infant. Complete chest breathing, where the ribs expand and lift, occurs only at times of maximum effort. It usually starts the moment we pull ourselves together for action, or if we focus our attention toward outer events. To put it in oversimplified terms: abdominal breathing goes with sleep, rest, inertia, letting things happen. Where it is disturbed, the inner life is disturbed; one is driven, unreceptive, and lives too intentionally.

On the other hand, those who cannot open their chest cage are often anxious, inhibited, self-conscious, and tend toward feelings of inferiority. In between, there are endless variations and combinations, slightly different in rhythm in each individual. Where the pattern is reversed, the chest is lifted abnormally high, which means that only the auxiliary breathing muscles are used, those we need for maximum adaptation, as in the effort of mountain climbing. The diaphragm is excluded and becomes flabby, so the circulation is disturbed and the inner organs suffer. By relearning the use of the diaphragm, the warmth of returning circulation can be sensed in different areas of the body when one concentrates on them.

II

Instead of correcting faulty habits one takes as the point of departure the individual breathing pattern, disturbed as it may be. One concentrates on the act of breathing, observing its inner movement until the breath, left to itself, can find the way back to its own rhythm. This kind of playful attitude counteracts purposive, directed movement, so that one learns to experiment with one's nature and harmoniously trains the body for its own purpose. This is very different from training for any kind of performance or outward goal such as sports or other competitive exercises.

The technique lends itself to self-exploration by concentrating in an introverted attitude upon oneself. The mind is set aside, so that quiet contemplation can allow for awareness of one's inner state. One may, for instance, suffer from too spastic or too atonic (flabby) conditions in his system, or from both. Since these are often below the level of consciousness, we tend to feel these disorders only when they have already done some damage. Experiments are therefore set up by which we learn to feel and sense ourselves before a symptom is forced upon us. Gradually we recognize that every physical rigidity is simultaneously a psychic one, *that relaxation is not collapse, but the appropriate degree of contraction, the life-giving tension called tonus.* Through subtle movements, we discover for ourselves that in the simplest motion there are always two opposite muscle groups involved, which balance each other in their opposition. If an arm is stretched, one group contracts, the other extends and holds; both work, so there is a "yes" and a "no" in each action. Instead of making arbitrary corrections, we look together ingenuously for the simplest, most natural ways of making small movements.

Many intelligent people have developed in a one-sided manner, to the extent that they live without using their senses. Some do not taste the food they eat or see what is before their eyes. Some are unaware of the state of their own body.

Everyone knows that he can sharpen his perception, simply by having observed that he may not hear the ticking of a clock in a room or the singing of a bird under the window unless he concentrates on the sound. The sound is there all the time, but one becomes conscious of it only if he focuses his attention on it. Otherwise, the sound does not really exist; it is unconscious. The same is true of our physical sensations, pulse or heartbeat for example; normally they are not felt.

The sensory cortex of the brain is the storeroom of past impressions which may rise to consciousness as images but which more often remain unconscious. A present sense perception may get linked to the store of earlier perceptions and evoke a response that belongs to the past. Memory can be held in the body and awakened by certain disciplines. A muscular contraction once caused by the emotion of fear or joy may exist long after the accompanying experience has subsided. With the physical release of that specific tension, the psychic experience may return, to become a steppingstone for further development. How far the message can be used in the direction of growth depends on the individual's psychological capacity. Here we enter the realm of psychotherapy.

All physical changes in this work occur spontaneously and may or may not lead to insights. The experience of a young musician illustrates that such recollections need not be highly charged events: This man recently returned to his vocation after having had to abandon it for a while because of external pressures. During his sessions, he visualized lovely sketches from his past life; these he looked at in a meditative mood and felt greatly enriched by them.

It all depends on the attitude of consciousness how the unconscious reacts. If one is in tune with the unconscious, as it seems that this young man was at the time, the psyche reacts in a favorable manner and compensates the outer life in a pleasant, rather than a menacing, way. The process often comes close to the work of psychotherapy, where this kind of listening is encouraged, leading to the needed associations and images from which healing occurs. While psychotherapy starts on an intellectual level by using words, *the approach through the physical sensations is predominantly nonverbal.*

Practical work with artists has taught me over the years that the need can be of another kind. Creativity is easily buried under ambition and the strain of being trained for a specific skill. Certain schools of dance and drama, in striving for top performance, are often unable to consider individual inclinations. The very different discipline of concentrating on one's genuine responses helpfully balances this shortcoming and may prepare for more genuine modes of expression.

It becomes evident that body and psyche act as a unit, so awareness can come by approaching one or the other. This is so because body and psyche are two aspects of the same reality, two poles of life, two manifestations of the whole of the personality that are in steady interaction. To bridge the gap between these two extremes, we may start from the point of view that *our physical behavior corresponds to a psychic pattern, according to the law of synchronicity, not of causality*. With this in mind we need no longer explain a symptom reductively, but can try to grasp what it wants to convey and can thus discard any kind of criticism or attempt at arbitrary correction.

A sunken chest cage, when expanded, brings a natural sense of self-assertion; legs tightly held together in the manner of a Prussian soldier speak their own language. No explanations are needed once a person becomes aware of such habits. *The distortion will correct itself when it has been experienced, since consciousness has been brought to it.* The different techniques applied in this work permit the mind to be a quiet observer while feelings and sensations are questioned and imagination is used.

In attempting to describe a method designed to lead one toward genuine experience much is omitted, since the living experience defies precise formulation. Therefore it may be helpful to indicate a few of the subtle, simple directions which are given in our sessions.

For example, one experiments with the weight of one's body (or its parts) by trying to give it over to gravity. This leads to the experiencing of one's heaviness and releases tensions.

One is asked to bend one's knees, to find the place where they are in balance, so that they have to be neither held in support of each other nor manipulated in any other way.

One learns to visualize an inner body space, while simultaneously concentrating on one's exhalation, as if the breath were sent into that particular space. This may change the blood pressure and lead to a sense of lightness.

One examines the distances between certain joints, or the relationship between one's limbs, which touches on the body image.

Experiments are introduced that involve contact with another person, by hand or by sitting back to back. By way of sensing the other person one learns to get in touch with one's own sensations.

One is asked to concentrate on scanning[1] a certain area of one's body and to combine this with one's inhalation. Gradually the two tasks will connect, as if one were breathing with that particular area, or being breathed by it.

---

[1] Scanning is defined as focusing one's energy on a particular part of the body—chosen at will. One mentally breaks up this area into small units or points and directs one's concentration progressively towards each successive point. This allows for a fresh sensory perception of the chosen area.

The ways people describe their feelings are of endless variety, since no two experiences are ever quite the same. Often the pleasurable sensation evolves, that the breath carries one upright so that no effort is needed for sitting or standing in good posture.

In the use of motion and breathing as therapeutic agents, one can roughly distinguish two basic tendencies. One is the rigid, tensely controlled attitude, "running on rails," incapable of spontaneous reactions, and therefore out of touch with the deeper layers of the personality. This picture reflects a life lived as a product of one's environment and upbringing, performed according to what is expected by tradition and convention.

Such an attitude was apparent in a young dancer who came with the intention of learning my methods in order to use them in her field of teaching. She suffered from severe anxiety attacks from which long years of psychiatric care had brought no relief. She was an overly intellectual woman who relied exclusively on her reasoning capacity. When I asked her to exhale gently, then wait and observe how the next breath came in, she became extremely anxious. She realized through this experience that she could not trust anything to happen of its own accord, not even respiration. Only what she controlled could occur. After an initial sense of confusion, this insight brought her great relief. It led her to the roots of her fears, which she felt went back to her childhood, in which no father was present to counteract an overburdened, domineering mother who knew no natural tenderness. She saw how far she had parted from Mother Nature and was glad to find this new channel through which she hoped to regain the lost contact with herself.

The opposite tendency is shown by the flabby, overflexible, unstructured dreamer with too little life-giving tension in his system, the person who is too close to unconsciousness and easily collapses into it. With this type, one may expect quietude without repose, phlegmatic disinterest, apathy, inertia, and depression. Whereas the rigid type has deviated too far from his nature, this type has not yet evolved. His ego got stuck somewhere between the womb, nursery school, and adolescence; the world is taken either as the benign parent who is supposed to provide for its child, or as the evil one against whom one must rebel at any cost.

One finds many less extreme combinations of both tendencies in most people, probably because the growth process itself contains the two alternating phases. Parting from the natural, unconscious state so that a differentiated ego can emerge, and periodically returning to it, constitute the cycle of human development.

The one-sidedness, with its loss of balance, which is so typical of modern man's development, may arise from two opposite tendencies: On the one hand, it can come about by overconsolidation of the ego, which blocks the reception of impulses and messages. On the other hand, it can come about by a state of unconsciousness that threatens concentration and the continuity of the ego by unchecked emotionality, daydreaming, or instinctive drives. In nature itself, the balance is not firmly established. A sexually excited animal may endanger itself, forgetting security and hunger while following a single drive.

The acting out of every impulse is often mistakenly taken for freedom. In practical work, it is important to know the difference between acting out and befriending the suppressed instincts. It is only after having made our first adaptations that, in order to become individuals, we find it necessary to rediscover what has been left behind. By definition, *individual* means indivisible, a separate unit, a whole; not split; in psychological terms, comprising both the conscious and the unconscious elements of the personality.

Education toward the goal of individuality must cope with the difficulty of trying to prepare people for life's tasks *with the least interference with their inherent nature, so that the desire for further growth can remain the motivating force throughout life*. Repeatedly, in the different stages of life, patterns which once provided security have to be renounced so that new potentials can take their place. Since this cannot be brought about arbitrarily, it requires that time and again we return to our roots. In the past, religions took care of this need by enacting the periodic return and re-emergence in the mystery rites of death and rebirth. Today there is confusion about this process.

We have to learn again that to contact one's depths is not to sink back into trancelike oblivion, but rather to submit to the difficult discipline of quiet attentiveness. This is a forgotten product of our culture that requires conscious effort. Culture means to tend to. Much as a gardener tends to the soil in order that his plants may grow in their own way and season, so attending to the depths of our own nature tills the soil in which, firmly rooted, we can develop into healthy individuals. The somatic approach of breathing therapy is aimed at providing the climate for this kind of growth.

4

Minor White

Extended Perception Through Photography and Suggestion

This essay contains outlines for three practical ways to extend perception through photography. All three are related to the canon of creative photography, "Be still with yourself." One relates to looking at photographs, one to making them, one to sharing with others responses to photographs.

First, however, let us meander into one of the peculiarities of the medium, namely, that photographers and members of their audience can be equally creative.

If cameras are for seeing, photographs are for looking.

If photographers can use the camera to extend perception during the period called "making exposures," viewers or members of the audience can extend their own perception during the period called "looking at photographs." If there is anything creative here (and where else does creativity lie in photography?) then seeing and looking are equally creative. That is, the audience can be as creative as the photographer, and in virtually the same way. The "exercises" outlined in this essay are devised to demonstrate the similarity.

If in the process of extended perception the photographer makes contact with the essence of what he is about to photograph, the viewer may make contact with the essence of the image. That is, both open themselves to any suggestions that originate in the essence by deliberately inducing a state or condition called "extended perception." In academic circles the condition is called "heightened awareness"; in today's slang, "turned on."

If the photographer may bring about a state of heightened awareness by his own efforts, *the member of the audience may also make deliberate efforts to make contact with images.* Audiences have been blatantly spoon-fed for so long that they have become a visually illiterate society. Until members of the audience become willing to make efforts to *look,* they will never realize that one of their nagging hungers comes from visual starvation.

If a photographer can share his experience of truth or beauty through photographs, members of an audience can share with others their *responses* to the same qualities in images.

If photographers can take a responsibility for their images, members of a group can be equally responsible for their responses communicated to each other. Perhaps more than any other one point, it is this last that caused the writing of certain exercises. (And the "exercises" may grow into a way of life for some readers.)

1. EXTENSION OF PERCEPTION BY LOOKING AT PHOTOGRAPHIC IMAGES

A. *The Simplest Exercise Possible*

Select a photograph that you can look at for a long time with pleasure. Set aside some time, a half hour or so, that may pass without a single interruption. Set the picture in good light and yourself in a comfortable position. Look at the picture for at least ten minutes without moving even one small muscle, or "giving in" to even one tiny twitch. Keep your eyes and mind on the image, instead of following long chains of associations; keep coming back to the picture. You can expect that many things will be found in it, not previously noticed. After ten or fifteen minutes, turn away from the picture and recall what you have experienced, step by step. Make this as visual as possible; review the experience visually rather than with words. After the thirty minutes have elapsed, more or less, and the experience has become a kind of flavor, go about the day's work, trying to recall the taste when you can.

No one can predict what you will experience. The trick is to accept whatever the experience is for *what it is*. Then one will face a moment of truth, tiny though this moment may be, relative, limited or even negative and unexpected. It is only when one anticipates explosions, ecstasy, breakthroughs, thundering visions, that an actual, real moment of truth will be overlooked and therefore missed. If you habitually bring the notion of God into your activities, listen for the whisper. To our weak perceptions even thunder may reach us but faintly.

B. *Elaboration of the Simple Exercise*

The exercise above can be elaborated as far as one wishes. A model of one elaboration follows. It is for persons who are willing to prepare themselves and to make efforts to look at photographic images either alone or with others. The exercise is also for the photographer in his periodic role of audience to his own pictures, also by himself or in the company of others.

There are four stages, each with a few steps: *Preparation, Work, Remembering,* and *To Share.* That is (1) becoming still with oneself in order to make contact with a *worthy* photograph, (2) working in a self-induced state of stillness of a special kind that engenders active perception, (3) the return to the usual state while remembering the visual experience or journey, and (4) sharing sometime later with others the interaction between image and self. The last stage really works best in company; hence we will treat the "to share" stage as a separate exercise in looking at images, for several people at once.

PREPARATION

The selection of a photograph has a bearing; so choose one that you like but suspect there is more present in than you have found so far. Photographs of water, snow, ice or clouds are fine to start with.

By being still you can make yourself voluntarily receptive to the suggestions coming from the image.

Remember that being still with yourself is a phenomenon possible in man which is an invitation to the unconscious to well up into the conscious. By being still with yourself you can help the wisdom of the psyche to infiltrate the commonly conscious mind.

Place the photograph in good light. Plan to hold it either in the hand or on a chair or other support. Seat yourself directly in front of the picture, *erect* and comfortable. It is of considerable wisdom to make certain that no interruptions will occur that might disturb your efforts.

Be prepared to postpone judgment of "good," "bad," "like," "dislike," until much later. The actions that these words call up, if allowed to remain in the mind while working with the picture, destroy any possibility of extension of perception.

Preparation continues by closing the eyes and starting to relax in a specific progression. Start by relaxing the muscles around the eyes, then the muscles of the whole face, then the shoulders, upper torso and arms, letting the arms and body begin to feel buoyant as the relaxation progresses. Next relax the lower body, the thighs, the legs, and finally the feet, always allowing and encouraging the whole body to become buoyant and receptive. A more or less weightless body is ready for impressions of all kinds.

During this relaxing period the body will have been motionless; and in the three, four, five minutes that elapse energy will have collected that the body usually dissipates by needless and heedless movements. This energy becomes available to the mind as it is about to cross the threshold of perception, and the mind needs additional energy for just this purpose of perception.

Relaxing is purposefully directed from eyes to feet, while, on the contrary, the gathering of energy is deliberately directed from feet and hands to head. As the energy begins to activate the mind, prepare yourself to project some of this energy to the photograph and be further prepared to sustain such projection of force.

When you feel that there is abundant energy, open your eyes. The first flooding of the eyes with the image is a crucial moment. Your energy is projected as force without a shape; the image gives the energy a form and bounces it back to you with a shape. Furthermore, at this moment the "total image" may or may not be perceived by the "whole man" in a single strong impression.

Sustain that first strong impression. It may be necessary to close the eyes quickly to retain it. When you have a grasp on that impression, re-engage the image. What follows, that is, *the work period*, may be said to consist of your efforts to bring into the ken of the conscious mind what the psyche in the unconscious found in the image. In most humans it is as if a kind of "forgetter" is wired into the circuit between psyche and conscious mind.

WORK PERIOD

The work period may be held as long as you wish or are able. The work consists mainly of overcoming the effect of the aforementioned "forgetter." The fact that a work period has arrived may generally be recognized from a certain clue. When the perception of space in depth within the image suddenly increases, one is in a working state. Some persons, however, experience other changes in the image, an increase of overall brightness or a change in size, usually larger, or a brightening of colors, and so on. This clue usually occurs shortly after the eyes are opened, and sometimes almost instantly.

After the first impression has been solidified for yourself in some manner, the work can start. Start active work by scanning the image in narrow bands: top left, across, and then back. Go back and forth until everything in the photograph has been seen and noted. Next scan the image according to the suggestions of flow and direction and relationships within the whole photograph. This is to make sure that you have seen all the relationships. When everything has been observed, start to study the images with whatever "tools" you can bring to the experience—tools such as previous knowledge of design and composition, the techniques and composition peculiar to photography, the philosophy and metaphysics of image-making regardless of media, the knowledge of the subject from either long acquaintance with humanity or specialist knowledge of the subject photographed.

In addition you can also let associations flow—flow on and on, far away from the image at hand, and into the personal body of compulsions at that moment prevalent in yourself. The associations that flow up in you while looking at photographs seem to originate in the images themselves, but actually the associations originate in yourself. Consequently the associations that flow while looking at what are frequently called "abstract" photographs or any otherwise ambivalent images transform the photograph into a self-mirror. And the strangeness that arises in such instances is not a function of the image so much as a fact of yourself.

The photographic image as a mirror of the self is a contemporary experience. Oliver Wendell Holmes, literary American of the last century, once called the photograph a mirror with a memory. He referred, however, to the photographic record of the scene, which the camera does superbly well. For many members of society today the ambiguous photograph functioning as a mirror asks the man to remember himself. The ambivalent (that is, suggestive of more than one meaning) photograph can mirror the angel in us, the demon, the goblin, the saint, the matriarch, the harlot, the child or the man, whatever is uppermost at the time. In a long work period, in a state of stillness, with ambivalent images, not only what is uppermost will surface into the conscious mind, but sometimes deeper hidden faces of ourselves will slowly drift into view.

THE PASSIVE MODE

Activity is not the only way to work in a state of stillness with a photograph or to remain sensitive to the suggestions that rebound from the image. Similar rewards may be anticipated if one remains passive. Sit in stillness, waiting, waiting patiently, without anxiety, waiting in readiness to receive suggestions and impressions; sooner or later the image will "speak" to you. It will even use your own words; how else, for who else is speaking? Some persons actually hear words. (This is the experience of the present writer.) Others hear colors, or sounds and music, or gestures, or other manifestations of the physical body. Whatever form the "speaking image" takes, the moment has the ring of conviction. A tinkle is about as much as the conscious mind can hear of the cosmic symphony, even when working in a state of stillness with both the self and the image.

To "turn on" the passive way, a certain word related to hearing helps some of us. This is the word "listen," and it is applied during an active work session. This does not mean to listen for sounds but to listen with the eyes to visuals or sights. The word is not to be taken literally, but allegorically. When this device works, the result is as if

the sense of sight were relieved of the deficiencies of its own characteristics!

In due time, try both the active and the passive modes.

REMEMBERING

You may find that there is nothing new for you in these exercises.
Most of us have experienced extended perception or concentration
when something fascinated us, devoured our attention. The purpose
here is to provide procedures and disciplines by which states of
extended perception can be induced whenever one chooses, that is,
by will and personal volition.

At the end of the work period the state of stillness is turned off.
This is to be done on purpose, when you decide to. Both turning the
state on and turning the state off are to be considered as great
opportunities to exercise will. So choose to.

The return to our usual state of mental numbness and physical
twitching is to be done in brief steps. Start by looking at the totality
of the image; in other words start to undo the spell by taking a final
impression. Close the eyes, let the buoyancy out of the body, and it
will soon move in its commonplace manner. Then turn away from
the photograph and look elsewhere. Try very hard to hold on to the
experience that has just been stopped. Try to hold on to it in silence,
no words, not even to yourself. Review the various things seen, not as
laundry lists, but as related visuals.

During this period of recalling the experience the intensity of the
experience will diminish slowly or rapidly as the case may be, and
the experience may begin to distill itself until only a taste or flavor is
left. Even after the actual physical appearance of the image has
disappeared, the "taste" of it may linger, and remain. The taste is
amazingly persistent! If you are still compelled to judge something,
evaluate the photograph from the taste. Judgment from "taste" has
at least a slim chance of objectivity.

Though, I suppose, something like judgment must eventually be
undertaken, what is more important than judgment and evaluation
is tracing the effect of the image on yourself. Was some kind of
change brought about? If so, where in you? Or what in you was
affected? Was something added? Was something taken away? Was
your energy dissipated uselessly, or gathered purposefully? And so

on. Few enough images add anything to our inner life. The rest are millstones and albatrosses around our necks.

Images of any kind may be compared to physical food. When images add something or direct our energy to higher levels, they nourish us. Poisonous images are those that lead us into useless or frustrating stimulations or misinform or otherwise degrade us. Nourishing images are food of a special sort for something else in us. Most of the time we do not know whether a given image is poison or nourishment for this something. In states of heightened perception, viewing images in stillness, sometimes the person can realize which is taking place in him: something fine in him is being destroyed during an encounter with a photograph, or something coarse in him is being made finer. The wisdom of the psyche is able to distinguish.

2. EXTENSION OF PERCEPTION FOR SEVERAL PEOPLE AT ONCE

THE "TO SHARE" PERIOD

We may not want to share our intimate encounter with a photograph, especially if it has pushed a skeleton of ours into our face. Not all images can be expected to affect us this way unless, of course, our inner lives are almost exclusively a hodge-podge of skeletons and closets. More often when the interchange between ourselves and a photograph moves us, we have a considerable urge to tell someone. This urge to tell can be extended into a real communication with others, a communication that may be quite as effective as the photograph itself.

An exercise in sharing can be arranged easily enough. The preparation consists of gathering a small group of persons who have tried out the "simplest possible exercise" outlined above. One photo is quite enough for an evening's work. The following procedure is to be explained to everyone before the image is brought out.

After the picture is in place and each has found a comfortable place to view it, without any glare of light, each induces in himself the state of stillness of body and intensified activity of mind in the manner and steps described earlier. To facilitate working together someone should be charged with the duty of starting the relaxation, timing when to open the eyes and later to turn off the state of activated stillness. He will never be able to judge the various times required for each of the stages for each person, and so becomes something of a nuisance; but for group work everyone will have to bear with him.

It has been found that if the person charged with timing the successive stages uses certain phrases of a permissive nature, everything goes more smoothly. The points below may be used as a kind of check list to start. If the exercise is performed more than once or twice with the same people, abbreviations will arise of their own accord.

1. To start the relaxation period he may say, "After you have closed your eyes, allow the muscles around the eyes to relax." This is given in a quiet tone of voice.

2. When the coach thinks that everyone is relaxed, he can say, "When you are ready, encourage the energy to flow upward."

3. When he thinks that everyone is about to engage the photograph, he says, "Whenever you are ready open your eyes." To help gauge the work period time, he notices when the last eyes are opened.

(If there has been any hypnotic effect during this presentation period, from the moment the eyes engage the image all suggestions come from the picture.)

4. After about ten minutes have passed the coach can start the disengagement process with some such statement as, "That is probably enough for now." After a short pause of maybe a minute or so he gives the next directive.

5. "Whenever you are ready, take a last impression, close your eyes, and turn your head to one side."

6. When all heads are turned, "Let your body come back to its normal weight, and let it move as it usually does." This is said in a crisp tone of voice or manner of speech.

7. When all are stretching he adds, "Face your chairs away from the photograph."

The procedure outlined above should be explained (as was said) to all present before the session starts. It is especially important to caution members of the group to remain quiet and motionless after the head is turned away from the photograph, so that those who are still engaged in the photograph will not be disturbed any more than necessary. Actually, turning the head at this time is only a signal to the coach so that he will know everyone is through and bring the disengagement with the photograph to a kind of official close.

After the engagement with the image, the period of remembering is a private affair and is to be respected as such. Actively remembering, letting the experience distill into a taste, should be done in silence; and a relative quietness of body should persist for at least ten minutes. Because the group has met to share experiences and tastes, each member of the group will be expected to try to formulate during this period some way by which he can communicate to the rest his "trip": observations, understandings, or maybe the taste itself.

It should be arranged beforehand that approximately a ten-minute period will be given to this activity, and if no one has volunteered by then the coach can call on members.

To share experiences may prove to be a period of extended perception high in quality and of long duration. Someone of the group is likely to arrive at an understanding while he talks, and all will have their experience of the image enlarged. If each listens intently to the overtones as well as to the words, it may soon be realized that as each talks the spoken words are coming from a different place in the speaker than usual. The words may come out slowly, there may be a noticeable effort to speak, as if a translation from visual to verbal were in progress. These are all clues that a heightened awareness continues.

There is one type of occurrence to watch for during this period of sharing. As each person tries to tell what he saw while engaged with the photograph, almost every one of the rest will notice that the image seems to change and suddenly correspond to what is being pointed out. It is as if the image makes an actual move or transformation. Obviously the image does not really move or change; so the change must be in ourselves. Because we wrongly attribute the change to the image, we forget to look at what is really happening to us.

If we repeat the exercise with another photograph and with this event to watch for, as each person's experience "changes the image" we may get briefly the sensation that we are seeing with the eyes of the speaker. If so, the experiment will be worth the effort, because *for an instant at least we are given the opportunity to see objectively,* that is, to see with another person's eyes.

Gathering other people's responses to images, our own or those made by other photographers, can help us add to the meaning of individual images. As each person talks about his experience, our own journey through the photograph is enlarged. A question may be raised about the problem of everyone seeing something different in the photograph, and the familiar objection will come up, "But aren't photographs 'supposed' to convey just one thing to everyone?" So few photographs actually convey but one "meaning" that it is more realistic to accept the fact that everyone is going to get something different—and make the most of that reality. As one gathers responses from various types of people, the "image itself seems to grow" in meaning for everyone present. The opportunity to work with an image in the company of a few responsive persons is indeed rewarding and stimulating.

So important is "getting out of ourselves" and helping others do likewise, that communication of responses should be developed to the stature of a creative act in its own right.

THE RESPONSE

To help those who wish to undertake "sharing responses" for the first time, a few points to avoid or omit will be helpful. Omit the words *good, bad, like, dislike, ought, should* and *interesting* from the vocabulary of the group. Discourage obvious substitutes for these words. Avoid describing the image; everyone present can recall it. Recognize that one's prejudices at least color response and usually make response impossible. Curtail descriptions of long journeys that have ended in some pet compulsion that in turn has no bearing on the photograph. Look at the fact that each different response adds something to everyone's experience of the image. *Forget the popular cliché that photographs "should" mean the same to everyone. They do not; people are too varied.* In a group the experience of images is enlarged in a way that can happen in almost no other situation. When the photographer of the image being studied is present, his own concept of the image can also be enlarged, altered and magnified—that is, if he is willing to accept the truth of a response and not throw out all responses that do not agree with his notion of what his image evokes or communicates.

To further help the people who will undertake sharing responses, we must clearly define both what is included in and what is excluded from this word "response." A "response" differs from a "criticism" in that it describes the journey or experience without evaluation of any kind. The journey may be delightful, oppressive, downright horrible, *all of which emotional evocations are simply treated as the facts of the journey and not evaluation of either the image or the person*. To exaggerate, a "response" is to be thought of as anti-criticism. A "response" is a fact; and no matter how limited the truth, that modicum of truth—"this is what took place in me"—is given in full confidence that no evaluation will be made by anyone present

Sometimes to be able to speak freely of what one has experienced is an extension of the state of extended perception. Certainly each person's knowing that his "response" will be respected as a sliver of a truth will help him achieve a higher degree of awareness in the first place, and, better still, will assist the mode of extended perception to sustain itself during a period of sharing with others.

A "response" differs significantly from a "reaction," too. *A reaction is to be thought of as an accidental, uncontrolled and unmanageable, more or less compulsive, happening that took place during the event of looking at a photograph*. A "response" is intended to indicate that a dialogue took place between you and the image— that is, if you are not overwhelmed by the image and so lose sight of yourself, but work as if with a colleague or a peer, and both parties are fully cognizant of each other, the image and the self in you. In other words, *something of yourself is recognized as present* in the interchange. This particular and special self-presence is something that will be particular to your response. And sharing with the group this special presence is exactly what members of the group can bring to each other in turn.

VISUAL RESPONSES INSTEAD OF VERBAL

For the sake of presenting the exercises with simplicity, responses have so far been treated as being only verbal. Actually, responses need not be verbal at all. If there is a dancer in the company, he can probably show something of his experience by making a gesture or a movement of the whole body. Any other dancer in the company will probably grasp the response in a specific way. A musically minded member of the company might go to the record collection and find a passage that corresponds to his experience. A painter or sculptor could dash off a sketch of his experience, and such a sketch need not be a simplified imitation of the photograph, but a new manifestation of his own private response.

Though most of us might not think so, all of us can make a workable sketch with a piece of charcoal pencil and a huge newsprint sketch pad. To demonstrate this, provide charcoal pencils and sketch pads to the members of a group, and at the sharing period have each person put down some kind of marks on the paper that correspond somehow to his experience. When they are completed lay them out on the floor for everyone to see. Probably most of the sketches will be rather meaningless. Here the person serving as coach can ask each person to explain with as few words as possible what the sketch stands for. Again, it is amazing and rewarding to see a meaningless few lines suddenly become the window into another person's mind and vision. The window also gives a view to the person's experience with the photograph. If there are experienced draftsmen in the group, often no words at all are needed. For those who may be putting pencil to paper for the first time since they were children, a few words will bridge the deficiency.

3. EXTENSION OF PERCEPTION AT THE TIME OF PHOTOGRAPHING

Add a camera to the exercises previously tried out for looking at images. This exercise is best done with equipment that allows the photograph to be seen on the spot. Select an object: a branch of flowering dogwood, a chair, or an object that appeals to one and can be moved into comparative isolation. Have a hand-held type camera within arm's reach.

Set object and self into position similar to that used with an image. Prepare yourself to make contact with the object in the same manner used for making contact with an image; that is, relax, let the energy gather, and direct it into increasing mental activity, and then outward to the object when the eyes are open. The same kind of experience of increased sense of depth or other noticeable changes again indicate that a state of stillness is present.

Sit quietly, working actively by bringing everything you know or feel or sense into the act, or conversely by simply sitting quietly and completely open to any and all impressions the object might arouse. When you have felt somehow a resonance between your own life and the vitality or life of the object, contact is established.

Sustaining the contact, bring the camera into the line of sight between you and the object, and make an exposure. Slowly, very slowly, lower the camera while continuing the contact and while maintaining the state of stillness. The tendency here is to be so eager to see the results that the state of stillness is broken in the rush to operate the camera. This exercise is one that is intended to allow movement of the hands and arms while the state of contact is maintained with deliberate effort and the state of extended perception continues to exist. With plenty of practice one can learn, if one wishes, to sustain contact while making many exposures in a fast-moving situation.

When the operation of the camera during development of the picture demands looking at it, do so slowly, in order not to break the state of heightened awareness. Then study the photograph also in a state of extended perception. *A photograph made during a state of heightened awareness is frequently best seen in the same state,* by both the photographer and, as already pointed out, the audience.

Photographers reading this will have experienced that damnable gap between seeing and photograph. Closing this gap is a long, hard course in craftsmanship, that is, learning to see as a camera. Meanwhile, the photographer can slip into the role of audience and make "contact" with his own image as if it had been made by another person. Photography is so generous and so mechanical that often a photograph that fails the *seeing* proves to be an image on *looking* at it.

IMPLICATIONS FOR FURTHER EXTENSION

The various exercises are presented and intended to be used as starting points for future growth of the individual. Consequently, doing these exercises will suggest many other applications. For example, the efforts required and the state of stillness obtained to "make contact" with photographs may be extended at any time to include all kinds of objects, art, music, dance, and the more intangible world of thoughts and ideas. In fact, by the same methods one can make contact, by eliminating all thoughts and thinking, with the inner movements of forces and energies that go on in us all the time, but out of range of sight, hearing, taste, and so forth.

It is hoped that the reader has observed that this essay deals with the total movement of photography; and the exercises, if performed, might *involve* the performer with the same. This total movement is a complex interaction involving the separate elements of medium, photographer, subject/object, camera, and audience. The total movement unites these various elements and the various interactions with life-as-a-whole, when that in turn is in gear with the world of spirit-as-a-whole.

5

Herbert A. Otto

Sensory Awakening Through Smell, Touch, and Taste

Man today is surrounded by a physical environment that anesthetizes much of his sensory equipment. Carbon monoxide and chemical wastes from factories and processing plants are added to the fresh air we breathe if we live in or near a metropolis or industrial complex. The quality and quantity of noises (many beyond hearing level, vibrations that nevertheless leave an impact on the human organism) have risen steadily over the years. Doctor Igho H. Kornbluen, physician and professor at Pennsylvania's Graduate School of Medicine, in an address to the American Association for the Advancement of Science in 1965, reached the following conclusion: "Urban living is leaving its stigma on the physical and mental capacities, creativity and productivity of the inhabitants.

"The questionable cultural achievement culminating in a lifetime in an artificial environment and punctuated only by rare escapes to the mountains or the seashores may lead to urbophrenia (city jitters), a composite of organic and functional syndromes or social behavioral disorders."

Multiple noxious stimuli constantly assail the senses of the man who moves in a structural environment not designed according to the principles of sound engineering. (The placement of building structures and the construction of façades and external facings is often such as to magnify and increase sound volume in cities.) Our sense of vision is continually assailed by the ugly proliferation of the concrete jungle and a myriad of advertising messages which, through alternating color and rhythmic sequences, seek to capture our eye—and succeed. At the same time our sense of touch is outraged and dulled by the fleeting and impersonal nature of daily contacts with the thousands of surfaces that we handle and feel with our bodies and fingertips.

We have also formed the habit of either making the meal a hurried, mechanical refueling routine for the human machine or turning it into a gluttonous, wholesale assault on the tastebuds—so that the very range of complex flavors and tastes leads to a defensive masking of the sense of taste and smell. The closing or restricting of our senses to what is being communicated to us cripples our communication system: much that needs to be expressed and communicated never finds birth, for our muffled senses keep it from being born.

Our swaddled and weary senses restrain us in a mysterious land of suspension and removal which has the qualities of distance and separation. We let nothing really touch us and become slaves to *automatic living,* paying very little notice to what goes on around us. Thus, we deny ourselves the fullness of *living* in the now, which requires that we must be able to open fully our senses and to direct our awareness.

Finally, one road to communion with the infinite lies through the removal of obstructions that cloud our senses. By extending our sensing, by becoming more sensitive and sentient, we can begin to open a door into the unknown. As William Blake put it, "Learn to apprehend the world with unobstructed senses. . . . If the doors of perception were cleansed, everything would appear to man as it is—infinite."

Through entering into a series of experiences designed to revitalize your sense of smell, touch, and taste, you can extend your horizon of awareness. Participation in experiences designed to foster what has been called Sensory Awakening can enhance your capacity for *selective awareness*—so that you can open yourself to awareness either at will or spontaneously.

As a part of the Human Potentialities Research Project at the University of Utah, a number of sensory awareness experiments and studies have been conducted, largely within a small group setting. It has consistently been found that for maximum effect *experiences designed to foster such sensory awakening should be shared experiences.* Not only is it more fun to have these experiences in a small, congenial group, *but individual growth and change appear to be more intense and lasting.* The principle of reinforcement and mutual interstimulation and enrichment seems to play a significant part in this process. It is also advisable not to use any alcoholic beverages preceding the sensory awareness experience. Alcohol not only dulls the senses but in many instances seems to interpose a barrier to the growth processes. Oftentimes a single drink seems to set off deep-rooted associational (and behavioral) processes, so that the person cannot seriously enter into the experience but has to "write it off" as a means of spurious (unreal) fun. There is also some evidence that both consciously and unconsciously any change or growth in the quality of perception and even the vividness of the experience *will be credited to the alcohol* rather than to the person's expanding state of awareness.

It has been found that one type of experience such as *either* a smell *or* a touch experience is sufficient for an evening. Overloading of the senses is thus avoided. If properly entered into, it usually takes the better part of an evening to conclude such an experience. It is a good idea to call a rest if a dulling of the senses takes place. In order to have a rest in the middle of an experience, one group used a seven-minute period of complete silence and meditation. Another group preferred to move around, to stretch and exercise spontaneously as a means of relaxation.

AN ADVENTURE WITH YOUR SENSE OF SMELL

The sense of smell is one of the most primitive of our senses and one of the most potent. It is also one of the most deeply repressed.

Discussing our "proximity senses" (smell and taste) Herbert Marcuse in his brilliant volume *Eros and Civilization*[1] makes the following observation:

> . . . they (smell and taste) succumb to the rigidly enforced taboos on too intense bodily pleasure. The pleasure of smell and taste is "much more of a bodily, physical one, hence also more akin to sexual pleasure, than is the more sublime pleasure aroused by sound and the least bodily of all pleasures, the sight of something beautiful."[2] Smell and taste give, as it were, unsublimated pleasure *per se* (and unrepressed disgust). They relate (and separate) individuals immediately, without the generalized and conventionalized forms of consciousness, the effectiveness of organized *domination*, with a society which "tends to isolate people, to put distance between them, and to prevent spontaneous relationships and the natural animal-like expressions of such relations."[3]

There are tribes in parts of the world whose members have a sense of smell almost as keen as that of a hunting dog. Indications are that even in the absence of conscious awareness we perceive the changes in body odor that take place in persons around us, and these form an important part of the total human communication system. It is well known that many animals smell fear and other subtle nuances of emotions. We also have this ability and, more often than not, both consciously and unconsciously exercise it. The widespread use of perfumes and deodorants and the considerable sums spent on these items reveal that, despite a certain squeamishness, our sense of smell plays a very basic and important part in our communicative behavior and responses.

We have found that to reawaken the sense of smell, the principles of ambiguity and surprise must be introduced. As in the regeneration of the other senses, this is best achieved in the context of a congenial, small group.[4] A creative group experience designed to reawaken the sense of smell involves both group consensus and

---

[1] Herbert Marcuse, *Eros and Civilization* (New York: Random House, Inc.) First Vintage Edition, 1962, pp. 35–36. Copyright, 1955, The Beacon Press.

[2] Ernest Schachtel, "On Memory and Childhood Amnesia," in *A Study of Interpersonal Relations*, ed. Patrick Mullahy (New York: Hermitage Press, 1950), p. 24.

[3] Ibid., p. 26.

[4] The series of sensory-awakening experiences easily lend themselves as the focus for a number of informal parties that have as their theme the actualizing of human potential. These could be an "odor enjoyment party," a "touch party," and a "taste party."

preliminary preparation. The group should first discuss whether they *wish* to enter into such an experience. On reaching a consensus and depending on the depth of communication and closeness within the group, members may then wish to explore with as much frankness as possible *why the sense of smell is so deeply repressed in our culture.* In preparation for the experience at this initial consensus meeting, the group may also wish to share *the most vivid smell experience they have had in the course of their journey through life up to the moment.*

The next step is for each group member to assume some responsibility of preparing for the experience. We have found it most effective if odors are divided into five categories—*natural* (crushed leaves, fresh herbs, flowers, etc.), *artificial* (kerosene, gasoline, ether, drugs, cleaning fluids, etc.), *spices* (nutmeg, cinnamon, oregano, marjoram, etc.), and *perfumes* (women's perfumes and also the range of recently developed men's perfumes and toilet waters); a final possible grouping is *incense,* including Indian joss sticks, Chinese incense available in a number of types, and the Japanese variety. We have found it best to use the incense experience in the beginning as a "door opener." Joss sticks or lighted pieces can be passed around individually (unlighted incense also has a very distinctive and pleasant odor). A very delightful and different experience can be enjoyed by burning dried leaves from various trees (the smell of burning pine bough is familiar to many) as well as burning various herbs, dried flowers, etc. It is necessary to allow some time to elapse before embarking on other parts of the adventure with your sense of smell.

We have found that leaves, flowers, and herbs are best placed in a small white paper bag, which should be rolled down and pressed together leaving a smallish opening for the nose. (Brown paper bags often have a distinctive odor which interferes with the experience.) The objective is to eliminate as much as possible all sensory clues as to content *so that the only stimuli presented are to the nose.* It is important that everyone clearly understands that the preparation of each discrete smell experience should be such that no one except the person preparing the experience be able to identify (by a marking on the receptacle) the nature of the content. Perfume bottles and spice containers should be well concealed behind multiple wrappings so that no clues are offered by color, shape, etc. If one desires to

undergo the experience alone, it is well to have someone else prepare
selections from each category of odors.

When the group has its next meeting following the initial consensus meeting, it is recommended that containers of odor categories
(natural, artificial, perfumes, etc.) be well mixed *so that members
are not overwhelmed by a series of experiences stemming from one
category.* The bags and containers are then passed around with the
instructions: "Don't think of anything—associate out loud—share
your fantasies and thoughts." "What do you recall as you encounter
a distinctive smell?" Emphasis should be on letting associations and
memories flow and letting the mind wander—letting it follow the
paths and byways of images, dreams, and memories. Spontaneity and
spontaneous sharing are an important aspect of this experience.

Participants may wish *not* to tell others the identity of the various
receptacles or to speculate about their identity as they come their
way. However, some groups have preferred to share identity clues
out loud. (Such comments are often heard as, "This smells wonderful—is it heather?") The danger is, of course, that the experience
deteriorates into a competition to see who can identify "the most"
and with the greatest accuracy. Emphasis should *not* be on establishing the identity, nor on labeling or categorizing, but *to flow with the
experience*—to let an unfoldment take place and to reawaken a
basic nature and perception. *The content of memories, fantasies,
and associations provides clues that can deepen insight and self-un-
derstanding, and offers a chance for synthesis and integration.* Participants in the sensory-awakening experience are also provided an
opportunity *not* to attach value judgments to smell experiences
("good" or "bad," pleasant or unpleasant), and to utilize the experience creatively, constant with both inner necessity and the realization of possibilities. Smell, as one of the most basic and primitive
senses, can put man in touch with the very wellsprings of his being
and the core of his becoming. Regeneration of our sense of smell can
add avenues of communication, deepen the dimensions of our identity, and make us more clearly aware of our at-one-ness with nature.

THE SENSE OF TOUCH—AN OPENING DOOR

The sense of touch is one of our neglected senses precisely because
we use it continually throughout the day while often being only

marginally aware or totally unaware. In our everyday activities our sense of touch is constantly exercised; but our minds and attention are so predominantly on other things that we rarely let ourselves have a pure, unalloyed touch experience. We seem to avoid fully entering into a touch experience. A contributing factor in our unwillingness to participate fully in a touch experience may be that *more and more the natural materials are being withdrawn from direct contact.* The overwhelming majority of contact areas in our living environment consists of artificial materials. Perhaps this is symptomatic of our identification with a culture where people are increasingly isolated and unwilling to let anything touch them. Is it possible that our unwillingness to let ourselves be touched by people or events is in a measure related to the quality of superficiality and noninvolvement that characterizes our daily touch experiences?

The sexual or erotic touch is, of course, widely used. On the other hand, the communication of love and tenderness, of support and understanding, of gladness and sorrow, by an exultant or gentle touch, is much less common. Yet the deeply meaningful physical touching of one person by another is for both a source of authentic being and joyous becoming. Much more transpires through touch than we recognize. A touch is always an exchange, if not a sharing. We grow through touch, and through touch *enable others to grow.*

Again, growth through touch experiences seems to take place more readily if undertaken in congenial company rather than in isolation. Touch is both a means of learning about the world around us (and learning about ourselves) and a way of communicating (don't we "keep in touch" with people?) .

As a result of sensory-awakening experiments with group members interested in actualizing their potentialities, a modus operandi for touch experiences has been developed. Again, touch experiences can be divided into categories:

A. With natural objects—wood, bones, leaves, stones, parts of twigs and branches, etc.
B. Cloth, fur, etc.
C. Artificial objects, i.e., plastic, iron, aluminun, etc.
D. Special effects—such as a piece of liver or semiliquids in a plastic bag, placticine studded with small rocks, etc.

As previously stated, agreement to have a touch experience must first be obtained from the group during an initial "consensus meeting." Members at that time can be asked to volunteer to provide touch experiences in specific categories. Again, flexibility is desirable; and it should be stressed that over and beyond the category for which a person is responsible, he may wish to use his creative capacities and prepare additional "offbeat" touch experiences for the group.

One of the most available receptacles for touch experiences is the large, brown grocery bag. It is better not to place more than five objects in one bag. Emphasis in the selection of objects should be not only on the surface or feel of the object, but also on the shape. In category C, artificial objects, and some of the other categories, it is better to avoid common or easily identifiable objects such as household implements, etc. We have found that it is stimulating if one or two "mixed bags" are supplied containing objects from different categories. However, the majority of bags should each contain *only one category* of objects.

To initiate the experience, one or both hands are inserted into the brown paper bag; and each object is explored separately using only the sense of touch. The purpose is *not* to identify the object *but to become keenly aware of the range of tactile sensations that occur while exploring the texture, shape and dimensions of the object.* Everyone should be encouraged to share freely his associations and memories while exploring objects by touch. *Fantasies should also be shared, and vividness of imagery and description should be strongly encouraged.*

A different type of touch experience can be initiated which has consistently produced excellent results: this is the use of finger paints while in a group. Users of the finger paints (a set can easily be obtained for a small sum at most variety stores) *are urged to focus on the tactile sensations associated with this experience and to pay particular attention to what goes on within them rather than focusing on the end product.* After completing their first sheet of paper using finger paints, participants beginning a new sheet can be urged to "do the opposite of what is your usual inclination—if you usually take little gobs of paint, now take big gobs—if you make circular or curvilinear marks with your finger on the page, make side-to-side movements—etc." To provide a varied tactile experience, each hand can be worked in a different rhythm; and knuckles, the backs of fingers, and the backs of the hands can be used. Selected background music also can be provided during this experience. *Participants should be encouraged to describe and share their feelings and to associate out loud while using finger paints. They should also share fantasies and memories at this time.*

Body massage is an interpersonal touch experience without peer and the royal road to sensory awakening. However, it must be *loving* body massage done with an understanding and a sensitive "feeling out" of the personality's massage and touch need *with the focus on developing individual potential.* This is vastly different from the impersonal meat-pounding, muscle-kneading efforts one encounters in many massage parlors.

Interpersonal touch experiences with group members often have considerable value as growth catalysts and growth stimulators. For example, participants can form a circle, either sitting or standing. They should then hold hands and observe a period of silence while having loving and compassionate thoughts about each other. Following this, group members can share the feelings engendered in them and explore the implications of this experience as related to their life philosophy and the meaning of existence.

It is also possible for group members to be paired (by choice or arbitrarily); they can then be asked to place their hands gently on the cheeks of the opposite partner, framing his face. The eyes are then closed. After a period of silence, partners share what was communicated by the other partner's touch. ("What did my touch say to you?" "How did it make you feel?" "What went on inside you?") *It is usually best to have an interpersonal touch experience after exploring the gamut of other touch experiences and only after complete group consensus has been reached to have an interpersonal touch experience.*

Our revitalized sense of touch at one and the same time helps us to be aware of our in-touch-ness and at-one-ness with all persons and things and with all being, while at the same time reaffirming our isolation and aloneness. To touch deeply means to let ourselves be touched deeply: it is a form of outreach and both a giving and a receiving.

A touch can also be a glance, a gesture, and a sound. We speculate that touch is an as yet unrecognized form of energy transmission between people. It is also a form of communication and a way of exploring the self and the world around us. Perhaps most fundamentally, through touch we are enabled to dissolve the barriers between us and others while demolishing the walls we have erected within ourselves.

UNFOLDMENT THROUGH TASTE

A sensory experience with taste can also yield some surprising results. As usual, consensus for such experience should be obtained; and, through the volunteer method, members should assume responsibility in the preparation for the experience. The use of spices offers a wide range of taste experiences. Members volunteering to provide taste experiences should place a good-sized pinch of each spice on a square of white paper, and these squares should then be numbered. A separate list should be kept of the number identifying each spice, as you may wish taste identification at the end of the meeting. (Health-food shops offer an amazing number of interesting taste objects such as dried kelp, dehydrated bananas, etc.) In order to clean the palate and to minimize the confusion of tastes, it is best to provide some bland cheese cut into squares, which can be used when needed.

In all instances, emphasis should be on letting oneself fully experience the taste sensation, minimizing outside distraction and interference. *Associations, memories, and fantasies should be shared, whereas identification of the taste sensation should play a secondary and minimal role.* It is best to flow with and in the experience and to let it lead you where it may.

Very simple "multiple taste experiences" can also be furnished. For example, a variety of breads (Jewish rye, Swedish bread, Bohemian bread, sourdough, etc.) can be cut or torn into small pieces and served with ordinary table salt. This is the age-old symbolic token of hospitality and friendship still used by many nations and tribes. Also effective has been the "taste exploration party" held by one group. Each group member brought a rare or novel taste experience to the group with the preferred emphasis on simplicity, i.e., a single taste object. Each member was pledged to secrecy not to reveal what he had brought. This secrecy was to be broken only at the conclusion of the total experience *and if indicated by group consensus.* To minimize identification, taste objects were served individually by group members (usually out of bags or carefully covered containers) with the admonition, "Close your eyes and open your mouth."

A truly amazing variety of taste experiences was offered and thoroughly enjoyed by each group member despite the revelation (after a consensus) that the taste objects included octopus, roasted grasshopper, smoked rattlesnake, etc. This experience successfully served to eliminate firmly established food prejudices in a number of members who admitted that they had enjoyed their experience and would never have tasted a given article had they known its identity.

The objective of a taste experience should always be to enlarge our tolerance for ambiguity, to open new doors of perception, to flow in and with an experience in an effort to lend new flexibility and new dimensions to the self-system. Many of the ideas and approaches to sensory awakening described in this article have been referred to as "kicks" by members of human potentialities groups. It is of interest that the designation "kicks" is characteristic of an underlying theme in a culture that retains strong puritanical elements. We must denigrate and devalue enjoyment by referring to it as kicks, i.e., receiving the boot, booting or kicking ourselves. *I would like to propose that we celebrate joy by using instead of the beat term "kicks," the word AFFIRMATION.* For joy is affirmation. It is life affirmation. We can thus say, "Let's do it for affirmation"—"like affirmation, man, affirmation." Affirmation, which is the positive acknowledgment of gladness, delight, and felicity, can be a road to growth and a means of unfoldment.

Touch, taste, and smell can be placed in the service of actualizing your potential. The world about you will be communicating with you in ways unknown before, and you in turn will be able to communicate more meaningfully to the world—thus you will have embarked on *growing* to achieve more of your potential.

6

Bernard Gunther

Sensory Awakening and Relaxation

Life is change, a flowing process in which nothing is ever the same. Even in ritual or routine there is never real duplication. So-called objects, people, and events are dynamic, subtle experiences, and only seem to be static because we tend to become excessively tense, to conceptualize, to freeze existence.

"Wake up—you're dreaming!" is one of the basic themes of all the Eastern ways of liberation. Much of this so-called dream is caused by desensitization—the inhibition of emotions through chronic muscular tension, and by the categorization of life through the misuse of language and imagination.

If you carefully observe your behavior, you will find yourself seldom making direct contact with reality, and much of the time conceptualizing your existence. By verbalizing, analyzing, and imagining, you filter the unique, evolving differences of each event. Most people react to new situations in established patterns, allowing past experience to dictate or color the actual. Rather than being in contact with what is, they continually operate from a frame of reference of how things were, how things should be, how they would like them to be.

Words ultimately become hypnotic conditioning, a series of expectations, leaving little possibility for the excitement of what might be or really is.

This is not to condemn language, which is a useful communicative tool, but only to recognize the imbalance that the educational system has produced in our society. Talking and thinking have become compulsive in many instances, a defense against feeling and the world.

Desensitization of the organism is caused by excessive muscular tension. What Wilhelm Reich called "body armor" is a way of avoiding intensive excitement and overwhelming emotions. Often started in childhood, this holding against reaction may at one time have been a semi-conscious mechanism that later became automatic. No longer serving any productive function, this defense against experiencing affect limits behavior and hinders many of the spontaneous functions of the organism. Obsessive thinking is in many instances a reflection of this withholding, producing a state of chronic self-consciousness. Numbing whole areas of the body, thereby inhibiting breathing and the flow of energy, often leaves the person with a feeling of dreamlike half-aliveness, of being separate from himself and the world.

Sensory awakening is a process that leads to heightened awareness, contact, and experience. Temporarily, at least, it allows the individual to let go of some of his defenses, experience the intensity of open experience and, to some extent, the potentialities that lie within. This process consists of different experiments designed to shift attention from symbolic or verbal interpretation to the actual. Too often people *think* they feel rather than feel. Ignoring primary processes, they freeze situations and themselves so that there is no sensory contact with the richness of each event.

Sensory awakening is a method for rebalancing the nonverbal aspects of the organism with the intellect, focusing attention on simple bodily functions. Some examples are relaxation, breathing, listening, movement and touch. These, used separately or in various combinations, help bring an individual back to his senses. By distributing attention throughout the organism rather than localizing it in the head, the person is often able to make contact with his muscular tension, to learn how he creates it, and experience what it is like to gradually let go.

Derived from many sources, sensory awakening is an amalgamation of sensory awareness, yoga, Gestalt therapy, and Zen Buddhism, among others.

The first step in the reawakening process is relaxation. Though only one of the basic aspects of sensory awakening, it is primary in the facilitation of experience. Because of the fundamental nature of relaxation, it will be the focal point of all the experiments done in this chapter. Try this experiment:

Close your eyes. Become aware that you are thinking, and for a few moments observe your thoughts. Then move out of the realm of conceptualization into the area of sensation and become aware of how you feel right now. Allow whatever comes. Make no choices. Stay with this awareness for at least thirty seconds. Keep your eyes closed. Feel what your feet are resting on without looking at or moving them; experience the chair you are sitting in; bring your attention into the tip of your nose. Try doing this not with your imagination but by coming into actual contact with these sensations. Now bring your eyeballs down to the bottom of your eyes. Let them remain there for approximately thirty seconds. Spend half a minute listening to the noises in the room you are in. Become aware of the air that surrounds your body, especially in the exposed areas: your hands, neck and face. Finally, experience the results of this experiment.

The preceding experiment is one of the many ways in which you allow yourself to let go of your tensions and relax. To be at ease is one of the basic states of existence. To be unable to obtain this balance is to be in chronic tension-disease.

Relaxation is not sleep or sagginess, which are but opposite poles of hypertension. Rather, to be relaxed is a state of aliveness in which there is only the necessary expenditure of energy desirable for optimum functioning. The best example is a cat, sitting at ease, completely alive, ready in an instant to spring into action. Even in movement, there is a lack of excessive tension, allowing the organism to operate with a minimal expenditure of energy.

To be at ease facilitates functioning, enhances health, increases learning, and permits a more joyous existence. When a person is relaxed, he expends only the amount of energy necessary to perform what he is doing. This not only allows him to carry out his activities more successfully, but conserves energy, which can be used for various other tasks or enjoyments. Being at ease, the entire body operates more effectively: the flow of blood is unhindered; nerves respond with alertness to each new situation. This openness makes any task easier, especially learning, and does not block or distract it by abnormal tightness. In fact, every activity is more pleasurable, because you are able to get with the experience rather than fight it.

The first step in learning how to relax is to become more aware of your tension. Tightness is a message telling you to "let go!" Yes, "telling you," for the next step is to become aware that it is you who are causing the tension. Though it may be done automatically, below the level of consciousness, it is still your own doing. The third phase of discovery is to find out how you hold and create these tensions: are you rigid in your chest? are you exerting too much pressure in your jaws? The final stage is to "let go." This is done best by not avoiding the tension but by experiencing it; moving toward and feeling it, *find out what it has to say to you.* If you really perceive and *allow*, the tightness will disappear.

This is one of the most natural and direct ways of working with tension. There are many others. It is important to know a number of different methods, since some people respond more to one approach than to another. Individual conditions, the nature and area of the "holding," are also important considerations.

When doing these experiments try not to expect certain results, even though you may get them. Each time you do the experiments, the experience will be slightly different, sometimes imperceptibly so. There are no correct or incorrect experiences.

The eyes are often a source of tension, quite subtle and unsuspected, affecting the entire organism. One of simplest ways to get rid of eyestrain is:

Lie down on your back or sit on a chair. Bring your consciousness into the area of your eyes; become aware of whatever feeling you have in this area without doing anything about it. After about thirty seconds of effortless concentration bring the palms of your hands over your eyes. The heels of your hands rest on your cheeks, your fingers over your forehead. The palms do not touch the eyelids; if you are sitting, rest your elbows on a table or on your knees. Remain in this position for a full minute, and then slowly remove your hands. Take about thirty seconds after each application to feel the result, allowing whatever may still want to develop in you as a result of this touch to manifest itself. It is desirable to repeat this process two or three times.

Seeing in our culture is too often replaced by staring: overfocusing rather than using peripheral vision, concentration on the figure to the exclusion of the background. In this manner of using our eyes we often miss more than we see. The eyes, like any other organ, operate best without unnecessary strain. To see is to allow, to be open.

Breathing is a very direct and useful method for relaxing the mind/body. When the breath is calm the organism is necessarily quiet. One of the most effective methods for the release of tension is:

Lie down and close your eyes (this experiment can be done in a seated position but is more effective lying down). Take a few moments to experience your body and its relationship to the floor. Now bring your attention to your breathing, and for a few moments become aware of how you are breathing. This is a passive process in which you make no effort to change; just watch and allow. After half a minute, place your hands on your upper chest, above the breasts, so that the palms are flat and the fingers of one hand do not touch the other. Feel the movement that goes on under your hands. After approximately one minute, take your hands away and slowly place them at your side. Take a few moments to experience the results of this touch. Then place your hands on the solar plexus, the area just above the navel. Become aware of what motion is taking place there. Again, after one minute put your hands slowly down at the side of your body and feel what is happening. Finally, place your hands on your lower belly, just inside of your frontal hip bones above the pubis. Experience what movement, if any, you feel in this area. Again, after a minute, bring your hands to the side of your body and become aware of how you feel.

Natural breathing is a function of the entire organism. It is not something that you have to do; rather, it is to be allowed. The oxygen/carbon-dioxide balance can have a great effect on how you experience the world. Minute changes can cause amazing differences in feeling and perception. As Gestalt therapy points out, holding your breath is one way to avoid emotion and excitement, but the price is the creation of anxiety.

Focusing your awareness on the breathing process is another valuable way to relax:

Sit or lie quietly. Note your breathing. Stay with the inhalation and exhalation. After a time, become aware of the pause between letting the air out and the next breath. Bring your awareness to your nostrils and experience the air as it moves in and out. Five or ten minutes spent in this silent meditation is sure to be effective.

Moving slowly is an easy way to let go. Try this:

Close your eyes and feel your hands; now, slowly stretch your fingers out as wide as they will go, like a cat stretching its paws. Use some pressure to go as wide as you can without its being in any way painful. Stay in this position for fifteen seconds. Then, very slowly, allow your fingers and hands to settle back where they want to go. Repeat three times. After each stretch, become aware of any change that may take place in you.

Large movements of the body are even more satisfying. An example:

Close your eyes and feel your shoulders. After taking a few minutes, slowly begin to hunch them as high as you can. This must be done in slow motion. When you reach the extreme position, hold the shoulders there for a few seconds, then slowly let them down. It is important to experience each aspect of the motion. Allow your shoulders to settle where it feels right for them to go. Experience the effects, taking plenty of time. Repeat the movement two or three times.

Hunching the shoulders in this way can produce not only a release of unnecessary holding but can improve posture as well.

Bending over slowly and reaching for the floor with your fingers may be done in conjunction with the last experiment or may be done separately. The point is to do it slowly and get the feel of it. It is not an exercise to be got over as quickly as possible or a contest to see how far down you can go:

Just close your eyes and let your body communicate to you where and how it would like to stretch. Don't rush into movement until you really feel it from the inside of you. Allow yourself to stretch as long as it feels desirable, permitting any sighs, moans or yawns that want to, to come out from within. Let your feelings indicate all the areas that want to be loosened. Periodically, take time to experience the effects of your stretching.

A fine method for combining stretching, relaxing, and keeping the wrinkles out of your face is a modification of the yoga exercise called the "lion." This yoga technique can be done in front of a mirror, though this is not necessary:

Lean slightly forward with your shoulders; allow your eyes to widen as much as possible. Open your mouth wide and stick your tongue out as far as you can. Don't be inhibited. Be ferocious! Tense and tighten the neck muscles and cords, as well as those in the face. Hold this position for fifteen to sixty seconds. Then, as slowly as possible, allow your face and neck to settle. Repeat two or three times.

This experiment will increase circulation and, if done correctly, will remove fatigue that has settled in the eyes. It is important to concentrate on slowly creating the tension and slowly letting go.

As children we are taught not to stretch, as it is not good manners. However, it is good biology. Stretching is a natural method for letting go of excessive stiffness and improving muscle tone.

Still another vehicle for letting go is sound. The following method is also effective in ridding oneself of minor muscular stiffness and is suited to being done in bed before rising:

Exhale completely. Take a deep breath, and, as you let the air out, make the sound "Eeee" as highly pitched as possible. Push the sound and air out through your mouth until you have completely exhausted that breath. Concentrate on feeling the vibrations centering in your head. After letting all the air out, allow a couple of natural breaths. Then, either repeat the "Eeee" sound once or twice more, or move on to the next sound, "Aaaa" (pronounce as in "play"). Concentrate on vibrations in the throat. Follow the instructions as given for the first sound. The next sound is "Aahh." Concentrate on the chest. Now move to the belly and make the sound "Om." The sound "Om" requires a little more attention because it is divided into two syllables. The "Oohh" uses the first half of the breath while the "Mmmm" uses the second half. The final sound is "Uuuu" (pronounce as in "true"). It is to be felt in the region of the hips.

These sound vibrations cause a massagelike effect over the entire organism. Strong exhalation cleanses the respiratory system of residual air, creating deeper breathing, and brings an entirely new supply of fresh air into the lungs.

A gentle touch is a most soothing experience. A sensitive laying on of hands will produce relaxation in the area touched and will be felt throughout the body. It is important to touch substantially, but without excessive pressure. Allow the hands to remain for some time. When removing the hands, it is essential to move away as slowly as possible. Though most parts of the body lend themselves to a gentle/firm touch, the head and shoulders are particularly well suited to this experiment:

Place your hands easily on some area of the body. For this example we will use the back. Let your hands remain on the back for about a minute. It is important not to talk during the experiment. Take your hands away as slowly as you can. Wait a few seconds for the effects of this touch to become complete. Then, make another application, making contact in the same place or some other part of the back, with another completion of this touch and a rest period. Finally, make a third touch, and sense this experience.

The preceding experiments are not just words about relaxation; they are methods. If you are willing to take the time to do them, they will help you to remember something that you already know but have forgotten: how to let yourself go and *be*—relaxed.

Comments from students about these experiments range from "I haven't been this relaxed in years." to "I feel at one with everything." Some experimenters indicate heightened feelings of warmth, brighter colors, sharper images. "I feel in the floor, rather than on it." is not an uncommon reaction. "I feel more natural, the way I would like to all the time." is another. "Nothing special," beamed a knowing Zen student after one class, understanding this open living to be his birthright.

Psychologists and patients have expressed the feeling that these experiments would facilitate the therapeutic process. Indications in both individual and group work have been most gratifying. Educators, too, have felt the possibilities of this work as an enhancement to learning. Writers and artists have found the experiments stimulating to the creative process.

The results of this work are seldom permanent. The experiments do, however, allow the individual temporarily to experience the vast possibilities of his organism, pointing out a direction in which to work. For these exercises to be ultimately rewarding, they must be done more than as experiments; they must become an integral part of daily living. At each moment, tension or relaxation reflects your basic attitude toward life and yourself—whether you are for or against, asleep or awake.

7

Gerhard Neubeck

Sex and Awareness

Lovesong[1]

How shall I withhold my soul so that
it does not touch on yours? How shall I
uplift it over you to other things?
Ah willingly would I by some
lost thing in the dark give it harbor
in an unfamiliar silent place
that does not vibrate on when your depths vibrate.
Yet everything that touches us, you and me,
takes us together as a bow's stroke does,
that out of two strings draws a single voice.
Upon what instrument are we two spanned?
And what player has us in his hand?
O sweet song.

We are what we are, endowed on the one hand with the most sensitive nerve endings and the most potent muscular force driving us to orgasm, to the time and time again exquisite explosion of our physical energies, and on the other hand with a most complex brain that generates vast amounts of thought proc-

---

[1] *Translations from the Poetry of Rainer Maria Rilke*, New York: W. W. Norton & Company, 1938.

esses without any appreciable interruption. What women and men have to do with each other sexually is governed by the results of this interaction. Freud described the process in terms of id, ego and superego, but no matter what one uses for a conceptual framework the intricate relationships between "body and soul" are a matter of fact, even if the facts are not too well understood—and they are not.

So to learn about sexuality in the "how to" manner, that is, what nerve endings are meeting other nerve endings, is learning as little as the idea that sexual behavior is a function of an emotional quality called love or of a spiritual quality called sacrament.

But we must make one assumption when we discuss sexuality, and that is that we talk about it as sexual relations between a man and a woman—leaving out homosexuality here—and that these behaviors are more than self-gratifyingly oriented. To make love is the act in which both are making love to each other. Not only does one "get laid," "they are getting laid," "they are making it with each other," there is a contract of sorts so that they are using each other for their own purposes but are also interested in each other's purposes. The line of demarcation is not always well defined between where one's satisfactions are primarily or solely for oneself and where one's satisfactions come in addition by satisfying the other. Harry Stack Sullivan said that "lust implies a willingness to destroy the other for the satisfaction of the self, whereas love implies a willingness to destroy the self for the satisfaction of the other," and on another occasion defined love as, "inner acceptance of the interests of another as being as much my interests as are my own interests." This may be going to extremes, but the Talmud says, "If I am not for myself, who is for me, but if I am only for myself, who am I? . . ."

That much I must assume then for my readers. In this context, I am writing about those who are not, in Lester Kirkendall's sense, "commodity-oriented." Commodity-oriented individuals simply desire some form of sexual excitation for themselves and try to obtain it from any possible source. They do not care much about other personal factors; their sole interest is in a steady supply and flow of sexual goods.

The dispenser of these sexual services is divorced from total humanness, neglecting, not sensing, not experiencing—either by design or by default—feelings, desires, of the other. Kirkendall rightly looks at this problem by examining the communication process, and observes that in the commodity-oriented sexual episode, participated in by either two such commodity-oriented persons, or just one, there is a minimum of verbal exchange. In this case then the contact between human beings is to the largest degree a nerve-ending one. What each touches in the other are the physiological tips.

I am writing about those who are, again in the Kirkendall sense, person-oriented; those who are aware of, conscious of the fact that (1) sexual responses in humans are linked to other mental and psychological processes and do not take place in a vacuum, and (2) the other person is not simply a dispenser but a participant whose total humanness is to be respected in and out of the context of the actual sexual episode.

If this sounds very ideal, I know that persons behave differently at different times, that our needs and our commitments fluctuate; but it is necessary to set some basic structure into which sexuality can be placed. This then is written about those who most of the time are person-oriented in their sexual encounters.

So there you are and here am I. What do you sense? How am I in your awareness? You hear me with your ears, you talk to me with your voice, you see me with your eyes, you feel me in your nerve endings, you smell me with your nose. But you also take in an "all of me" in some form or another, sometimes more consciously than at other times, and your brain computes all of these impressions into some formula that brings forth some action. And this goes on uninterruptedly for both you and me. How rich we are, having been endowed with this equipment of excitation, this storehouse of sensations, this arsenal of awareness. But how do we use it? How well have we been trained to make use of these riches, to understand them, refine them, mobilize them, propel them into action?

First of all, we differ in the ways in which these sense organs have developed. For some there may have been physical impairment or extremely slow development. But even considering that, we must understand to what a large degree our practices are a function of our upbringing and our learning.

Take demonstrativeness in physical affection, for example. When I compared groups of Scandinavians with American college students,

I found the Scandinavians to be less demonstrative. It was apparent that Danes, Swedes and Norwegians received less physical loving from their parents than Americans—less hugging, kissing and touching. Unfortunately, I did not study verbal affection, though my impressions are that the Scandinavian parents are less affectionate in this area as well.

It is likely that Americans differ among themselves in the way that sense organs are utilized. Our social and cultural background undoubtedly has produced different patterns of affection—but nothing needs to remain static.

So you and I who are in encounter come with our senses in motion—our senses as they have been conditioned over time which, if we speak about today, includes time of our previous encounters. From these experiences we have gained some knowledge that enables us to make some predictions about each other. When I look at you with that tiny crook in my smile at 10:30, when I put down the book, you receive a message, don't you, and you comprehend the message, don't you, and you can predict that the day will end in a union. There are many kinds of messages that contain sexual agreements: some quite obvious, some even more subtle than the one just mentioned. There is much comfort in this predictability but also a seed of trouble; that we are too complacent and take things for granted. For those of us who need departures from routines, changes from well-established patterns, some ambiguities may need to be introduced that will necessitate clarification and the invention and introduction of new signals and cues. Yet we remember how painful were our first fumbling sexual encounters, when we had misread messages, or found that ours were misread and our sexual senses, poised for fulfillment, were thwarted.

But now we have learned. We have learned how to hear, how to speak, how to see, how to feel, and how to smell. We know because we have slowly and painfully, but also joyfully, taught each other. And we taught each other by using words. We had made up our minds that we needed a vocabulary that would develop better understanding of each other's psychological and physiological makeup, our fantasies, our thoughts and bodies. Words, words, words. Where were they hidden, where had they been overlooked? I learned the laboratory and the locker-room language, and you had read Henry

Miller and listened to your gynecologist; but with each other why did we hesitate to use words we had learned—to recall their meanings? Why was our tongue so reluctant while our face was so flushed? But we had made up our minds, and so we tried. To say "your nipples" was much easier the tenth time around and hardly an effort the twentieth. To you, "That's a pretty prick" was almost impossible to pronounce at first (even though you had been thinking it for a long time). But after all, there were more ecstasies to come and opportunities to repeat. So we learned. Some of our words were borrowed from the locker room—they gave us a bit of a thrill at first when we had mastered them but succumbed to the dulling process of repetition after a while. Some we invented, but we tried to make sure that we both understood their meanings. We were learning how to say the words that contained sexual meaning, and we learned to hear those words. Our lives became somehow more complete. We had opened up avenues to each other that had been blocked, avenues ready for use but through which we had not been able to reach each other. When we saw that film where the man's legs were outside the girls's legs—and that is all the screen showed—we could say to each other afterwards that "it seemed that she was going to get a good shot at her clitoris." And also that there was to be a similar occasion later on in our evening.

And we learned the seeing. Here we both started from the beginning. Our childhood rested heavily on our eyelids. Nakedness was not the mode in either your or my home. Nudity is all around us today, and it takes no great courage to look at pictures. In fact, many of us get feelings of excitement from looking at bodies, half dressed or undressed; the follies, the striptease shows, the Playboy girls, the out-and-out pornographic scenes. (Of course, there seems to be a sex difference here, since men enjoy stages of undress in women more than women do in men.) All these seem to provide some thrill of a commodity nature; but you and I, here in our charming chamber, are having a tough time opening our eyes to see the forbidden territory of bosoms, bellies and balls. Our sexual excursions had taken place in the dark (remember the wedding night we even went into the closet to take our clothes off?). While they turned out to be pleasant enough, after a while I wanted to see, and asked you if you would mind keeping the light on. And you said you did mind, but then on that Sunday morning the sun peeked through the curtains; and you didn't suggest blindfolding, and there we were, peeking. There was a hesitancy to look up and down and left and right, and vision would be blurred unless we could focus on a tiny detail at a time. But we widened our vision, and after a while the curves and the elevations, the valleys and the grooves, the hair and the skin, the color and the angles became familiar landmarks that remained in our consciousness at lingering speeds or at a hundred miles an hour.

Even more difficult was it to look each other straight in the eye. It seemed at first a terrible, accusing look we gave each other. After a while this yielded to a kind of conspiratory smile and then to an exchange of looks carrying a message of contentment or joy or relaxation or excitation or disappointment, according to the moods we produced. So we trained our eyes, sometimes to roam, sometimes to rest, sometimes to thunder, sometimes to soothe. Seeing is believing, all right, but seeing is also extending the genital thrusts into the optical realm.

Touching was one of our easier tasks. After all, some touching we had practiced all along. Lips do meet when we kiss, nipples come in contact with nipples when we embrace, and I have brushed by your fanny in a playful moment. Some touching has become perfunctory, and the nerve endings in our fingers hardly notice the impact of touching skin any more. But do you remember how excited you became when I touched your wrist when we first were lovers? Some dulling has taken place; but when we have initiated a period of sex, our nerve endings are tensing up marvelously; and there are many places that welcome you, your finger, your mouth, your toe, your elbow, your chin. My ears and my lips, my bottom and my thighs, you have found those places all right; you have wandered as I have wandered, and explored and found grounds of glorious sensations everywhere. Not all of us are that lucky; some of us are less sensitive in these nerve endings; but luckily for us your body is full of responsive spots and I, too, have my share. You never did slap my hands, but in the beginning you thought my finger to be naughty until you trusted it to be a part of me, of the all of me. These individual contacts of our flesh are the prelude to the final movement of orgasm. The uniting of our bodies makes the "one flesh" out of us; and the synchronized vibration momentarily makes us lose our individuality, and we are truly in touch.

And smelling. Here our training did not help at all. Odors came from decomposition and decay, and they were bad. Some foods, however, delighted our noses; and those smells we learned to call "fresh" we associated with pleasantness. There was Mother's perfume and Dad's after-shave lotion, for instance. Also, deodorants were introduced into our personal hygiene to cover up, erase and avoid body odors, which our nostrils were trained to revolt against. Yet our glands are part of us, and what you excrete affects me. It is impossible to be neutral about it. You are there—I can smell you. But we also differ in our reactions. Sour sweat offends me, it pleases you; pubic odors excite us both. Other men and women have different responses from you and me.

But when we breathe the air of each other, it does "send" us. What did the troops in "South Pacific" sing longingly, "Nothing stinks like a dame"? Men should add, "and we stink the same." We found out then what was pleasing to us and what was offending, and we came to appreciate finally that these full-bodied odors came from bodies that we knew were good and that belonged to us. "Humani nihil a me alienum puto," said the Latins. Freely translated, this means, "I accept all of your humanness, or nothing of you is not acceptable."

So we are what we are what we are. But we are never the same. No matter how well we have trained ourselves, sometimes our senses seem to pick up nothing, our antennae are receiving very fuzzy messages, and our radar system goes on the blink. But our intellect also has days of dullness; that cerebral machine will sputter and misfire. The next day, though, our senses are working again, and my touch will again "send" you, send you into a state of openness into which I can come, into which you will receive me.

Our practice has paid off most of the time; yet there are moments when our surroundings seem to stifle us, and lovemaking has lost its appeal for the time being. By "appeal" it may be taken that it has lost its novelty, its freshness—is there such a thing as compulsive copulation? Our bodies are meeting because that's the way it has been and not because we are seeking each other's substance. We were next to each other, yet we did not feel close; we united, but only parts of us made a connection. Sometimes we were too rushed or under too much outside pressure and strain, so that most of our senses had no time to fully extend, and only the sexual organs expanded into some external ecstasy that left the rest of us behind.

What a relief then to move into a quiet place where we could block out the rest of the world and be exposed only to each other. What a marvelous feeling, this concentration on just you, as if I wore blinders that restricted my senses to you, a center of saliency—and the total spectrum, while undoubtedly around you, could not be perceived. We had time then to try to see what we had not looked at before, to say what had not been spoken, to stroke what had not been touched. This is called play. No great pressures, no competition, just a meandering along a road of pleasantries, stopping here to relax, turning off there to explore, and returning again to the journey that leads to our ultimate accord. Sometimes there are detours and sometimes we end up at a dead end. Yesterday you seemed untouchable; and tomorrow we may, either of us, be moved to adventure. But we know that there are other tomorrows when we will again be curious for each other's texture, and our meeting will run its course.

To know—we understand the biblical term now—is to understand intellectually and to perceive sensually. It is total impact; it is complete integration. So you and I have grown away from our mere selves, separated by physical distance, to a togetherness of alert responsiveness so that, at any time, you and I may move to each other, onto and into each other.

We are what we are, a complex system of thinking and feeling. But we don't need to be alone. Luckily for us, most of the time we are ready to feel and communicate, so that we can bridge that distance. You shall have all of me, and I shall have all of you.

8

Herbert A. Otto

Developing Family Strengths and Potential

I

A number of exciting methods designed to strengthen the family have been developed as a result of a research project in human potentialities conducted at the University of Utah. The methods have been field tested in experimental programs for five years, and families have been exceptionally enthusiastic about using these methods.

Early in the research it was discovered that every family has latent strengths or capacities which are not being used, and that in many instances family members are unaware of these resources. Every family has a large *family potential*, which can be identified and used for more creative and productive family functioning. Just as families are able to plan and follow through with outings and special events, such as birthdays or vacations, so *families can develop family strengths on a planned basis combining the best elements of thoughtful selection and spontaneity.*

Research has disclosed that very few families ever undertake a systematic evaluation of their strengths and resources. Conversely, families are much more aware of problems and difficulties than of their capacities and potentials. It was one of the early discoveries in this work that, if a family began to look at its strengths and potentials, *this process in itself was experienced as strengthening.* Using these newly developed methods families were also able to identify strengths and family resources of which they had been unaware. Not only does the discovery of such hidden strengths often result in a feeling of accomplishment and satisfaction, but the identification of strengths has a positive effect on the self-image of the family and enhances family pride and functioning.

Before using any of the methods to be described parents and children should acquaint themselves with all the methods. This can be done by means of a "family round table" during which each method is briefly summarized and discussed. *One method is selected that would be most fun for all concerned and in the judgment of all will "do the most for the family."* In the event opinions differ as to which method (or "action program") would "do the most for the family," select the one that would be *most fun* or enjoyable. Activities that are enjoyed are most likely to be repeated, and families get most out of the methods and action programs when they enter into the experience in the spirit of adventure and fun. Once the family has decided to develop family strengths and potential it is important to remember that the emphasis should always be on *nurturing creative imagination and spontaneity.* The mother of one family, for example, reported: "We had a good time discussing what we would do and had just about reached a decision. Our five-year-old, who had not said a word, spoke up at this time with a different suggestion. At first we laughed at him and were ready to override him. Then my husband said, 'It's an original idea and it's different. Let's look at it.' The upshot was that everyone thought that with a little change it was the best plan, and we adopted it. Was Jimmy proud! But, if my husband had not remembered the instructions about spontaneity and creativity, we would never have listened to Jimmy, because we had made up our minds what to do before he spoke up."

It is best to find out if the family is interested in having an adventure in developing family strengths at a time when everyone is in reasonably good spirits and not tired out by a long day's work or play. Generally family-strength sessions should be less than an hour in length, and it is best to stop the session while the interest is still high. This assures a readiness and eagerness to resume the experience at some future convenient time. Finally, it is helpful if one member of the family will take responsibility in providing leadership and general direction during the first strength experience together. Another member may wish to volunteer to do this for the next session.

II

Research has disclosed that very few families ever sit down together to take a look at family strengths and resources; it has also been found that *this process is in itself strengthening*.

Taking inventory is quite simple. There are three steps to taking inventory of family strengths:

1. The family sits down together; someone gets a pencil and a piece of paper and volunteers to write down the strengths. The question is then asked, "What strengths do we see in our family?" Everyone is encouraged to participate and to contribute any idea, however wild, that may have something to do with strengths and the family. If children are too small to understand what is meant by "family strengths," the following question can be used: "What are all the things that make us glad to be a member of this family?" Problems and shortcomings are not brought up at this time, and any such discussions are gently but firmly discouraged.

As family members call out strengths, these are written down using the exact words of the person as nearly as possible. A list of family strengths is compiled. Sometimes an element of friendly rivalry can be injected by asking family members to compete to see who can think of the most family strengths.

2. When it becomes difficult to think of further strengths, the next step is reading the list. Following the reading of the list, everyone is urged to say what he considers to be *the most important family strength and to give reasons for his choice*.

3. As a final step, the following question is discussed: "What additional family strengths do we need to develop?" (or "Which of these strengths do we want to develop further?") A separate list of these is made and forms the basis for action programs.

Family strengths are found in relation to many areas. In the Otto Family Strength Survey,[1] developed to aid this general process, fifteen such areas are identified. They are:

1. Strength through family physical and other resources
2. Family traditions
3. Family participation in local and national events
4. Fostering curiosity and interest
5. Family recreation and leisure time
6. Meeting family emotional needs
7. Building friendships and relationships
8. Providing an environment of honesty and integrity
9. Child-rearing practices and discipline
10. Spiritual life
11. Developing creativity
12. Relations with relatives
13. Giving encouragement
14. Family management
15. Other family strengths

III

One of the most successful methods for developing family strengths is through action programs. After the family has taken inventory, they may wish to discuss which particular strengths should be developed further. Once a specific strength area has been selected, everyone is invited to submit ideas about what the family, individually or as a whole, can do to build further strengths in relation to this area.

Action programs are any planned activities or experiences that the family undertakes to build or develop a particular family

---

[1] The Otto Family Strength Survey is designed to help families gain a clearer idea of the range of their strengths in relation to fifteen strength areas including a total of 106 strength items. The survey is filled in by the whole family together and is especially useful in the identification of latent or hidden strengths.

strength. The essence of this method is contained in the two words *planned* and *action;* a family does not develop strengths by sitting around the table talking about them but by making plans for concrete ways to develop strengths and translating these plans into action. For example, a family may decide that creativity as a family strength should be developed further. They may then decide on ways to put into effect one of the following action program ideas:

A. Husband and wife help each other to discover the hidden creative capacities and creative sparks present in every person. Husband and wife help to find these creative sparks in children.

B. The family spends a series of weekends exploring whether they can have fun by painting, using clay, carving wood, making jewelry, playing music, etc.

C. Specific fields of art are explored through museum visits; discussing art, craft, or hobby books together, etc.

D. The family recognizes and explores the implications of the fact that a person can be an artist in human relations.

E. Specific ways and means are discussed to encourage the expression of creativity at home or at work.

F. The family discusses and plans concrete ways through which the creative spark in every family member can be nurtured and brought to further flowering.

It is by means of working out and following through with a specific set of action programs that outstanding gains have been made by families in developing further strengths and resources. To illustrate the range of possible action programs that might be undertaken, a series of additional action program ideas are presented in relation to a few of these areas. Action program ideas are kept general so that families can work out individual and unique ways of implementing these ideas through planned action.

The importance of action programs cannot be overestimated. To undertake action programs means that the family is willing to become actively engaged in the process of building strengths. Although it might be helpful to talk about family strengths, planned action and effort are more likely to lead to positive change and growth. Action programs are one of the most valuable means available for tapping family potential.

IV

Extensively tested, "strength bombardment" is of particular value in helping family members to obtain increased self-confidence, self-esteem and self-assurance. The method also contributes to the formation of stronger family ties, as various family members in turn participate in the unique and deeply moving experience of having their strengths recognized. As one mother noted, "The bombardment helped me to get a more well-rounded picture of myself and to discover some strengths I never thought I had. But, above all, it made me feel how much I am really appreciated."

Strength bombardment is voluntary, and no one is forced to participate as a "target person." The process of strength bombardment is first explained in detail. It is usually best for one member of the family to be in charge, explaining strength bombardment and directing the process. After the directions are clearly understood, all those wishing to participate as target persons write their names on a slip of paper which is folded and dropped into a hat. (Children too small to write can make their mark on a slip of paper.) A person is blindfolded and asked to draw a slip from the hat. The one whose name is drawn is the first target person.

The target person begins the process by telling everyone what he sees as his strengths. (With smaller children the wording can be used, "What do you like about yourself?") When he has finished listing his strengths, the target person should turn to the group using the following or similar words: "What other strengths do you see that I have?" *Strength bombardment does not begin until the target person has thus asked the family group to start the process.* All now begin to bombard the target person with what they see as his strengths, abilities, capacities, assets, resources, talents, etc. The discussion of weaknesses or problems is firmly discouraged. Small children participate freely if asked to tell what they like about the target person or by using such questions as: "Why do you think he is nice?" or "Why do you like him?" Bombardment should be as spontaneous and free-flowing as possible, with everyone calling out strengths as they see them.

When the bombardment is slowing down and when everyone

present has contributed all the strengths he sees in the target person, the person in charge asks, "Can anyone think of any further strengths?" If no further strengths are forthcoming, he can suggest: "Now that we have seen John (or Mary) as having all these strengths, let's have a dream (or fantasy) about him (or her). What do we see John (or Mary) doing five years from now if he (or she) uses all these strengths?" *Everyone in the family is encouraged to use his imagination freely in this shared dream or fantasy.* Sometimes the deepest wishes and dreams the target person has about himself are mentioned, and he is encouraged to work toward the realization of these goals. The target person can then be asked, "What is your own dream for yourself five years from now? What do you see yourself doing if you were to use all these strengths?" With this shared dream the strength bombardment comes to an end, and the name of another person is drawn from the hat.

It is advisable that only two or at the most three persons be bombarded at one time and that other family members wait until a subsequent occasion. Bombardment should be conducted in a spirit of fun and adventure for the whole family, and refreshments can provide a festive touch.

V

This again is a voluntary method, and only those volunteering should have strength roles assigned to them. The method is first explained in detail by a family member who takes responsibility for directing "strength-role assignment." In this as with other methods it is important that the family enter into the process in a spirit of adventure, enjoyment, and relaxation.

Each person wishing to participate in the method should write his name or make his mark on a slip of paper. Before drawing a name, the person in charge should carefully explain that the purpose of strength-role assignment is not to correct a person's shortcomings, weaknesses, or problems by asking this person to do something he may not wish to do; the purpose of the method is *for everyone to help the person to work out a strength role that he will enjoy carrying out and that will strengthen him.*

The person whose name has been drawn should ask the family the key question: "What are some of the roles that you think would strengthen me most?" (It is best to have older children and grown-ups volunteer first. With smaller children leave the initiative entirely to them, i.e., let them ask to be included in the process.) After the key question has been asked, everyone should contribute his ideas as to what role would most strengthen the person. The following are examples of strength roles:

1. You are a person with a good sense of humor, who likes to tell jokes, recite, and entertain people.

2. You are a very honest person, who never holds back the truth as he sees it. You are completely honest with people.

3. You are a very kind person, able to give much love, affection, and understanding to everyone. You go out of your way to anticipate their needs and do things for them.

4. You are thoughtful and somewhat retiring. You like to deliberate and think about matters carefully.

5. You are outgoing and extroverted. You like to share your ideas and thoughts and to take the initiative.

6. You are very alive and spontaneous. You like to do things on the spur of the moment, and you share your ideas and your feelings freely.

7. You are a very creative (artistic) person who thinks up new ways of doing things (or who lends touches of beauty to the home and the times the family has together) .

Strength roles should be made up and tailored to the specifications and needs of the person to whom the role is assigned. A wide variety of choices is possible, limited only by the imagination and perceptiveness of those present. All members of the family should participate as much as possible in discussing the strength-role assignment of a member. However, *his wishes should prevail in deciding on the assignment.* He should *want* to enter into the strength role assigned to him and should be able to enjoy the role. Coercion or forcing a strength role on a person through family pressure should never be attempted.

Assigning strength roles is most effective for adults and children eight years or older, although smaller children can participate successfully if their limitations are recognized.

Strength roles are discussed with a person in detail, and *particular actions and behavior characteristic of the assigned strength role should be spelled out in detail.* One member of the family can be asked to take notes and should list each individual strength-role assignment together with behavior and actions characteristic of a specific role on a separate sheet of paper. The sheet of paper that lists specific behaviors and actions is then given to the person to whom the strength role has been assigned. For example, Strength Role #1, "a person with a good sense of humor," might have the following list of behaviors and actions:

1. Tells jokes at mealtime and whenever possible.
2. Helps others see the humor in a situation.
3. Laughs often and gets others to laugh.

It is well to limit assignment of strength roles to one or two members at a time. Strength roles are "lived" or followed by family members for a two- or three-day period. At the end of the agreed-upon time, the family meets together and discusses the high points of the experience. It is of value to discuss the following questions at this time: How did it make you feel to carry out the strength role? In what ways has it helped you? How do others see it has helped you to make better use of your strengths? Emphasis is on the gains and the positive aspects of the experience, *and criticism is discouraged.*

Strength-role assignment can be repeated if two weeks or longer are allowed to elapse before the method is again employed.

After trying some of the described methods, families find it fun to develop their own variations and original ideas, which serves to strengthen the family functioning. A new spirit of family fun, adventure, and growth can be developed through the use of new methods. Compatible families of relatives, friends, or close neighbors can also be invited to participate. This serves not only to deepen relationships, *but the recognition of diverse and differing strengths in the families leads to an exciting cross-pollination of ideas and efforts.* Developing family strengths can be an absorbing and vital adventure—a journey into happier and more productive times together.

[9]

Gerard Haigh

The Residential
Basic Encounter
Group

The residential basic encounter group can provide
a setting within which intensive personal growth
may occur. Participants often describe personal
impacts of profound significance. The results suggest
the value of exploring what happens in these groups,
with the possibility of discovering principles that
might be applied to other situations for enhancing
their growth potential. I will attempt to explore the
dynamics of a residential basic encounter group by
presenting and discussing the typescript of a critical
incident that occurred in one.

The incident constitutes an intensive crisis both
in the life of the participant centrally involved and
in the life of the group. Condensed within this
incident can probably be found most of the major
forces operating within residential basic encounter
groups for fostering change in behavior and
experience.

This incident occurred at the end of the first week

of a two-week sensitivity-training laboratory.[1] The group of fourteen people had completed a twelve-hour marathon that had ended at 9:00 P.M. Ella, the central figure in the growth experience, had been an active participant during the marathon. Near the end of it she had talked of her own need to be mothering to her two boys and her sense of being lost from contact with her own mother. The group dispersed with instructions to get some rest and to return at midnight for a feedback session on each person's experience during the marathon. After a few people had given reports, the group leader became aware of Ella's trembling and crying softly. She began to talk in a quavering voice that was almost inaudible. As she spoke, her voice slowly gained a little strength. There were many long pauses, many sighs, many periods of crying, most of which have been captured in the following typescript:

Ella: (very low, almost inaudible) It's almost too much to open my mouth. I feel drained. Not anything. Breakfast seems like such a long time ago. I feel like I've been on a long journey. I don't know where. (voice quavering) I keep thinking of the image of going through the bowels of the earth. (long pause) I stopped in the lounge on the way down here. I wanted to see Al or somebody I knew away back then . . . I felt as if I'd been gone such a long time. (pause) It was almost as if I didn't know where I was or even . . . He said I looked like a little girl, and I felt like I was. I was looking for somebody to run to . . . And I feel like I'm looking for that person I left back there this morning. I need to make some kind of contact . . . It's a very strange thing and I don't know how to describe it. It's as if, you know, I'm at one end and I'm at the other end and I'm trying to get together with myself . . . Does that make sense?

Leader: Who are the two different people, Ella? Who are the different parts of you?

Ella: Well, the very violent person who was talking this afternoon . . .

  (Joe arrives, interruption takes a few minutes.)

Leader: The part of you you have to get back with the old part of you is the new violent part.

Ella: That seems to be it. (long pause) I can't find any words.

---

[1] Western Training Laboratory, Lake Arrowhead, July 1965.

Leader: Mmh. Can you express how you are feeling? Are you feeling kind of lost?

Ella: Yeah, I feel kind of lost. Usually I can think in images and words . . .

Leader: What kind of images?

Ella: Everything seems sort of dark inside . . . I felt like, I was trying to tell Al, I was walking in slow motion. It's unreal, there's something unreal about me right now . . . And I . . . He didn't understand and . . . I couldn't make much contact with him either. He was trying but he didn't understand. (tears)

Leader: Is it frightening to you?

Ella: (pause) Yes . . . It's awfully dark . . . The sky seems so far away tonight. (crying) I didn't want to start all over again tonight. I was thinking in terms of theory and trying to make some sense about all this . . .

Leader: What if you let yourself go into the darkness for a while?

Ella: I guess this morning when I came, I had this sort of exhilarated feeling like Jean did. Like I was going to ask . . . I did, didn't I? I asked you all to hold hands with me. I felt very strong and sure of myself, and I was going to go into that underbrush again so that I could see the sun at the other end. And I knew where I was going although it was a gray morning and I hadn't been there for years. It was pretty well covered over. But I knew where I was going, and I wanted all of you to come with me . . . (sigh) I think I lost my way . . . I can't see the sun. Sorry (crying) . . . I wasn't going to do this tonight, I was going to talk very sensibly and not get all emotional . . .

Leader: When did you get lost, Ella?

Ella: I'm not sure when. I told you that I kept losing or not being able to concentrate, not being able to follow things that were going on around here. And I thought it was because I was tired and couldn't concentrate. But I don't know, I seem like . . . I think, now that I look back, it's almost as if I went on ahead too fast and I kind of lost you.

Leader: Where were you? Where did you go?

Ella: It was dark. My mind was dark. And everything was so clear to me this morning. I knew the whole process of what we were doing and where we were going and . . . I think I'm stuck back somewhere.

Leader: Do you think that the darkness had anything to do with trying to find your mother?

Ella: . . . I lost her so long ago. I don't know where I lost her. (crying) I don't know . . . She was such a . . . I get little, quick images of her. She was . . . she always seemed so sad, and yet she was always smiling. And I can see her smiling . . . And I'd feel sorry for her . . . She was so lost . . . Why don't one of you start talking? (crying)

Alice: Would you rather put this away for a while, Ella?

Dotty: (comes over to sit beside Ella) You said you had a lot of mothering to do. That was how you finished up. You wanted to go back and pick up.

Ella: I don't know how. I don't know how I can be a mother. She never taught me how.

Dotty: I want very much to hold you close but I don't know if you want me to. (puts her arms around Ella)

Ella: She never helped me. I don't ever remember kissing her . . . I can remember one time when I was in high school I went to the library and she seemed so lonely. I thought maybe she would like to read as much as I do. We had a small library and they had a collection of books from other countries, and I picked out two books for her . . . She tried to read them . . . I guess they just didn't interest her or something . . . She really was awfully lost. (sigh) . . . She didn't know English very well. She was very friendly and everybody loved her. (sigh) . . . She never gave in. She never complained, she seemed to take things . . . I don't remember her, well once or twice, she got very exasperated with me. I remember she spanked the hell out of me once (laugh) when I was about four because I wandered off and got the kids lost and myself lost . . . She's starting to come alive to me again . . .

Leader: Does it seem quite as dark as she starts to come alive?

Ella: No. No. I remember her coming home in the morning after an all-night dance. I must have been about four or five and she seemed so happy . . . She was. I think she really had a good time. I was so pleased. And I wish she had gone on having good times . . . We used to clean the house together when I was small. I was the oldest, so she and I would do all the housework together . . . She taught me how to embroider . . . She made such beautiful things with her hands. She used to sew my clothes and make all sorts of things for the house. She would give me things all the time . . . I couldn't talk to her, but I knew she loved me because she always brought something home for us even if she just went to the five and ten. (crying) . . . She was lonely when I was young, when I was little, but she was sort of peaceful, too. She wasn't in any great turmoil. I guess it was me, how I felt, you know, that she ought to be miserable and unhappy. But she was very peaceful. I'd come home after school and look for her. I didn't like coming home from school if she wasn't there. She used to make bread . . . When I came home there'd be hot bread and butter . . . The kitchen was so bright and it smelled so good. (sigh) She was a good mother. (sigh) I lost touch with her as I got older. I guess that was it. I started going away from her and wanting to be something different . . . I wanted to go places and do things. And suddenly she was caught in a trap. And I put her there, sort of. She was so helpless. I don't know how she ever survived. I mean she wasn't, she could do things, she wasn't helpless in that way, but she was so gentle. (sigh) And I was in such a hellish turmoil. Stupid adolescence. And I wanted to go places and I wanted to do things, and I wanted to leave home. Everything I wanted, she didn't understand what the hell hit me. So the more restless I got, the more confused she got, and the more my father pulled the reins. And so I was straining to get out, and I turned on her because she wasn't standing up for me enough. And I . . . She and my father had a pretty good relationship going. And I sort of pulled them apart, I think . . . Because she wanted me to do what I wanted within reason, and yet she couldn't disagree with my father either; she never had. There didn't seem any reason for her to disagree with him. She had her place, and he had his; and they seemed to understand each other, now that I think about it. I was the one who didn't understand her, and I resented his wanting to keep me back . . . Then the gap got bigger and bigger between them and, oh, I was such a brat.

(sigh) Such a bitchy brat . . . It's not so dark now . . . (long pause)

Leader: Should we stop now, or do you want to go on?

Ella: Well, I wonder what the rest think. I feel like I've taken up a lot of your time and attention . . . (Group nods to go on.) Well, there's just a little bit more and I'll finish . . . Well, I guess I gave the whole family a pretty hard time. I was the oldest and I couldn't let myself get married off like so many of my friends had been. They didn't really try too hard, you know, to marry me off. At least it wasn't an old man. They didn't know any different, you know, this is the way people did things; and they wanted me to get married and have children. It seemed like a reasonable thing to them. But anyway, I didn't want that. I wanted to leave and go to school, do a few things. I did. And she used to come to the hospital to see me. My father wouldn't let me come home after I left. I always remember Jim, he's my youngest brother, he was born when I was fifteen, so I didn't really know him too well. After I left home one day (I came home whenever my father was away working) and I remember Jim saw me coming around the corner and he took off like a streak of lightning, ran to me and said, "You wait here and I'll go see if Daddy's home and then you can come in." So I'd sneak home when he wasn't there. It was awfully hard on her and she'd come up to the hospital to see me or we'd go to a movie together . . . And that first Christmas after I left home . . . I thought, I had three days off, so I thought I talked with her. She wanted me to come home. It was the only time she ever (crying) . . . Well this was the only time she ever stood up to my father. The way she said, "I want you home." (crying) So I went home those first two days and helped her bake. My father would come in and he'd go in the next room. He was very angry that I came back and he didn't know quite what to do about it. And I guess, well I thought he's beginning to accept me back again so I took a chance and went home for Christmas dinner . . . And he got so furious. (crying) . . . He made me leave . . . she cried. (crying) . . . And I remember saying, "I don't know what he's doing to you, I don't know what he's doing to you." (crying) I don't know if I even remember when I saw them again. I remember feeling numb that next day . . . I felt drained and numb . . . She started to get sick after that. First it was kidney stones. Then it was diabetes. Then it was breast tumor . . . And then it was cancer . . . In five years, she was dying. I finished my training. I got married and I left and went to New Jersey with Ted for three months. When we got back, she had lost so much weight. She was so thin. She was still walking around. She could hardly breathe. She had been for a walk with me to my aunt's, it must have been a mile and a half. She could hardly walk . . . Ted had a Fulbright that summer. We were going to go to Paris. This was the ultimate for me, to be able to go to Europe to be with Ted. And I was pregnant. When my father found out she was dying, he was so furious. He was so furious with God, with himself. And he didn't want me to leave her. I think now, he didn't want me to leave him. And I was torn between staying with her, she only had another month or so, and going with Ted. She realized this and she . . . I didn't ask her what to do. She looked at me and she said, "He's your husband, and you go with him. You can't leave him. You can't let him go alone." Well, she made it easy for me to leave her. And she never got in bed as long as I was there. That summer she was in the hospital for a while but she came home. She was up. And I left her at the end of August, I went to Europe. And she died in October . . . (crying) I never cried for her. All these years I never cried for her . . . I guess she gave me more than I thought. And she did it so quietly . . . And I thought she was weak . . . Maybe it's her strength I've got, not my father's. Maybe a little bit of both.

Leader: Can you feel her strength in you now?

Ella: I never did before. She always seemed so fragile. And maybe weak, I guess. I always thought of her as sort of weak. That's strange.

Leader: What about the mothering you have to do?

Ella: I have to let myself be as gentle as she was to me. I've tried to raise my boys the way my father raised me, not like she did. I've had to be more of a father to them than a mother, I guess. Because Ted wasn't much of a father, and I've had to do more of the disciplining. And I've been, I couldn't be like her. I guess that's it. I had to be like my father. And, I don't know, I don't want to be like him, not completely . . . I think I see that little patch of sunshine. (laugh) It looks like I did find it and I didn't get us all lost. (laugh) . . . I think I've found a little bit of my mother in every one of you women. (sigh) Lucy's got her eyes and color. Jane has her smile. Jean has her bubbling . . . When she came in that morning so happy. And even you (to Dotty), your hair. She had long hair. I lost touch with Irene this evening . . . But I'm aware of you now.

Irene: I'm here, Ella.

Ella: I don't think I was aware of Jane before. There was something that I was saying that seemed to make sense to you.[2] I knew I had something of all of you in me, but I didn't know why. I didn't know what it all meant. But I think it's this. I think you've made her more alive for me. (crying) . . . More than I ever let myself think before. And I feel very grateful . . . I might never have found her . . .

Leader: You're a very beautiful person, Ella.

Ella: She was beautiful, she was. She always looked ten years younger than her years.

Leader: Like you, Ella.

Ella: And she was a little bit of a child . . . A helpless little child.

Leader: Like you, Ella.

Ella: And she was very giving.

Leader: Like you.

Ella: And I said she never taught me how to be a mother! Oh, I was blind. I was so blind. I feel full again. I feel like I'm finding out . . . I feel whole again . . .

This moving human document depicts both a personal growth crisis and a peak group experience. The two, in fact, interweave in a reciprocal interaction between the individual, who offered her panic to the group, and the group, which offered its healing attention back to the individual. Within the context of this therapeutic reciprocity, Ella seemed to achieve an integration of previously repressed emotions and their concomitant memories with her present identity as a

---

[2] Jane had been sobbing along with Ella for a long period during the session.

mother and as a woman. Furthermore, she also seemed to integrate these combined elements with the immediately felt relationships within the group. Another kind of reciprocity is reflected in the apparently authentic response of group members to Ella's self-presentation, thus providing a direct payoff for the risk she was taking in disclosing herself. Elements in this growth experience include a working through of previously unexpressed grief, a nonprojective acceptance of responsibility for previous conflict with parents, and an assimilation of mother-image fragments into her own identity. The group session as a whole might be seen as a reliving of the traumatic Christmas dinner with an accepting rather than rejecting father and with the possibility of union with rather than separation from family members (mother and, to a lesser extent, siblings).

There were many indications during the second week of the lab that Ella held and integrated the growth that she experienced during this midnight session. One reflection may be seen in the following poem, which she wrote near the end of the second week, during a period of solitude in the woods:

Thought Fragments

1.

I am
Alone with myself
In the underbrush of my life
Surrounded by the raging stillness
of the trees.
The sun creeps through
The treetops in the distance.
Pain and joy
Rise to meet the sun.
I think of what has transpired.

2.

I reached for the stars
In the exuberance of my youth.
The stars stretched forth and
Lifted me into the warm brilliance
of their light.

Gently they sent me back again.
My search for that moment
has ended here
Where I have crawled through
The depths and caverns of my soul.

3.

I am dark still earth
Soaking the rain of your touch.

Dry leaf curled in yourself.
The blood of life gone from your veins
I feel close to you.

4.

I am the sea spray and the wind
Howling in my ears.
I become the rainbow in the depths
of the gray green sea.
I am cold in the warmth of your
touch.
I am warm in the chill wind of
your breath.

5.

I am lost.
I stand on the abyss of separation.
Ghosts of forgotten memories
Rise to enfold me in their sweet
Bitterness.
I return to the unknown and
Familiar world of noise and bluster.
I am afraid and glad.

AFTERTHOUGHT

The underbrush is not all darkness
and cold.
There is lightness and warmth,
Delicate weeds and soft bird feathers.

> *Excruciating joy*
> *Of being.*
> *I am.*

PREDISPOSING FACTORS

Assuming that the foregoing is a valid account of a growth experience we may ask, "What are the factors that made it possible?" Three major antecedent factors are worthy of note: One is the fact that Ella had in her past received several years of individual therapy, so she was relatively open to exploring the dark recesses of her mind; during her therapy she had become *skilled in free association,* which she used almost in poetic fashion during the midnight session.

Another predisposing factor was the prior history of the group, extending back for a week, in which Ella had participated. A fair degree of trust had developed in this group, so that *intimate self-disclosure had become an accepted norm.* Ella had developed *emotional involvements with other group members, and they with her.* These involvements became an essential part of the unfolding. She had developed a *trust* in the group leader, which made it possible for her to accept his support in facing a fear that amounted almost to terror. One of the women in the group was able to offer Ella her nurturing attention in a motherlike role, and Ella was able to accept this during the early part of her journey through the dark underbrush of her life. Through her emotional attachments to each of the women in the group, feelings were stirred in Ella that reawakened memories of her relationship with her mother.

The third major predisposing factor with regard to this incident was the twelve-hour marathon. This sustained period of continuous contact, with its mounting intensity of emotional involvement and its progressive relinquishing of defenses, led to increasing depths of self-disclosure. The openings that occurred for Ella during the marathon included some that induced a panic state immediately following the termination of this session. And it was this panic state that eventually generated the growth experience described above.

LEADER RESPONSE TO EMOTIONAL DISTRESS

Several aspects of the leader's behavior were of central importance in the development of this growth incident. One was his willingness to cope with Ella's emotional distress as a phenomenon that might be examined within the group. This reflected a triple trusting: in himself as leader, in Ella, and in the group—a trust that the three together would be able to work through whatever might emerge. The leader had some initial uncertainty about going into Ella's feelings with her. She was obviously very deeply upset at the beginning of the session. Her first attempts to talk were vague and almost incoherent. Her description of the sky as seeming very far away, and of the world as being very dark, suggested perceptual distortions on the borderline of possible decompensation. It would have been possible to summarize these conditions in the judgment that Ella's ego was not sufficiently intact for her to be able to tolerate exploration. The leader did not make this judgment, but instead offered Ella the choice of exploring her distress. His own willingness to risk whatever might emerge made it possible for him to offer Ella the choice.

A number of alternative leader responses could have emerged from treating Ella's distress as a pathological symptom. One such response would have been to turn group attention away from her distress and focus on someone else, permitting Ella to "recover," (i.e., to re-cover). Another might have been to remove Ella from the group until her emotionality subsided. A third might have been to sedate her, so as to chemically reduce the intensity of feeling. These responses in the sequence presented represent an increasing depersonalization of treatment, increasing to the extreme in which the recipient of the drug is no longer a person with whom the leader and the group are engaged in dialogue but is instead a body or an object to be worked upon.

The choice that a leader makes between interpreting emotionality as pathology or as a potential ground for growth is of central importance in influencing the direction in which the emotion develops. A cohesive group will usually accept the leader's interpretation and will support him in fostering either the expression or the suppression of the emotion. *The leader's choice of the pathology interpretation confronts the distressed individual with a choice between achieving alienation from his own affect or being alienated from the group.* Both of these states are stressful and tend to foster further pathology. *The choice of a growth interpretation* makes possible the exploration for meanings in the emotionality so that it may eventually be integrated into the individual's identity and into his intragroup relationships.

The significance of this point of choosing, in leader response, is heightened when the distressed individual is in a state of near panic. Such a state may be a precursor either of psychosis or of a peak experience.[3] It is characterized by an overwhelming loss of meanings, by a breakdown of familiar roles, precipitating the individual into unidentified and therefore chaotic emotionality. If no congruent meanings are found for this emotionality, it may persist as anxiety and perhaps lead to psychotic reconstruction. If congruent meanings are sought and found, the anxiety gradually comes to be experienced as excitement and may develop into exhilaration or even ecstasy. If the group leader identifies the emotionality as pathological, mobilizing group resources against its expression, the attainment of congruent meanings is precluded and the development of psychosis is fostered. But *if the group leader accepts the emotionality as amenable to congruent interpretation, then group resources become mobilized in the search for meanings, and a peak experience may ensue for both the individual and the group.*

Thus, leader response may strongly influence whether an individual's state of intense excitation becomes the ground for either psychotic decompensation or for a peak growth experience.

THE SEARCH FOR MEANINGS

The group leader repeatedly turned toward rather than away from the fear with which Ella began this session. Prior to the session Ella had felt lost, out of contact, not understanding her own anxiety nor being understood by anyone. She had sought out a friend from another group during the interlude between the marathon and the midnight feedback. But he failed to understand her, and this failure seemed to increase the intensity of her fear. By the start of the session, Ella was so afraid of her dark feelings that she hoped to turn away from them, and talk, when called upon, somehow "sensibly" about something else, perhaps anything else. But the group leader

---

[3] In his book *Toward a Psychology of Being* Abraham Maslow defines *peak experiences* as the most wonderful experiences of a lifetime, i.e., the happiest moments, the most ecstatic moments, the moments of greatest rapture. Such experiences arise from being in love or from listening to music or from suddenly being hit by a passage in a book, or from giving birth to a child or a painting, or from some other great, creative experience.

repeatedly offered her the choice of turning toward and exploring these dark feelings. She was able to accept this choice and thus, with the group supporting her, enter into the search for meanings.

GROUP ATTENTION

The search proceeded within the context of intense group attentiveness. This somehow seems to act as a powerful healing force. *Whenever group attention vacillates, the person journeying falters, hesitates, usually stops.* A number of times Ella checked to see if the group wanted her to continue. She required their consent before she could go on.

EMOTIONAL INTERFLOW

Repeatedly, during the intensely tearful parts of Ella's unfolding, one of the other women in the group sobbed along with her. At times, more than half of the group were crying along with her. This sharing in an intense feeling is a kind of primitive understanding and acceptance that can only happen when the other is deeply stirred in a personal way by what is being communicated. The leader did not have and could not make this kind of response to Ella during this particular incident. The problem with which she was dealing did not stir him in a personally intimate way. While he could understand in an empathic way what Ella was going through on her journey, he was not able to identify with her as if he were on a similar journey himself. One outstanding value of a group experience is that there is often at least one member of the group who is personally stirred by the expression of deep feeling and who closely identifies with the person expressing the feeling.

IMPLICATIONS FOR FAMILIES

Abstracting from this critical incident some of the factors that seem to have supported growth suggests a number of interesting hypotheses for individuals or families seeking to maximize personal growth.

The impact of the preceding marathon session suggests that the sheer duration of sustained and focused contact is important. How might families provide for such duration of contact? Would it pay off in release of growth potential of members?

A key factor was the willingness of the group, under the leader's influence, to turn toward rather than away from emotional distress. To what extent would it be possible for families to follow this principle? What might be the results? A related factor was response to emotional distress by searching for meanings. To what extent might it be practicable for families to invest themselves in seeking out the meanings of emotional upset as an alternative to either comforting or moralizing the distress away?

The value of group attentiveness seems clear-cut, but the task of applying it to family life with its myriad distractions will call for great ingenuity.

The amount of emotional interflow might be used as a barometer to measure the extent to which a family group is enhancing the personal growth of its members.

Jack R. Gibb and Lorraine M. Gibb

Leaderless Groups: Growth-Centered Values and Potentialities

I

People can grow. Man's potential for growth is vast and, as yet, relatively unexplored. In his inner depth—in his *essential* reality—man is capable of giving and receiving warmth, love, and trust. He is moving toward interdependence and confrontation. Growth is a kind of freeing of this inner self of these internal processes—an emergence and fulfillment of an unguessed inner potential. Growth is a process of fulfilling, realizing, emerging, and becoming. It proceeds outward from within. Fundamental changes can and do occur at any age in personality, inner motivation, life style, and ways of coping with the world. In his basic core man is loving and lovable, trusting and trustworthy. People are to be trusted, and thus are trustworthy. People are to be loved, and are lovable.

This is an oversimplified statement of one view of man and his potential. A similarly oversimplified statement of a more common alternative view follows below.

Man's potential for growth is relatively fixed, determined by strong hereditary factors that in large part determine the direction and degree of development of the person. The limitations of growth are pretty well set in the early years by an interaction of these hereditary factors with our relatively stable environment. A person does change his behavior from time to time and can learn a great deal within the framework of his largely stable personality. But fundamental changes in personality seldom or never occur, particularly after early youth. Change, when it does occur, is a matter of teaching, indoctrination, and training. People do not change, but *can be changed* within relatively predictable limits by manipulation of environmental controls and by programming of relevant rewards and punishments. Change proceeds inward from without. Man's essential core being is destructive, self-preservative, defensive and, unless he is well trained and adequately socialized, basically untrusting and untrustworthy. Hence, people are to be feared, and thus are fearful. People are to be distrusted, and thus are distrusting.

The viewpoint described in the first paragraph we shall call a "growth view" of man. For purposes of discussion we shall call the second view a "defensive view," because it is rooted in the fears and distrusts of man and is essentially an intellectual projection of these fears and distrusts. These two views, as we shall see, have significant and antithetical implications for many aspects of modern life.

For a number of years the authors and their associates have been involved in a program of research and development designed to examine man's potential for growth. We have looked at man in groups and in organizations in a natural setting: committees, management teams, families, classes, neighborhood groups, and clubs. We have also looked at groups whose conscious purpose has been to grow and develop into more effective groups, in effect, to test man's group potential. We have led, observed, and participated in group therapy, sensitivity groups, marathon groups, and action groups which in various ways have realized greater potential than more typical groups seen in natural settings. We have also seen and helped set up innovative management and work teams in industry and in educational and volunteer organizations with the explicit purpose of seeing what groups can become within ongoing organizational life. *In general, our research has tended to confirm the growth view of man and his potential.*

In this research we have obtained a revealing and even inspiring view of man as he might become, and occasional glimpses of groups in peak experiences of sustained creativity and trust. These group experiences have most often come when (a) groups have been in sensitivity training in semiweekly sessions for eight or nine consecutive months, (b) groups have been in around-the-clock "marathon" sessions for thirty or forty hours with little or no sleep, or (c) groups have been in twelve-hour sessions daily for twelve or thirteen consecutive days. In our experience this optimal growth occurs most frequently in groups that have no professional leader present and in which, possibly because of the absence of a leader, emergent and interdependent strength is maximized.

Under these conditions groups are qualitatively different from the groups usually met in the natural setting. The groups attain and often maintain states of creativity, excitement, depth of communication, and trust that are impressive and memorable both to those participating and to those observing. We have seen this state of affairs in occasional natural groups in the organizational setting, usually after the group has undergone a training experience of appropriate duration, intimacy, and intensity.

Behavioral scientists in evaluating potential have looked at persons and groups in the natural setting and judged what they might become. It is as if in wishing to determine how well men could hit golf balls, we lined up fifty average adult males at a golf tee, had each take two swings at the ball, measured the distance each ball traveled, and concluded that the average man's golf-ball-hitting potential was 15.5 yards. After practice and effort, under the same test conditions, the average man could hit the ball approximately 155 yards. This does not take into consideration that after applying new theory to the training process the average person can be trained to hit the ball perhaps 255 yards. Our impression is that the above analogy is relevant to the examination of the potential of groups for creative growth. There is a similar gross qualitative difference between the average discussion group or management team operation in the usual natural organizational setting, and the same group or team performance after the kind of training that is now possible. This phenomenon has led to a new look at human potential in persons and in groups, to new organizational theories, and to new theories of personal and group development.

The group, *qua* group, in its significant process aspects, is a relatively recent object of scientific study. Because, at least as we see it, *human growth is essentially a social and interdependent process,* this new look at the nature and development of groups makes possible new insights into the extent of human potential and also into ways of achieving significant new functional levels of living. Knowing little about groups and often fearing them, man has sometimes felt that groups were a deterrent to human growth. *It now seems likely that man can reach his highest moments of creativity and satisfaction in group action.*

From our research and group experiences and from an examination of the growth literature, we are evolving a theory of group growth and human potential. The structure of the theory is diagrammed in Table One. A brief statement of the theory follows below.

TABLE ONE

A GROWTH-CENTERED VIEW OF SOCIAL PROCESSES AND VALUES

Primary social processes	Basic personal needs	Primary growth processes	Antigrowth	Primary personal values
Membership	Belonging	Trust, love	Fear, distrust	Trust
Data flow	Clarity	Openness	Façades, filters	Openness
Goal formation	Fulfillment	Self-determination (Autogenic life)	Apathy, frenetic overactivity	Integrity
Control	Freedom	"True" interdependence	Dependency	Freedom

There are four basic processes that seem to occur in all social structure. People work on these processes both in natural groups and in the training groups we have constructed for study. Group members work continuously on the problems of relating to each other, communicating with each other, forming goals, and developing control systems. These primary processes are related to four basic needs that seem to be common to all persons and that direct and sustain human growth. As people get in depth communication, these needs appear most clearly. A person has a need to love and to be loved, to belong to the human race, and to have an emotional relationship to some significant group of relevant others. A person needs to have emotional and intellectual clarity, to know where he stands and where the world is, and to know how he is seen by relevant others. He needs to grow to self-realization, to become what he is to become,

TABLE TWO

THE FOUR PRIMARY ASPECTS OF GROWTH

Personal growth is toward:	Group growth is toward:
1) Trust and love of self and others	1) Full membership in love and trust
2) Communication in depth with self and others (awareness and spontaneity)	2) A functional feedback system permitting consensual decision-making
3) Integration of a self-determined goal system into creative action	3) Integration of and creative movement toward group-determined goals
4) Emergent freedom in creative interdependence	4) Spontaneous, participative, and emergent structure and function

to have a sense of emergent worth and achievement, to feel fulfilled, to feel that all parts of his life have integrity and wholeness, and to feel that his motivations and inner self are congruent with his behavior. A person needs to be able to mingle satisfyingly with others in personal relationships, share in their lives, influence and be influenced, live in interdependence.

Growth is a primary property of human organisms, a unitary process the basic correlates of which are a reduction of fear, the development of trust, and the removal of defensive states. Table Two describes in some detail the primary aspects of growth as specified by our theory. Growth is a process of reducing fears and defenses and freeing oneself to love and to trust and to be loved and trusted. In the process of interacting with other persons we learn to fear and to behave defensively—behave in a way that will defend ourselves from perceived or anticipated attack. As defenses increase, people lose psychological contact with themselves and with each other, and make fear/distrust assumptions about each other and about themselves. As people get an intimate psychological contact with themselves, they come to trust themselves and to love themselves—to see themselves as they *really are*. The same things happen in our contacts with other persons. As fears increase and defenses are built, the person becomes lost in the role; and the growth-necessary processes of love and trust are decreasingly possible.

Growth is a process of increasing the depth and validity of communication with the self and with others. The growing person is increasingly aware of incoming data from his social environment and increasingly able to emit valid data. He is better able to tell the world how he feels and how he sees things. In one way or another, all barriers to intimacy are matters of defensive fear and distrust. Communication in depth, genuine intimacy, is possible to the degree that people reduce fears and distrusts.

Growth is a process of identifying one's own intrinsic emerging motivations and of maintaining his life activities in congruence with these motivations. As one grows, his life directions stay in tune with his own becoming, as motivations emerge and change with one's experiences. Self-determination, self-generation of activities, and self-assessment of progress toward his goals are earmarks of growth. As fear and distrust lessen, one is able to communicate his motivations both to himself and to others. There is a growing awareness of one's unconscious motivations and a greater harmony or merging of one's unconscious life and his conscious goal systems. Life is a quest, a searching; and becoming, a fulfillment. As one becomes more free from defensive fears, life becomes more creative, spontaneous, directional, and full of zest.

Growth is a process of achieving interdependence. People who fear and distrust become chronically dependent or aggressively independent. With love and trust people can achieve creative freedom in interdependence. Trust, the primary ingredient of human growth, is a social process. For trust to grow, communication in depth and intimacy must occur. One cannot grow in isolation from loving and being loved. One must frequently communicate in depth of feeling with other growing beings. In order to grow, people must care, must be in psychological contact, and must live in depth.

In our experience there is an impressive similarity in the emerging values of people who are experiencing growth as we have defined it above. As people grow they come to value themselves, to value growth, and to value the emergent correlates of growth. Certain emergent and enduring values are congruent with the personal needs and the social processes as listed in Table One, and with the growth view of man as stated earlier.

Trust is the central process of growth and the resultant central value. The inevitable correlates of trust are openness, integrity, and freedom. Growing people prize for themselves and for others the processes of open, honest, spontaneous communication in depth; the integrity that accompanies congruence of motivations, feelings, and behavior; and the love that can occur among people who are truly free to live in interdependence.

When intensive intimacy training has been conducted in the Scandinavian countries, and in Japan, Austria, and France, researchers have been impressed with many cultural differences in expressive behavior but also impressed with the similarity in the basic processes and values described above. Though well aware of the immensity of differential cultural influence upon social processes and upon personal values, we are impressed even more with the evidence that the values described above are residual in the nature of man. These values are inevitable outcomes of psychological intimacy, reduction of fear, communication in depth, and interdependent goal creation. Love, honesty, integrity, and freedom are, not accidentally, central to most of the enduring moral philosophies that constitute our cultural heritage.

II

What are the implications of this growth view of man for the reader of this chapter? The authors have been developing for many years, largely as a by-product of a series of researches sponsored by the Office of Naval Research, a program for personal and organizational growth that has been tested in a variety of educational, industrial, religious, and other organizational settings. Our program implies at least three things that the reader might do: (1) engage with others in creating an intensive, depth experience in an "autogenic group"; (2) examine with the group your theory of living, and begin constructing a personal theory that will help your life to become more congruent; and (3) engage in a number of miniature experiments with your relationships that will test your emergent theory and force you to grow.

1. *Create an autogenic group.* We have performed enough experiments and studies of leaderless, emergent, group-directed, or "autogenic" groups to satisfy ourselves that any group of people who have enough motivation can get together and form an intensive, intimate, compelling, and meaningful learning group. An experienced group trainer, leader, or therapist can often be helpful; but our experiences have indicated that the strongly motivated leaderless group is even more powerful in producing personal and group growth and especially in showing the person *how he can create a comparable atmosphere in his own personal relationships.* The space here is too brief to indicate in full what happens in such a group experience. The autogenic group provides opportunity for at least the following outcomes:

You can examine your own fears and distrusts. When people are committed to stay together and look at themselves, they begin to express fears to each other: that we will hurt ourselves if we are left on our own, that we will go too far into therapy without someone to restrain us, that we will not go far enough or do anything, that we will only do what the least of us will be able to do, that we will not be able to control the vigorous or aggressive ones among us, and that we will reveal too much to each other and not be able to look at each other again. People usually learn that their fears are groundless, exaggerated, self-fulfilling, and related to their distrusts. Their fears are related to their theories of life, their child-rearing practices, their managerial behavior, and their life style.

You can confront your own inner being. The intimate group affords an opportunity for each person, at his own pace, in the warmth of growing group trust, to come to look at himself *as he is,* as he sees himself, as he is seen, and as he wishes to be seen. People often find, especially after experiences in depth, that they protect themselves from looking at themselves by many defenses and that what they first see is sometimes disturbing. As far as we are able to tell from our interviews, however, after groups have stayed together long enough to create a satisfying experience in trust, persons come to like themselves better, and to find that they are better able to trust and love others. People usually learn to enjoy all aspects of self better—to accept, incorporate, appreciate, savor, and expand some of the aspects of self and manifestations of self that are discussed in this book: images, body feelings, sex, play, meditation, dreams, smells, worship, prayer, conflict, anger, loneliness, and art.

You can confront your own control needs. As the group gets started, people are immediately confronted with problems of influence, decision-making, goal-setting, and other activities that bring out control needs. The autogenic group provides an ideal opportunity for persons to look at the control elements of their lives. People often look at how their own growth impulses and creative motivations are covered and inhibited by denial, self-control, discipline, guilt, a sense of duty, and self-sacrifice, and how impossible it is to create a group consensus around a zestful goal when these defensive controls are present. Group members learn that they not only control themselves, in response to their own fears and distrusts, but that they control others for similar reasons. With these control needs and behaviors visible, members are often able to examine them and relate them to the problems of group living. Members see for themselves that intrapersonal and interpersonal control needs diminish with greater trust, learn under what conditions they can develop trust and reduce control behaviors, and learn how to exercise influence productively when it is appropriate. This aspect of the learning is particularly important. Members learn how satisfying it is to create a powerful group that is at once influential and docile and that they can personally influence. This experience is particularly meaningful if the group does this without a formal leader or trainer. Members learn the meaningfulness of reaching consensus on a goal that is not a compromise but is what everyone wants deeply. A truly interdependent social situation is a new experience for most members of the autogenic group. To find that spontaneous freedom comes through genuine interdependence and that group action can be creative and freeing and not frightening is potentially the most valuable learning that can come to the growing person.

You can confront dissonance in your own internal world. Health and growth come through confrontation of dissonance on the road to new levels of creative integration. In the open society of the auto-genic group, members are faced with disparities in their internal systems: beliefs, behavior, values, feelings, motives, and theories of action. Members see inconsistencies between their Christian ideals and their actions, between how they feel and what they say they feel, between what they want and what they say they want, between their impulses and their behavior, and among all aspects of the world of which they are becoming increasingly aware. Confrontation of this dissonance can cause anxiety, learning, growth, and endless and productive group work.

You can get a glimpse of what man can become. The autogenic group in its advanced stages comes nearer to a utopian ideal than any other experience in which we have participated. Members often get a deep emotional experience with new aspects of life that they have not previously experienced. Members may see the deep and loving inner core that is present in all human beings. Members may experience a deep emotional consensus that they did not think was possible. Members may experience sustained periods of peace and tranquility that they had only read about. Members may see and experience creative conflict and fight that they had always avoided. One minister said in such a group: "In all my years in the ministry I have never before had a truly religious experience." Perhaps the range and diversity of meanings and emotions is the most significant aspect of the autogenic group.

2. *Verbalize a personal theory that will add congruence and direction to your life.* All persons make assumptions about life that are more or less conscious and articulated. We find that it is helpful to growth for participants in the autogenic groups to examine their assumptions, look at how their experiences jibe with their "theo-ries," compare theories with other members, and make deliberate attempts to formulate a consistent and satisfying set of assumptions that can guide their lives. This informal theory construction occurs as a subtheme in most group interaction but takes on greater signifi-cance in the openness and confrontation of the depth group.

It is our experience that reading seldom changes behavior or values. It is equally true that systematic reading motivated by a genuine quest for understanding *after* a deeply emotional group experience can lead to a meaningful reorientation of a person's life.

*For productive personal growth, persons must confront the issues
implicit in the statements earlier in the chapter that contrasted the
growth view and the defensive view of man and his nature.* Man *must*
confront the issues implicit in Table One: how trusting and loving
can I be? how open and honest can I be? how do I set my goals in
relation to the goals of others who are important to me? how do I
exert influence upon others, and how do I receive influence from
them? Each person has an explicit or implicit "theory" that covers
each of these primary problems of man. Inevitably in the process of
group formation the members of the autogenic group face these
problems again and again at increasingly deep levels of interaction.

3. *Experiment with your life.* You can transfer your group
learnings to all phases of your life. The autogenic group is a proto-
type of all groups that you have experienced or will experience.
There are a great variety of group experiences available to the
interested person: group therapy, sensitivity training, basic encounter groups, religious retreats, group counselling, etc. It is useful and
often productive to go to these groups for learning or to add members to your autogenic group who have had experience in process-
oriented groups.

There is ample evidence from our research and from a great
variety of other studies that people can learn, grow, change, and
modify all aspects of their personalities and motivations. People can
take responsibility for their own lives. People can become happier,
more creative, more zestful, and more productive than they are. A
person's potential is so great as to continually surprise even the most
experienced observer. One is limited largely by his fears and his
distrusts, on the one hand, and by his inadequate and invalid theory,
on the other. One can set up experiments with his life that will
remove his fears and that will improve his theory.

You can test your trust level. You can measure your trust by
examining how open you are, how much you allow others to set their
own goals and be what they are or what they may become, and how
much freedom you are able to give yourself and others. People who
are distrusting tend to exhibit this distrust in their social roles as
parents, teachers, supervisors, or managers by being closed, secretive,
and strategic; by being persuasive, coercive, manipulative, and guiding; and by being controlling, paternal, formal, and hostile. You can

determine for yourself how trusting you are and how trusting you wish to become.

You can try being more open. You can try being open in ways that seem appropriate and reasonable to you—that fit your personal theory. People who experiment with openness usually find that they get rewarded for greater openness. Assessment of the hidden rewards and punishments for closed behavior is difficult. A certain amount of open communication in genuine intimacy is necessary in order to test the effects of openness! If you *want* to become more open, you can push the limits of your own openness a bit to satisfy yourself that your openness will be rewarding to *you*. Try expressing a genuine positive and warm feeling to a friend. Try telling someone a secret about yourself. Try telling a friend your real reason for turning down his invitation. Experiments in openness need not be drastic but by definition must be genuine!

You can allow others to set their own goals. Within the natural boundaries of your own fears and distrusts you can make open and deliberate attempts to give your children, your spouse, your subordinates, or your pupils a greater opportunity to set their own goals in wider and wider areas where their lives overlap with yours. You can see for yourself where rewards for this behavior will come. You may find that others make better decisions than you would have thought in advance, that others are more committed to their own goals, that you spend less time in supervisory and counselling activities, that relationships improve between you and self-determining others, and that in general permissive behavior is rewarding for all concerned. As with openness, changes in this aspect of your interpersonal life will cause upsets in the system and apparent immediate effects may be disquieting. Persistence is required in bringing adjustment in your own comfortable need-systems, theories, relationships, and predictions. The long-term rewards of behavior-change are great.

You can allow greater freedom. A good place to start in examining your own authority and control behaviors is in attempting to set boundaries by interactive discussion with the persons concerned with you (i.e., your family, your work associates, your group members). You will experiment only within the limits of your own well-stabilized need-systems, because your experimentation will be limited by your fears and by your theories. We have found it surprising both to ourselves and to experimenting group members how little change is necessary in behavior to make big differences in satisfactions and in relationships.

You can experiment with groups in which you hold membership. If you have some degree of influence upon a group that is important to you, you can exert influence in the direction of helping your group to become more effective and to grow along one or more of the dimensions specified in Table Two. We have seen successful efforts toward satisfying growth in family councils, discussion clubs, work groups, management teams, home demonstration clubs, classes in elementary schools, staff meetings, research planning teams, Sunday school classes, therapy groups, and a wide variety of natural group settings. Efforts often meet with initial failure, strong resistance, misunderstandings, paranoidal mistrust, and little change. Efforts often meet with encouraging success, however. Occasionally, startling success occurs. If our analysis of the growth process is approximately true, the rewards of success are great.

Growing groups differ in degree. In experimenting with groups of which you are a part it is helpful to recognize some of the characteristics of growing groups. As indicated in Table Two, the healthy group is growing toward full membership in love and trust. Persons begin to feel loving toward and loved by other members of the group. The healthy group is growing toward a functional feedback system that permits consensual decision-making. A member begins to communicate in depth with other members of the group about matters that are relevant to the group and begins to feel free to say exactly what he thinks and feels about himself and about other members of the group *in the group.*

A growing group moves toward the integration of group-determined goals. A member feels that his most significant goals are creatively achieved in the group, that he does not sacrifice anything for the group, loses nothing by compromise or sacrifice or duty, and is able to feel fulfilled and satisfied by creative work toward goals that the total group has come to value. The healthy group is growing toward spontaneous and participative structure and function. Members begin to feel powerful in the group, feel that they can influence and be influenced by the group, feel no sense of discipline but a sense of freedom and release, and feel that controls are exercised only by confluent and emergent desires of the group.

An examination of the above criteria faces all of us with the wide disparity between the many groups in which we hold memberships, on the one hand, and the realizable potential of all these groups. We invite the reader to participate in an exciting effort to improve the groups of which he is a part, thus improving the lives of all of us as persons and changing the society in ways that will bring greater congruence between our lives and our potential for growth.

[11]

Paul Bindrim

Facilitating
Peak Experiences

INTRODUCTION

Peak experiences are the most wonderful experiences of a lifetime (Maslow 1962). They are the moments of greatest happiness, ecstasy, and rapture. They occur under a wide variety of circumstances, from being in love or giving birth to a child, to listening to music, creating a work of art, or climbing a mountain. In addition to being wonderful moments in themselves they also help us to grow emotionally. They may cure our neurotic symptoms, improve our self-image, and increase our regard for people and the world in general. They may open new horizons, giving us enriched values by which to live and releasing our fuller potential. In general they are spontaneous occurrences that are difficult to induce synthetically.

The procedure that follows is designed to actualize and intensify any potential toward peak experience that may be present in a group of individuals. It is therefore desirable that it be employed when a group is spontaneously approaching a peak state of experiencing, as in the final phases of a workshop or marathon, when the participants begin to express a deep appreciation for one another (Mintz 1967), or when an ongoing group has reached a similar degree of interpersonal closeness. It may be used by groups of any size, from two persons upward. Large groups should be divided into twenty-person subgroups that will work together throughout the session. A minimum period of two hours is required to complete the process. The leader should be prepared to work with fairly intense emotional releases, which often accompany peak experience. It is best to begin by giving the group a detailed description of the procedure. Participants maintain silence at all times after step 2, making further discussion impossible.

STEP 1. DISCUSSION OF PEAK EXPERIENCES

Each participant is asked to recall a peak experience that he can relive in fantasy in a later part of this exercise. This is best done by general discussion, since one person will stimulate another. To start the discussion, ask all participants to think of the moment in their lives that they would rather relive than any other moment they have experienced. Ask them to briefly share this experience with the group, emphasizing how they felt at the time rather than giving a lengthy description of the circumstances leading up to the experience. If a participant cannot recall a peak experience he should be encouraged to select some time, for use later in the exercise, when he felt reasonably happy. When a number of participants have related specific peak scenes that they can relive in fantasy, go on to step 2.

STEP 2. SELECTION OF PEAK STIMULI

Distribute the form "Selecting Peak Stimuli," which is found at the end of this article. It is self-explanatory. It can be given to the participants prior to the meeting so that they can come prepared. If it is distributed at the meeting, the remainder of the exercise takes place at the following meeting. Another alternative is to omit sensory saturation in step 6 and instead play the recommended recording. While this lessens the effectiveness of the procedure it avoids the problem of asking the participants to select peak stimuli and makes it possible to do the exercise in one session without advance notice.

Number 5 in the form "Selecting Peak Stimuli" is for the use of couples or small groups who can agree on the music they would like to hear. With larger groups the leader selects the recording.

STEP 3. PICKING PARTNERS

Ask the participants to stand, and rearrange their chairs in two rows of equal length so that the chairs face each other in pairs. These rows should be close enough to each other so that when the participants are reseated facing each other they will be able to touch the fingertips of their partners' hands with their own without stretching or leaning forward. Ask the men or the women, whoever are the more numerous, to be seated in one row of chairs. Those who cannot find seats remain standing with the persons of the opposite sex. This divides the group as far as possible by sexes and will result in men being paired with women, making the eye-to-eye meditation in step 8 easier to do than with partners of the same sex.

Now ask the persons who are standing to file in front of the individuals who are seated, pausing for at least thirty seconds in front of each person to look into his eyes. Ask them to select the person into whose eyes they can gaze with the greatest degree of comfort, openness, and receptivity. Suggest that they disregard all other characteristics, such as age and physical attractiveness. Tell them not to select a person whom they already know well, and to have a possible second or third choice in mind. Complete quiet is maintained during this procedure and is continued throughout the rest of the exercise except for statements made by the group leader.

When all participants have completed this process, ask them to sit across from the partners of their choice. If the partner they prefer is already taken they are to go on to their second or third choice. Be sure that they are seated close to their partners and that their peak stimuli are at hand so that they can reach them without opening their eyes in step 6. If they begin to smell, touch or taste these stimuli, tell them not to, as sensory accommodation will occur and reduce their effectiveness when they are needed. Ask them to look at their visual stimuli so that they can imagine them later in the exercise and then to close their eyes and to keep them closed until asked to open them.

STEP 4. RELEASING TENSIONS

a. *Physical Comfort:* Ask the participants to become aware of their physical bodies and see if they are comfortable in all areas. Encourage them to be aware of even the slightest discomfort, as these feelings will be intensified as relaxation increases. Suggest that they loosen their belts if they are too tight. Some may wish to remove their shoes; other may require pillows; some will find that their ties need to be opened. Permit them to carefully explore their entire bodies and take care of these needs before proceeding further.

b. *Releasing Muscle Tensions:* Ask the participants to breathe deeply and slowly. Suggest that they imagine that their bodies are like balloons. When they breathe in the balloons are filled with air and become tense throughout; when they breathe out they are emptied and become limp. As they breathe out ask them to explore their bodies to see if any areas do not relax. Ask them to pick the areas that are most tense and become increasingly aware of them until they can exactly define their boundaries. Then ask them to slowly increase this tension by tightening the muscles in these areas. Suggest that they also tighten all the muscles in their bodies to further increase the tension in these areas. As the tension in the selected areas builds, encourage them by saying: tighter and tighter and even tighter (tensing your own body at the same time) until you cannot increase the tension any more, and then allow the areas to suddenly relax like a balloon that has been punctured by a pin (allowing your own body to suddenly relax). When participants are correctly following your instructions, they will go from a state of rigidity to sudden limpness while expelling air with a sound resembling *uh*. After a brief period of natural breathing ask the participants to again resume deep breathing and repeat the entire process. Tension may then be found in the same or in different areas. This can be repeated four or five times until a greater degree of relaxation is experienced.

c. *Releasing Breathing Tensions:* Ask the participants to allow themselves to breathe in a normal, natural way. Then ask them to become increasingly aware of their breath as the air flows in and out. They may discover that they breathe smoothly or hesitantly, deeply or shallowly, rhythmically or erratically. They are to make no attempt to alter this basic pattern but simply to become aware of what is happening. After a few moments ask them to particularly note the smoothness of the flow of air. Are the in-and-out breaths of equal length and do they flow smoothly, naturally, and without strain, or can they detect gasping and other forms of unevenness? When they are aware of irregularities in the flow of air, ask them to see if they can smooth the flow and balance the rhythm without straining or forcing.

After a little while ask them to become aware of the depth of their breathing: Are they using all of their lungs or are they breathing shallowly? When they are aware of the depth of their breathing, ask them to see if they can gradually increase the depth without forcing or strain. When their breathing is smoother and more rhythmic and deeper, ask them to become aware of the rate at which they are breathing. Are their in-and-out breaths slow and long, or short and rapid? When they are aware of the rate at which they are breathing, ask them to see if they can gradually lengthen their in-and-out breaths so as to slow their breathing without forcing or straining. Allow them to continue this exercise for a few minutes to establish a pattern of smooth, rhythmic, deep, and slow breathing, which will increase the degree of their relaxation.

Now suggest that when they breathe in they may be able to feel an inflow of energy that fills their entire bodies. Some may be helped by imagining that this energy is in the form of light emanating from a source directly above and in front of them and shining on their foreheads. When they breathe in they may visualize this light flowing into their bodies through the centers of their foreheads. At the termination of the in-breath they may imagine their entire bodies glowing with this light, and on the out-breath they may imagine this light flowing out through their fingertips. To feel this fully their hands should be on their laps, palms upward. You may then suggest that they further release their tensions by allowing them to flow out with the light energy that accompanies the out-breaths.

d. *Releasing Mental Tensions:* While the participants continue the breathing exercise, ask them to see if they are being disturbed by any of their thoughts and if so to observe how they are responding to this mental activity. Some may discover that they are trying not to think while others may find that they are being carried along by their thoughts. In both instances they are being distracted from their meditation. Ask them to allow their thoughts to take place without resistance, since trying not to think simply intensifies the difficulty. On the other hand suggest that they return to their meditation as soon as they are aware that they have been distracted. Ask them to imagine that their mind is a room with open windows and that their thoughts are like birds that fly in and out freely while they themselves remain inside. Suggest that they try releasing discordant thoughts when they breathe out, allowing them to leave through the fingertips in the flow of light and energy. Further suggest that they may imagine their mind to be a lake with the wind blowing across the surface causing thoughts to appear as ripples on its surface. Gradually the wind dies and the surface of the lake becomes clear and they can see into its depth. Now they can observe the reflection of trees and sky, and finally as the day ends and sunlight fades the silent stars are seen shining deep in the quiet interior.

STEP 5. DEEP RELAXATION

Inform the participants that you will now make suggestions that will help them relax more fully. You will tell them that various parts of their bodies are becoming heavy and that when you pause they are to repeat these statements to themselves mentally and then if possible feel the growing weight in the areas mentioned. Tell them at times you will also make the statement, "I am at peace," and that they are to repeat this statement to themselves, becoming aware of a central point in their being that like the deepest part of the ocean is always at peace, no matter what emotional storms or tensions may be occurring on its surface. Then make the following statement: "My left arm is heavy (pause), my left arm is heavy (pause), my left arm is heavy (pause), I am at peace (pause)." Repeat this sequence three times. Then make similar statements regarding the right arm, the left leg, the right leg, and then the arms and legs.

STEP 6. SENSORY SATURATION WITH PEAK STIMULI

Ask the participants to keep their eyes closed while their hands slowly move to their peak stimuli. They are to smell, taste, and touch them all at the same time and imagine their visual stimulus as though they were looking at it through the middle of their forehead. Ask them to allow these sensations to flow to the peaceful center of their being, which they discovered in step 5, and to imagine this center opening like a receptive cup and being filled to overflowing with the pleasant joy of these sensations. If they feel any emotion they are to let themselves respond openly and to continue focussing on the pleasant sensations coming from their peak stimuli. While the participants are experiencing their individual stimuli play at moderately high volume a classical or semiclassical instrumental record that is emotional in quality. It should be one that begins quietly and builds to a climax. The Prelude to Wagner's *"Tristan und Isolde"* has been found to be quite effective in this respect and is recommended (Angel SB-3610-2) .

STEP 7. FANTASY RECALL OF A PEAK EXPERIENCE

Suggest to the participants that every event that has occurred in their lives exists in their inner world right now and can be reexperienced. Ask them to imagine that they are a traveler in this inner world and suggest that they go to their peak experience. When they arrive they are to explore and discover the event as if it were happening for the first time, as though the experience were entirely new. They are to look at the scene and allow it to emerge and not attempt to remember it. As they look at the scene ask them if they can hear any sounds coming from the persons or things that they are seeing. Are any smells and aromas coming from what they are experiencing? As they look, listen, and smell, ask them if they can feel sensations coming from their body as they encounter the scene. Are they sitting, standing, lying, or walking? Can they feel their body moving? Are they touching something or is something touching them? Can they feel wind, warmth, cold, or physical contact with another person? If they are eating, can they taste the food? If another person is talking can they hear what he is saying, and then can they reply mentally and again listen to hear his response? Can they establish physical contact with him by putting their arms around him, looking into his eyes, and so forth? These suggestions are given slowly in order to permit the gradual emergence of the scene. When sensory contact with the peak scene has been established, tell the participants that there will now be a period of silence during which to enjoy the experience and that whenever they are ready to leave the scene they may open their eyes and begin the eye-to-eye meditation with their partner. If their partner is still in meditation, they are to wait quietly until he is ready.

STEP 8. EYE-TO-EYE MEDITATION

This procedure should be demonstrated in advance so that the participants can begin it as soon as they open their eyes, while they are still experiencing a peak state. It is designed to heighten the peak state and to add the dimension of interpersonal intimacy. If either partner is defensively isolating himself, the nature of his blocks often becomes apparent to both individuals.

Ask the participants to rest their hands on their laps, with their fingertips lightly touching, while they quietly look into each other's eyes. (In each pair one participant will have his palms facing upward and the other downward.) Ask them to avoid all movement, since it distracts from the intensity of the meditation. This includes extensive blinking, smiling, or shifting one's gaze or body position. Since participants are often unaware when they move, write what is happening on a pad and show this to them. Play a musical selection similar to the one used for sensory saturation with peak stimuli. Wagner's "Love–Death" from *"Tristan und Isolde"* has been found effective and is recommended. Maintain silence for the rest of the period. You may help the participants by suggesting that they let each other in through their eyes, merging and communing in a common peak experience. Suggest that they allow their emotions to express themselves openly, so that they may continue focussing on higher peak experiences. If they experience fear, hostility, shyness, or other forms of closure in their partners, they are to reassure them by talking with them mentally and allow the obstructions to dissolve as they continue rising to higher peak states.

Tell the participants that they may continue until they have reached the fullness of the experience. They may then bid each other farewell mentally, sit back, and remain quiet until the other participants are finished. When most of the participants have completed the process, ask the remainder to bid each other farewell and go on to step 9.

STEP 9. SHARING SESSION

Ask the participants to place their chairs in a circle and share their experiences. As these experiences are shared, there is a tendency for group members to reach even higher peak experiences. This part of the session should be allowed to evolve spontaneously. Interpretations and drawing out persons who do not freely discuss their experiences will inhibit the process and should be postponed until later in the session.

The material produced can be divided into two categories: 1) Many participants report what can be classified as spiritual, mystical, or religious experiences. These are characterized by a heightened sense of individuality, at times expressed in terms of self-acceptance, wholeness, and uniqueness, accompanied by a heightened sense of at-one-ness, at other times expressed in terms of belongingness, sameness, unity, and love. These experiences should not be explained away as hallucinatory but simply accepted as inner-world realities. They apparently are extensions of normal awareness and are usually highly integrative and ego-strengthening. 2) Some participants report experiences mildly resembling the "bad trip" phenomenon characteristic of some LSD sessions. This often constitutes the spontaneous emergence of repressed material that occurs when the participant approaches a peak state of experiencing. This material must be dealt with therapeutically if the participant is to experience higher peak states. It generally is quite varied in nature and fits many diagnostic categories. If it is sufficiently intense it must be worked with as it emerges. On the other hand if it is milder in nature it can be noted and returned to at a later point in the session. While this material may be handled therapeutically in various ways, the procedures of peak-oriented psychotherapy (Bindrim 1966) are specifically designed for working with fantasies of this type that have been facilitated by peak stimulation.

ILLUSTRATIONS

The following statements by participants are taken from a tape recording of a sharing session.

SPIRITUAL EXPERIENCES

—I kept looking—and it was all black—I kept looking and trying to find what I was looking for—and when I did find it, my whole spine was just going up and down—I was shivering up and down and there was lots of light.

—I found it to be a very tranquil experience. I got out somewhere on the stream of the universe.

—In the eyeballing it was as though I were looking into my own eyes—I felt he was very with me—practically every moment—there were times when we were just grabbing for each other—trembling—and it was very difficult to withdraw.

—I had a kind of vibrating, ecstatic, tingling sensation coming from my shoulder tips down to my spine—I felt so warm, and then it was like two lines of brilliant—the whitest light coming together—their inside edges were smooth and their outside edges were jagged—they came together blinding.

—I felt a terrific warmth and tingling sensation up the spine—and sometimes a sexual sensation with it—and as the experience built, I again saw the two experiences that I had in your office: the violet eyes followed by the light.

—Sometimes I would have a hard time telling whether your face was your face or whether I was there—rather than that it was myself, rather than any extension or anything else—just merely the self in the same way as any other part of oneself. In many ways there was kind of a relaxing feeling, almost iike being asleep for three years.

—I was looking at the sky and I thought—I've never been here before—and I haven't seen it—and my heart started pounding. I looked around and I hadn't seen any of you, I hadn't seen the floor. And at this point I thought, I'm really tripping out. And then the beauty of the whole thing came through. I feel like a kid!

—There was a complete other height of—as Lee said—his white light. I sort of had a white Nirvana, and then coming out of it and being more individuated than I was before, before I came here I was all over the place. After this peak experience I want to share this with everybody. I thought, if there was only some way to get in everybody's mind and give them a little piece of the beauty that I had felt.

BAD-TRIP EXPERIENCES

—I was looking at this lake and on the other side of the lake there were cities burning. The fire was just burning—just tremendous—and I had a terrible time not looking at the burning—trying to find where the peace was—trying to find the peace—and I kept looking back at the burning cities you know—it was terrible.

—I wanted to run—I really felt like screaming my goddam heart out—I had to control the scream—I would have disturbed the whole mess—I wasn't really with my partner and I didn't feel she was really with me—I still felt she was there because I was the only one left and she had to pick me. I had a very difficult time. But I never did clear myself up to the point where I could have the kind of eye contact that I wanted, and when I did get it I couldn't keep my eyes open. The first image was a bad image and it kept repeating in different forms.

WORKING THROUGH A BAD-TRIP EXPERIENCE

As one participant begins to describe her experience in the sharing session, she begins to pant and states:

—I have such a strange sensation—I feel as though I'm in labor.

The therapist responds by suggesting that she close her eyes and let it happen. The panting becomes more intense. She lies on the floor, assumes the position of giving birth to a child and moves as if in labor. She groans and is apparently experiencing considerable pain. She cries,

—Somebody be my baby!

A participant volunteers and lies in her arms. The labor movements and pains continue and then abate. She states,

—I feel like I created something—it didn't just happen to me—I guess God is always right here—I hadn't really believed it before—I just gave birth but I feel purged at the same time—it's like they're both the same—I am shook up but boy do I feel good (laughing) —I'd like everybody to hold hands with me—I want to stand up but I don't think I can do it on my own— (she is helped to her feet) —I feel like laughing and crying and everything all over—I never could thank anybody properly but I sure feel like thanking all of you for making this possible for me—without you I couldn't have done it . . . I am shaking all over.

SELECTING PEAK STIMULI

Peak stimuli are the things that you most enjoy smelling, tasting, touching, looking at, and listening to. When you experience them they tend to lift your mood and make you feel a little better than you normally do. Naturally, your tastes differ from other people's, so it is necessary for you to make up your own list by filling in the following blanks:

1. The three things that I enjoy smelling the most are:
   1 _____ 2 _____ 3 _____
2. The three things that I enjoy tasting the most are:
   1 _____ 2 _____ 3 _____
3. The three things that I enjoy touching the most are:
   1 _____ 2 _____ 3 _____
4. The three things that I enjoy looking at the most are:
   1 _____ 2 _____ 3 _____
5. The three things that I enjoy hearing the most are (if the leader is selecting a recording for the group this choice is unnecessary) :
   1 _____ 2 _____ 3 _____

Most people find that they have to give the matter considerable thought before they can fill in the blanks. While they may be able to think of many things that they like, it takes considerable thought to pick out what they like the *very most*. For example, many people find that they like listening to music, but may experience some difficulty in stating the exact selections that they like the *very most*. The closer you can come to what you like the *very most,* the more effective will these stimuli be in aiding you during the session. Take all the time you need in deciding. This is *very important*.

When you have completed the list, get one item for each of the five senses and bring it with you to the session. You will quickly note that some things that you enjoy cannot be brought into the session. For example, you may enjoy the smell of sea air but have no way of bringing in sea air. Continue working with your list, replacing the things that cannot be brought in with those that can. Some partici-pants find that it takes considerable time and effort to obtain the *exact* items that they need. However, they soon discover that it has been well worth the trouble.

Be sure to bring at least one item to smell, one item to taste, one item to touch, one item to look at, and one item to listen to. In the session you will be asked to experience all of these items at the same time. Although they may bear no relationship to each other, the final effect of experiencing them all at the same time is to lift your mood more than would be possible with any one of them at a time. For example, one participant experienced considerable mood eleva- tion by eating chocolate, touching fur, listening to "Scheherazade," smelling perfume, and looking at a picture of a green meadow, all at the same time. Lifting your normal mood level as much as possible is *vital* to the work we will do. The combination of items is strictly individual, and nothing that anyone else brings with him will work for you, so you must make your *own selections* and come *prepared*.

[12]

Claudio Naranjo

Contributions of Gestalt Therapy

I

Gestalt therapy is a label that refers to the psychiatric approach and procedures developed by Dr. Frederick Perls. This approach, practiced by his trainees all over the United States, is fragmentarily described in his books. Essentially a form of existential psychiatry,[1] it is also characterized by the relevance of the holistic and gestaltist conceptions, as well as many notions derived from psychoanalytic theory. Its most specific link with psychoanalytic therapy lies in its concern with body language. In this concern Perls has expressed his indebtedness to W. Reich. The

[1] Gestalt therapy is one of the three psychiatric schools that have arisen from phenomenology and existentialism, the other two being Frankl's logotherapy and Binswanger's *Daseins Analyse*. Of these, the latter does not and cannot claim to be a therapeutic procedure. Van Dusen, in his discussion of existential analytic therapy, claims, "There is a psychotherapeutic approach which most closely fits the theory. In fact, a close adherence to the theory demands a particular approach. The approach has been called Gestalt therapy, and considerable credit for it is due to Dr. F. S. Perls. . . ."

uniqueness of Gestalt therapy does not lie in a theory of personality or of the neuroses; nor, for that matter, does it lie in theory at all. It is essentially a nonverbal creation, an approach to people in the therapeutic situation which has developed out of understanding, experience, and intuition, and continues to be transmitted nonverbally.

I think that the essence of therapy is more than an application of ideas, a living fact to be explained *a posteriori*, and Gestalt therapy is no exception. I see a unity among its different devices, and can elaborate on their rationale, but somebody else might look at the same facts from a different point of view and in terms of a different conceptual framework. I will, therefore, in the following pages focus on therapeutic methods, restricting the more abstract comments to what is of immediate relevance to the description of procedures.

I believe the techniques of Gestalt therapy can very well be conceived as exercises for individual use. Moreover, it is in this context that Perls has described most of them in his books. When he describes "concentration on eating," "undoing of retroflexions," "body concentration," "feeling the actual," "sensing opposed forces," "attending and concentrating," etc., he is addressing the reader and not a psychotherapist; and he assumes that anybody can set himself to experiment with the procedures.

True as this may be, I have chosen to describe the techniques in the context of the two-person therapeutic situation, since the overt dialogue between patient and therapist lends itself well as an example of the inner dialogue in him who wants to be his own "therapist." I also believe there are advantages in the two-person situation, and I think the average person would be in a better position to proceed on his own after an initial contact with someone more "awakened" than himself, or who could at least supplement his own awareness. Parenthetically, I may here state that I also believe this to be true of all spiritual exercises: that though we can tackle certain inner struggles only by ourselves, we may get there faster with the help, support, and challenge of somebody ahead of us in experience. Nevertheless it is up to the reader to decide what he can do with the ideas in this chapter, and I would emphatically advise him to try them out at least twice before pronouncing judgment.

The immediate aim of Gestalt therapy is the restoration of awareness. *Its ultimate goal is the restoration of the functions of the organism and the personality, which will make an individual whole and release his potentialities.* It assumes that awareness by itself will bring about development and change.

It is an agreed-upon concept of depth psychology that the essence of healing lies in the process of becoming conscious of the unconscious. The emphasis of Gestalt therapy on "awareness," rather than "consciousness" or "understanding," points further to the importance of contacting the immediate ongoing process "here and now," and better suggests the sensory and feeling basis of such process. Accordingly, the intervention of the therapist is essentially noninterpretative and directed to the awakening of the patient's own awareness of what he is doing and feeling. The emphasis definitely does not lie in explaining behavior, in understanding *why,* but in perceiving *how* it proceeds. This awareness by itself brings about a new experience and a new challenge to awareness.

II

A basic procedure in Gestalt therapy is that of staying in what Perls has designated "the continuum of awareness." The patient here is asked to "simply" express what he is experiencing. Here the emphasis on *experiencing* makes the situation very different from free association of thought, in which not only abstractions but memories and anticipations constitute much of the verbal output. In fact, most persons will discover to their own surprise that they have enormous difficulty staying in awareness of their experience for more than a few seconds. At a given point they will inadvertently turn to thinking ("computing," in Perls's jargon), to remembering, or to fantasying about the future. All these, in a situation in which the task is to stay with the present experience, are considered to be forms of avoidance. It is important to contact the experience that led to the avoidance, by returning to the point at which there was an interruption in the awareness of the present. It will then be found that there was at that point some discomfort or fear that prompted the subject to establish a distance by thought or to escape from the instant. Furthermore, awareness may possibly extend into the underlying experience at the time of thinking, so that the patient notices that he is explaining himself in fear of not being understood, justifying himself to counteract his feeling of guilt, offering an "interesting" thought or observation to be appreciated, etc.

In the same way the awareness of fantasies can be deepened to the point of contacting what the *subject is doing* with them, and to the discomfort at the root of the urge to do what he is doing. Not only the activities of thought and fantasy are stimulated by the need of avoiding or counteracting an experience, but physical activity as well. Posture, movements of hands and feet, facial expression, intonation of the voice, all convey either the feeling that was excluded from awareness or the effort to ward it off or counteract it, or both. The function of the therapist here is to redirect the patient's attention to his experience of himself: Are you aware of what you are doing with your hands? I noticed your voice sounds different now; can you hear it? Can you see where you stopped and began to make a case? and so on. The expression of experience is not a matter of an "all or none" response. For example, the patient's form of reporting may be at any point between real expression and "talking about" himself as an outside observer, and he will be unaware of his implicit avoidance of identifying with himself (and taking responsibility for it). The therapist may choose to concentrate on this at the beginning, so that the patient becomes more aware of what is the basic experience and what is his elaboration or his diluting of it in irrelevant words and concepts. For example:

—What is your experience now?

—I feel there are several persons I don't know in the room and perhaps they may not understand what I say.

—That is a thought, and an expectation, not an experience. Try to express your experience now.

—It is like what I feel when . . . I guess it could be called fear.

—Can you describe what you are feeling now?

—My hands are trembling. My voice quivers. I am afraid.

Directness is often dimmed in English by recourse to "it" and related figures of speech on occasions in which either "I" or "you" are implied (and avoided). It may be fruitful to point out such alienated statements and ask the patient to reword them,[2] e.g.:

---

[2] "Every time you do apply the proper Ego-language you express yourself, you assist in the development of your personality." F. S. Perls.

—My hand is doing this movement . . .

—Is *it* doing the movement?

—*I* am moving my hand like this . . . and now the thought comes to me that . . .

—The thought *"comes"* to you?

—I *have* the thought.

—You *have it?*

—I *think.* Yes. I think that I use "it" very much, and I am glad that by noticing it I can bring it all back to me.

—Bring *it* back?

—*Bring myself back.* I feel thankful for this.

—*This?*

—Your idea about the "it."

—My idea?

—I feel thankful towards you!

Perls conceives personality as comprising three layers: the surface is constituted of the roles we enact in manipulating the environment, the "games" we "play"; when we do away with such "phony personality" we are confronted with an area of deadness, nothingness, emptiness (the "implosive" layer); and only by working through and giving in to that deadness can one come to real life—the "explosive" layer of true feelings and strivings. The exercise in staying with awareness will eventually lead the individual to an impasse, a nothingness in which the forces of resistance are equal to what he is resisting. So the next stage is working on the impasse. Here again the aim is to restore awareness to the activity that there *is* in the apparent paralysis. The patient that seems to be unmoved is being pushed or torn by opposing forces of equal strength and must be brought in contact with them. More than that, he has to recognize that these opposing forces are himself, his own potential. In psychological terms, the ego has to identify with the alienated functions or processes.

An example may make this more clear:

> When the therapist asks the patient to pay attention to his voice, the patient becomes aware of it and reports a sad intonation. As he does this there is a change in his facial expression. The therapist comments on this, too. "Yes, I feel some moisture on my eyes." The therapist then asks, "What would your tears say if they could

speak?" The reply is, "We feel shy. We would like to come out but we don't dare." Since a conflict has been exposed, the therapist now instructs him to alternately take sides in him with the desire to cry and "with the desire to resist the crying." This leads to a dialogue between the little tender baby and the "tough man" in the patient, and to an acceptance of both and to an understanding between them.

III

It can be seen in this example that each statement of the therapist leads the patient to *identify,* to *become* his unconscious and alienated activity: his voice first, then his tears, finally the desire to refrain from weeping. The greatest resource for this purpose is that of dramatization, and in this we find the second "tool" of Gestalt therapy. *As awareness leads to some action, so does deliberate acting lead to expanded awareness.* Through the attitude of "taking sides" and acting out any alienated movement, feeling or thought can be developed, contacted, and reassimilated by the ego. It can be one's own voice, a gesture, a fleeting suspicion, a figure of speech, an imagined attitude of the therapist, a fantasy. The therapist will typically propose this at the moment in which he notices an inconsistency between the verbal and nonverbal expression of the patient, suggesting to him to "be" his posture, to "develop" a movement of the fingers, to put into words a smile, or to impersonate the therapist and answer his own question. An illustration here may be helpful:

—I would like to understand . . .
—I hear a wailing in your voice. Can you hear it?
—Yes . . . there is a trembling . . .
—Be your voice, now.
—I am a weak, complaining voice, the voice of a child that doesn't dare to demand. He is afraid . . .
—*I* am . . .
—I am a little boy and I am afraid to ask for anything, can only ask for what I want by showing my sadness, so that mommy will have pity and take care of me . . .
—Could you be your mother, now?
—I *hate* that wailing voice of yours, always wanting to make me

feel guilty about you, poor victim! Can't you speak up and honestly say what you want, for once? etc.

Here we see the enactment in succession of the voice, of the child, and of the mother. A dialogue between the two eventually showed the actor how he was manipulating others by playing the helpless child and how he was hating himself for his deviousness. This awareness was not achieved by analyzing the past or "talking about" his present but rather by letting this behavior develop and, so to say, speak for itself. The individual is not encouraged to become an observer of himself (alienating himself further from his doings) and "compute" an "interpretation," *but to merge with his action and feeling, and have them say what they want.*

IV

The strategies discussed thus far—the exercising of awareness, and that of acting, impersonating one's self—are the two aspects (the contemplative and the active) of one indivisible process: we can become really aware of what we do or perceive only while doing it, and we can have the experience of being the actor, the doer, the perceiver, only when these functions are in our awareness. In other words, there is no real distinction between being "aware," "contacting" our experience, "becoming" ourselves, "entering" our bodily or mental processes, and "becoming one" with them. The alternative to this, the state in which we think of ourselves as "removed" from ourselves and our experience, is one in which we are creating an artificial boundary between self and non-self, and therefore asserting an illusory separateness from the stream of life—our life. *In this duality lies the root of all inner conflicts.*

We may be no more aware of the extent of our intrapsychic conflicts than we are of our sleepwalkerlike restriction of awareness or our estrangement from ourselves, yet the lack of unity in neurotic functioning is as pervasive as the lack of awareness or the lack of identification with ourselves. And again, it is no more than a facet of the same happening. In the same way that total awareness involves opening up to the bliss of the eternal Here and Now, and the end of our alienation involves the realization of the Upanishadic "That art thou," "Thou art God," *so the end of conflict—the synthesis of opposites—involves being one with life, surrendering to the push of its stream and being "it" at the same time, relinquishing any individual will other than the will of life through us, our true self.*

The strategies of Gestalt therapy in dealing with conflict—reversal and encountering—constitute an elaboration of those discussed thus far and are among its most original contributions to psychiatry.

Whenever a conflict is obviously experienced as such ("I would like to but I don't dare," "I am not sure whether I like it," "I feel like crying but I cannot," etc.), it is generally easy to "take sides" with the alternatives and become involved in the fullest possible experience of each at a time. It may be that either one or both conflicting tendencies are being experienced as "non-self," so it has to be reassimilated by the ego through the active effort to impersonate "it," to become "it" by living "it" from the inside. It is an assumption of Gestalt therapy that hardly ever or never will the solution be an either/or. Since both tendencies are living forces in the individual, "each element of the self style must be experienced so that the person can use it when necessary. Freedom is the choice and responsibility taken for the style element used."[3] In other words, the approach is not one of doing away with the elements of the personality (such as resistances or the commands of the superego) but of reassimilating them into the ego. Becoming aware of what "happens in us" is to become aware that *we do it,* and by so *becoming it* we have both the potential and the control. "Do not be tempted to give up your style until you have experienced it. Otherwise you give up one false God to worship another."[4]

V

Whenever a conflict is not experienced as such, it may not be so easy to act out and experience its sides; yet a therapist may see enough of the contradiction to point it out. If the patient smiles while being critical, for instance, the therapist may suggest to him to act critical and severe first, and then, after having experienced his

[3] Gene Sagan: unpublished manuscript.
[4] Ibid.

attacking side, to develop that ingratiating smile. Or if a patient is feeling critical towards her own relaxed, lazy posture, the therapist may guess that she is only avoiding the awareness of the other half of the experience: that she wants and enjoys this posture, since after all she is assuming it. So he may instruct her to exaggerate and give in to her laziness, until she is able to be one with her unacknowledged urge. In a similar fashion, he may propose to somebody who is feeling guilty, carrying the "well-deserved blame," to act resentful in face of "undeserved criticism," thus trying out a reversal in his perception of the situation and himself. Or he may tell a "little old lady" to say nasty things and yell, if it is obvious to him that she is not acknowledging and expressing her hostile reactions. *The princi-ple involved in all such instances is that of taking up attitudes that are opposite to those the person has been assuming.*

We live in only a fragment of ourselves, holding on to a pre-estab-lished self-image and rejecting as non-self all that is conflicting with it or that we expect to be painful. In this island of personality we feel impoverished and helpless, subjected to the pulls and pushes of impulses or compulsions. Gestalt therapy suggests that we regard the self-image as the "figure" in the figure–ground relationship that is involved in all perception. In order to regain from the background what has been rejected from the self, this therapeutic approach invites us to reverse the figure–ground relationship involved in this self-perception and start experiencing ourselves as the background: not the one that is being depressed, but the one that depresses himself; not the one that feels guilty, but the inner judge condemn-ing himself; not the one that feels half dead, but the one that does the chronic self-rejection and killing. *Only by sensing how he does this can a person stop doing it and put his energies to better use than engaging in fruitless battles.*

The principle of reversal can be applied not only to feelings but also to physical attitudes. Opening up when in a closed posture, breathing deeply as an alternative to a restraint on the intake of air or exhalation, exchanging the motor attitudes of left and right, etc., can eventually lead to the unfolding of unsuspected experiences. The following is an example of this kind:

> The therapist notices that while expressing his ongoing experi-ences the patient often interrupts what he is saying and feeling, and

in such moments he swallows or sniffs. He therefore suggests that he do the opposite of sniffing and swallowing. The patient engages in a forceful and prolonged exhalation through mouth and nose, that ends with what he reports as an unfamiliar and surprising feeling: ". . . somewhat as if I were sobbing, but also pushing against a resistance, and my muscles are tense, as when I stretch in yawning; I enjoy this tension while trying to exhale to the very end of my breath, which also feels somehow like an orgasm."

Later, he discovered that he had been living with this feeling for a long time without being aware of it: "It is like wanting to burst, wanting to explode from the inside, tearing down a sort of membrane in which I am wrapped and limited. And I am at the same time this strait jacket, and I am squeezing myself."

This short experience was the starting point of a spontaneous development that took place in the coming months. The muscular tension and concomitant feelings were always very much in his awareness from then onwards, and he felt more and more inclined to do physical exercise. He then discovered the pleasure of dancing and became much freer in his expression, both in movement and general attitude. Finally, he could sense the anger implied in his muscular contractions until he would be aware of it in his reactions to people to a degree he had not been before.

VI

"Taking sides" and merely experiencing the tendencies involved in a conflict may sometimes be enough to precipitate a spontaneous synthesis or resolution. If not, this integration of the opposites may be brought about by their "encountering."

The term "encounter" is being used with increasing frequency to describe a form of direct communication *between* people, but Perls has extended its use to include communication between intrapsychic entities or processes. These could be, for instance, the two sides of a conflict, or the experienced ego and any specific mental content, such as a fantasy, an urge, a feeling. To him, as to Buber, the essence of the encounter is the I–Thou relationship: one in which neither party is reified by "talking about" "you" or "me," but one in which the speaker directs his own activity to the other.

In the interpersonal situation the therapist may encourage the encounter by bringing to awareness all avoidances of the relationship, such as looking away, indirect speech, etc. In the situation of group therapy, the members may be encouraged not to talk in the third person of anybody present, but to express any feelings or thoughts directly to the person to whom they refer. Also, in the same situation, when faced with a question, individuals are encouraged not to "answer" but rather to "respond." Regardless of the answer to a question, we do have a response when confronted with it in a given situation: indifference, eagerness to answer, fear of being exposed by the answer, annoyance, etc. *Expressing this response is closer to self-expression, encounter, and the I–Thou relationship than an answer would generally be.*

Here are some examples of how the principle of encountering can be carried into the intrapersonal domain:

1. A lady explains she would like to remember last night's dream. She is instructed to call the dream, to address it directly, and she says in a very low, monotonous voice, "Come, dream, I want to remember you." When her attention is drawn to the lack of feeling in her calling, she tries again several times, with no success. In doing so she is able to experience the fact that she really does not feel an urge to remember. She feels rather indifferent towards the issue and has been misinterpreting herself, assuming she had such a desire. She can now see she has been playing the "good patient."

2. A woman had a dream in which she saw herself crawling across a room. Somebody asks what she is doing, and she answers: "I want to have a confrontation with that wall."—"Why don't you rather have it with a person, then?"—She answers, "People are walls."

Not only was the person replaced in the dream by a wall, but the wall itself was never reached and "confronted." When told to do so in a session, the woman did so in the same position as in the dream, on her knees and bowing. "I want to go through you, wall." Taking the role of the wall, now, her reply was distant, hard, and disdainful towards her meekness and docility, her posture and weak complaint. After several reversals of roles she stood up, and further, she adopted the attitude of the wall herself, firm, erect, and hard, so she was visualizing two walls in front of each other. This felt to her like the confrontation she was seeking. A week later she reported that she had for the first time been able to confront a man in the same attitude.

A great many and perhaps the most significant encounters are particular forms of one widespread split in personality: the "I should" versus the "I want." It may take the form of a dialogue with an imagined parent, with a disembodied self-accusation, with "people in general," etc., but the parties appear again and again with the distinctive features that inspired Perls (in his inclination for a phenomenological nomenclature) to call them Top Dog and Under Dog.

"Top Dog can be described as righteous, bullying, persisting, authoritarian, and primitive. . . .

"Under Dog develops great skill in evading Top Dog's commands. Only halfheartedly intending to comply with the demands, Under Dog answers: 'yes, but . . . ,' 'I try so hard, but next time I'll do better,' and 'mañana.' Under Dog usually gets the better of the conflict.

"In other words, Top and Under Dogs are actually two clowns performing their weird and unnecessary plays on the stage of the tolerant and mute Self. Integration, or cure, can be achieved only when the need for mutual control between Top and Under Dogs ceases. Only then will the two masters mutually listen. Once they come to their senses (in this case listening to each other), the doors to integration and unification open. The chance of making a whole person out of a split becomes a certainty."

VII

The procedures discussed thus far constitute the embodiment of three principles: (1) that of bringing the spontaneous activity into awareness, (2) that of identification or "taking sides" with such spontaneous activity, and (3) the integration of personality functions or activities by bringing them into a relationship or encounter. Though any experience can be the object of such approaches and procedures, a special place must be granted to our most spontaneous activity, which is dreaming. In fact "dreamwork" is one of the most original contributions of Perls to the therapeutic traditions.

As it is to things in general, the approach of Gestalt therapy to dreams is noninterpretative, and yet it views the dream as an existential message that is to be understood. "Understanding" in this context refers to the direct experience of the dream's content rather than to an intellectual inference, in the same way that "awareness" stands in opposition to an intellectual insight. The road to awareness here, too, is letting the experience speak for itself rather than thinking about it, "entering" the dream rather than "bringing it to mind." In accordance with this, it is important that the dream be not only remembered, but brought back to life. Only by experiencing it *now* can we gain in awareness of what it is conveying. It is therefore advisable to begin by narrating the dream in the present tense, as if it were happening at the moment.

The mere change in wording implied in the use of the present tense instead of the past may be enough to bring about a great difference in the process of recall, which now to some extent becomes a returning to the dream and the feelings that go with the fantasy. This may be an adequate moment to sense its metaphorical language by thinking or saying before every sentence: "This is my existence." Thus, saying, "This is my existence: I am rolling a peanut with my nose," made a dreamer aware of how in her life she was adopting an overly humble role, "kneeling down" and preoccupied with menial tasks and details instead of standing up and facing the important issues. Another dreamer, by saying, "This is my life: I am driving on a freeway and would like to pull off and sleep," realized how he was feeling caught in the conflict between a compulsive, stressful, and lifeless race for power, and the wish to relax, enjoy, and dream.

It may not be easy for some to produce anything more than a dry recall of dream images, in spite of the effort to re-experience, and *this only indicates the strength of the tendency to alienate the dream from the individual's "own" experience*. This alienation is to some extent present in every dream, so the task of Gestalt therapy is that of reassimilating it into the ego and having the person take responsibility for his unacknowledged forces, now projected "out there" as "strange" images. When the attempt at actualization and contemplation of the dream does not lead to more than verbal formulas, such reassimilation may be effected through the acting-out of the different elements in the content.

The "acting-out" of a dream necessarily entails a creative experience of interpretation or translation into movement, and as such it involves an extension of the creative activity expressed in the dream itself. But this is not the only way in which the dreamwork can be expanded. It may be fruitful to fill in the gaps with fantasy or finish the dream where it was forgotten or interrupted by waking up. In being faced with this task the individual necessarily turns into a dreamer again, and becomes one with his dreaming self. Or he may give words to characters that only felt unspoken emotions in the dream, so that they now engage in a dialogue. This is only feasible if the individual really "listens" to his dream by becoming part of it.

A man relates a dream in which he sees himself in a corridor full of lockers. He is looking for some books that he has kept in one of them, but he does not remember which. An attendant approaches him and tries to help him but with no success. Here the alarm clock rings and he wakes up. When told to "go on dreaming" he fantasies that he finally finds the locker and opens it.

When instructed to *sense* this image as his existence he reported that he was actually feeling as "in a corridor full of lockers." His life felt grey, enclosed, impoverished, boring, and unsatisfactory, as if he were searching for something with no success.

The following are some excerpts from the play-acting that followed:

(Here comes the attendant. He takes the key and wants to help me. *I* know better than he where I left my books . . .)

Therapist: Tell him.

—*You* can't help me. I know better than you and can do best when undisturbed. Leave me alone.

Therapist: What does he answer?

—I am sorry, sir, I only wanted to help you . . .

Therapist: Be the locker, now.

—Here I am, a grey locker. I have a number on me. People come and use me. They open me and close me; they put things in and take things out of me. I am pretty tired of this. I am sick and tired of it! How I would like to disappear, not to be found again! . . . I know now . . . I know I can play a trick on this fellow; I can have him be deceived so he doesn't find me! Yes, I will have the attendant "help" him, so he is misled and does not find me.

Therapist: Be yourself opening the locker, now.

(He goes through the movements in a pantomime and ex-
claims: "So it was you! *You*, trying to deceive me!")

Therapist: What does the locker answer?

—ha, ha, ha, ha, ha!

The patient ends expressing that triumphant mockery in a
dance, turning slowly and powerfully at the center of the room
while he laughs.

Therapist: Do you still feel grey and like a number?

—Not any more.

The illustration shows how meaningful it can be to identify with
objects, and not only human or animal characters, in a dream. This,
too, was an instance of a figure–ground reversal, by means of which
the patient came *to experience himself as the one playing hide-and-
seek with himself, and not merely the searching victim.* When his
self-defeating wish was enacted and channeled into the dance he was
not in an impasse any more but creatively expressing himself and
feeling himself as a living being.

"The integration of these selves—the full acceptance of how one
is, rather than how one *should be*—leads to the possibility of change.
As long as people persist in remaining split and not fully acknowledging (taking sides with and experiencing) what and how they are,
real change, I believe, is impossible."[5]

Although I believe all of the techniques described in this chapter
can be advantageously used by the individual, I think the procedure
that lends itself best to the self-therapeutic situation may be the
exploration of dreams. Not only is the dream "the royal road to the
unconscious," so that it can be a guarantee of starting off with a very
significant theme (however insignificant it may appear); it also
provides a convenient blueprint to follow when applying the diverse
exercises of Gestalt therapy. For the one who is willing to explore on
his own, here is an outline to follow:

1. When you wake up in the morning, write down the dream in
the greatest possible detail.

---

[5] Simkin, 1965.

2. Look in the dream for unfinished situations or anything that you have been avoiding, and finish the story in the spirit of *not avoiding*.

3. Say the dream aloud as if the action in it were actually happening in the present, and be aware of yourself and what you are feeling while you do so: Is the intonation of your voice compatible with the reactions you are reporting? What is your breathing doing? etc.

4. Go over the dream once more, still in the present tense, and contemplate it as a picture of your existence: Does it make sense?

5. List the elements in the dream: human characters, animals, objects, elements of nature (wind, earthquake, fire, etc.).

6. Act out the completed dream story from the point of view of yourself in it, placing special emphasis on the avoided situation (falling, dying, being caught, etc.).

7. Play each of the other elements, giving them a voice and letting them speak for themselves and of their wants ("I am a hard rock, a very old rock polished by the centuries," "I am the wind, powerful, free, invisible, unrooted," etc.).

8. Look for pairs of opposites and engage them in an encounter. In doing this you may want to write down a sketch and then play it to the best of your dramatic ability. While giving words to your characters (including yourself) do not just make up sentences, but try to impersonate them, enter the situation, and honestly express your reactions in each role.

9. While doing all this, *be aware* of your reactions.

10. Do you begin to understand the dream's message to you?

The "four visions" that I include as a final illustration are particularly relevant to the application of the foregoing suggestions outside the two-person therapeutic encounter. The poetess who wrote them had been deeply affected by some Top Dog–Under Dog confrontations in a few sessions with me, and was particularly impressed by the effect of reversing roles with a sadistic mother image. This reversal and becoming "the other" in the encounter, as well as the enacting of her fantasy images in general, soon became spontaneous attitudes in her, and led to an ecstatic merging with the elements while writing the following lines:

FOUR VISIONS

I

We swim together
in a clear pool of water
like two tadpoles
close to each other
face to face
ready to mate
and we stop swimming
and tread water
and the water slowly turns
blue blue blue
cerulean peacock blue
and slowly we too
turn the same blue
our arms our bodies
our necks and finally
our faces
and we merge with the water
into the water
and we merge with each other
into each other.

II

Among the big green leaves
of the plane trees
I make my bed
on blue sheets of air
the wind rustles the leaves
against my white voile gown
lifts the gauze
the leaves caress my limbs
through the thin veiling
enfold me in their hands
and I dissolve
to liquid smoke or fog
and merge into each leaf

become a flock of
small grey birds
that sing and sing and sing
from inside each leaf
with high thin delicate voices
the whole tree sings
with every leaf.

III

The eastern sky is pale
yellow air
and I a traced line
in morning sungold coming
with many other girl graces
toward the light
by banks of thin clouds
below the whole earth
where sleep all
now the rolling red ball
fire comes toward us
burns through our air bodies
reflects rosy below
sweats smiles
as he rises smiling giant
climbs to the sky
drops tears and sweat
of hot sungold
down on us we glide
down on it to earth
it becomes sunshine
our traces part of it
we fall with it
rest on fields of grass
and sway on each head
of wheat on each blade
and we become laughter
and pure light and color.

IV

A black tall slim shadow
against the blue-grey
water coming in small waves
in from faded sky
the shadow flat
not molded round like
sculpture or man
shallow or hollow
as a shadow
or a mirror dark
entrance to another world
where it is the beast
I come but do not fit
the shadow
my yellow hair flies soft
in the bare wind
my shadow white and round
against blue-black water
the shadow shrinks
down to my size moves
as if to embrace me
shrinks more
into my white arms
into my white thighs
into my belly
into my head until
I finally sink
into its dark beast shape
and become one
with its dark world beyond
fill the space and
finally am one with the world.

13

George Brown

The Creative
Sub-Self*

I

There is a film of the poet Theodore Roethke, *In A Dark Time*, made a few months before his death. In it he reads some of his poems; he talks about his teaching, and the writing of poetry, and the world he sees. Sometime in the film you go with him, through sun-spangled woods, on a cold, wind-swept ferry, to an eager-faced classroom where he teaches, to a coffee pot. In one scene, Roethke walks the pebbled edge of the sea. The shore is grey; the mood is dark. You see in the water a rock that would be lichen green but on film is black-covered instead.

"You stare," as he speaks, his words come slow, "you stare, until the object becomes you and you become the object."

---

* A part of this chapter has been drawn from "A Second Study in the Teaching of Creativity," *Harvard Educational Review*, Vol. 35, No. 1. Winter 1965.

The simplicity and the power of the thought make even breathing a distraction for the moment. You realize that you are proving his words. The film is so well done that not only has the crusted rock become Roethke and Roethke become the rock but you are now Roethke and Roethke is now you. And then and thus the rock is you and you are the rock.

The birth of this new you, the rock, is so subtle and so satisfying that you find nothing bizarre or strange in its genesis. You realize that circumstances could be such that you might become a tree, a bird, a building, or even the sea that pulses around the rock. You can become many things, and you are many things already.

Because you are many things you are also many you's. You are husband, wife, father, mother, lover, worker, voter, driver of a car, eater of food, drinker of fluids, reader of books, etc. Each of these selves though possibly possessing some characteristics of other selves has its own uniqueness determined by the nature or the function of the role or context perceived by you. This last mentioned "you" is the total you, the overall you, the you that embraces all the other you's, a you that is the summation of the multitude of increment you's that have ever been, are now, or ever will be. It probably seldom exists except perhaps during mystical experiences where timelessness or eternity becomes the context. But for most of us, we are driven to ask with Roethke, "Which I is I?" or to wonder,

> *In a dark wood I saw—*
> *I saw my several selves*
> *Come running from the leaves.*

Yet, if you were to accept the idea that each person is actually many selves, what difference would this make? After all, when faced with a problem, a decision to be made, it is I, Joe Doe, who must make the decision. Not a rock, nor a bird, nor a building, nor the sea. If the problem is a new one for me, what then? It is I, all of me, who must solve the problem. If the problem is new, if it cannot be solved with any of the old answers, answers I already know, and if I am the kind of noncreative person who finds it extremely difficult to apply any imagination, to be original, to think in any way but the cut and dried, the safe and sure, ways you can count on, the tried and tested—then where am I?

I am the way I am. Can I be changed instantly or overnight or even in a year? After all, my whole lifetime has gone into making me the way I am, and logically I would need another equal lifetime to work back through it. Even then to be the kind of person who can find the new solution a new problem demands I would apparently have to start all over again.

This indeed seems a hopeless dilemma. Unfortunately, the dilemma is even further compounded when we edge closer. If the problem is not a new problem, it has either been solved, in which case it should no longer be a problem; or if it has not been solved, it remains in the same condition it was when I first encountered it as a new problem—unresolved. Thus, as in the past, I continue being unable to solve old problems that are no different from the new ones I encounter now. They remain as new as the instant we first met. If I do encounter a situation I already know how to handle, or think I do, the situation as I see it contains no problem for me. On the other hand, any problem from the past that I continue to perceive as a problem is, whether I like it or not, still a new problem.

So here I am, unimaginative, lacking originality or the courage to be different, without spontaneity, freshness, or insight, facing problem after problem—they seem to come more rapidly and with increasing complexity—a pretty kettle of fish.

And as bitter frosting for the wormwood cake, some professor is about to propose that I become a kettle, or worse yet, the fish, or at the least some other self, and thus solve my problems.

There may be alternatives to this approach, but for most of us these seem somewhat elusive. On the other hand, if the approach or some modification of it has been demonstrated to work at times, then we may have dislodged a straw serious enough for grasping.

II

First let us look at a slightly more sophisticated conceptualization of human personality and then consider the results of experiments based on this theory to see whether there might be a possible strategy that can be used to climb out of our dark, deep dilemma.

We begin with what Combs and Snygg call the *phenomenal self*, and the part *figure–ground* relationships play in the phenomenal self. The phenomenal self includes "those aspects of the perceptual field to which we refer when we say 'I' or 'me.'" It features a highly dynamic series of continual modifications in figure–ground relationships. Something is in figure when it stands out or is in focus in the perceptual field, having been selected, segregated, or differentiated from the ground, which makes up the rest of the field. Thus a clock on the wall would probably be part of ground until someone asks for the time. At this instant the clock, or more precisely, the face of the clock, leaps into figure.

These figure–ground relationships govern the process of differentiation, the searching of one's perceptual field or perceived universe. *This search for personal meaning continues as long as there is life in the individual.*

ORGANIZATION OF SUB-SELVES

Behavior at the instant of action is completely determined by perceptions; these perceptions are the fruits, ripe or otherwise, of the search for meaning. As the individual finds himself in a different role or situation and as these roles and situations become familiar, a relatively predictable corresponding organization or structuring of the phenomenal self takes place. It is an organization that the individual believes most appropriate for the situation or role. As the organization becomes more crystallized and predictable, it can be thought of as a sub-self, not "sub" in the sense of "higher and lower" or "better and worse" but rather a self subsumed with others under the larger umbrella of the total phenomenal self. The phenomenal self, then, contains a plenitude of sub-selves. These all overlap to some extent, the degree of overlap probably influenced by the degree of similarity between the determining roles or situations as perceived by the individual. *The total phenomenal self may be thought of as a kind of dynamic multidimensional mosaic that continually changes in characteristics and modifies its organization as sub-selves move into figure, into prominence and dominance, replacing other sub-selves, only to fade in turn into ground or background as each is itself replaced.*

Ostensibly, one of these sub-selves might be a creative sub-self. In order to describe how it may be distinguished we introduce the *preconscious.* Kubie[1] describes the preconscious as existing between the conscious and the unconscious, a level of symbolic process whose function is to express "by implication the nuances of thought and feeling, those collateral and emotional references" that form a kind of coded language essential for creative thinking.

Sub-selves slice through a kind of layer cake of the conscious and the preconscious. (We will not consider the unconscious in the theory now, not from a de-emphasis of its influence, but because once we admit its power, especially in terms of compulsive behavior, not much more can be said that is pertinent here to the utilization of our theory.) The layer-cake analogy is imperfect, however, because divisions between a cake's layers are usually precise and distinct. The division between conscious and preconscious might more aptly be thought of as like that between the colors of the rainbow. Another imperfection of the cake analogy is the concept "slice," which has so static a connotation. More likely, as the phenomenal self palpitates unevenly with figure–ground changes while bumping against the universe, the modulating and imprecise dimensions of the sub-self vary considerably when more than one instant of behavior is considered. Not only do the relative proportions of the conscious and preconscious vary, but so also do qualitative aspects of the two levels. For example, the conscious level may be wide open to new experience or narrowed into a kind of tunnel-vision operation.

Whichever sub-self does become prominent, it dominates the operations of the individual: his differentiating, his perceiving, and ultimately his behavior. How long this sub-self will be prominent or dominant is determined by the individual's role, situation, or context, as perceived and differentiated by him.

Just as situations or roles can determine the prominence of sub-selves, so, too, can preselected symbols.

III

A symbol may be used to trigger a sub-self, bring it into prominence or figure within the mosaic of the phenomenal self, if the

---

[1] Kubie, Lawrence S.: *Neurotic Distortion of the Creative Process.* New York: The Noonday Press, 1961, pp. 32–39.

sub-self has been crystallized around the symbol. The symbol would be a central core of meaning about which a sub-self has been built. Thus, two functions are performed by the symbol, a kind of skeletal function with the symbol becoming the frame about which the sub-self is constructed, and a triggering function such that, when the individual encounters the symbol, the related sub-self is thrust forward into figure to become prominent within the total self.

It should be possible to find a symbol for creativity and to structure about it a sub-self characterized by originality, inventiveness, imaginativeness, spontaneity, experimentality, uniqueness, etc., of perception and behavior. Then the symbol may be used to activate the creative sub-self when creativity is desired. (An example drawn from an experiment will be presented subsequently.)

The creativity symbol would operate at both the preconscious and the conscious levels. In the preconscious it would become a symbol for all the many symbols lurking there and their ever-changing associations. Within the total self, including the conscious level, it would become a trigger for the kind of sub-self that is both relaxed and eager for novelty, a creative sub-self. This is a sub-self that would enjoy a minimum of the structures of threat and guilt, that would have available perhaps the deepest and widest perceptual field or personal universe that could be experienced by the individual.

The creativity symbol also can form a strong tensile link between the preconscious and the conscious. Kubie says this bipolar anchorage of the symbolic process thus has roots linked simultaneously with the external perceptual experiences of the outer world (conscious) and the internal perceptual experience of the body (preconscious). The linkage is necessary if the results of the preconscious symbolic process are to be transmuted into the conscious world to be used in solving problems.

Perhaps, more importantly, the creativity symbol can act as a facilitator or "inviter," allowing the creative sub-self to operate more within the preconscious level. And as the sub-self acts more *here* it has greater powers for free association, for making the analogies or metaphoric connections between the multitude of symbols in the preconscious that result in new patterns and relationships, possibly the root of the creative process.

Thus our theory leads us to believe that it should be possible to develop a creative sub-self built around a creativity symbol. When triggered by the symbol, this sub-self, permeated by much preconscious activity, allows the results of this activity to emerge at a hospitable, open-ended conscious level, ultimately to be transformed into creative behavior by the individual.

In two studies by the author attempts were made to develop a sub-self focused on creativity and built around a creativity symbol.

During the initial stage of the experimental procedure subjects were introduced to creativity as a psychological process and a philosophical value. These two facets of creativity were then "pushed" from an intellectualized understanding toward a more personal, internalized involvement.

The next step was to introduce the creativity symbol by reading a children's book, *The Very Nice Things,* by Merrill and Solbert (Harper, 1959). In the story William Elephant and Old Owl come across the clothes of a man who is swimming. William Elephant finds unique ways to use these very nice things. A pith helmet becomes a bath for his bird friends, the trousers when tied at the bottom become an excellent coconut bag, etc. Old Owl's chronic plaint is, "I don't think that's what these things are for," even when the man later appears and puts the clothes on. The two characters were continually referred to for the remainder of the procedure. *William Elephant became a symbol for willingness to think and act in new, unique, inventive, original, etc., ways, while Old Owl represented the antithetical behavior of conformity, resisting innovation, clinging to the conventional, fearing to make mistakes, etc.*

The personal and professional goals of the subjects (teachers-in-training) were examined and re-examined in terms of the symbols. There was a stress on emotional involvement in creativity as a way of solving problems, of living; there was also emphasis on intellectual and emotional commitment to creativity as an educational goal. As threat tends to narrow the conscious perceptual field and to interfere with preconscious activity, it was kept at a minimum by encouraging the subjects to share as much authority in decision-making as they cared to assume. On the other hand, experiences during the procedure were structured at a challenge level interspersed with opportunities for reflection and recapitulation. Subjects received encouragement for thinking and acting creatively. They were supported increasingly by fellow students for individual daring and apparent willingness to make mistakes.

This latter activity is crucial to counteract our puritanically, perfectionistically oriented culture. Many times the best way, in fact the only way, to learn is through mistakes. A fear of making mistakes can bring individuals to a standstill, to dead center. Fear is the wicked wand that transforms human beings into vegetables. No, perhaps not; even vegetables grow. A person trapped by mistake-fear becomes frozen, rigid, or worse, he may shrivel or shrink through his dehumanization.

Problem-solving, relating, all appropriate aspects of living, were cast in the context of an open system. The more open a system, the more vectors, tangents, and accompanying or related conditions and processes are acceptable, and the more change becomes the primary intrinsic quality of the system. In contrast, a closed system in extreme provides for the using of a very limited amount of information, only one way of doing things, one answer and nothing else no matter how relevant, and absolutely no change.

Throughout the experimental procedure the creativity symbol, William Elephant, and the noncreativity symbol, Old Owl, were increasingly used, apparently because of their appropriateness, attractiveness, availability, and capability for performing the symbol functions described earlier.

The instruments used to test for change in the subjects were measures of preference for complexity and asymmetry. These dimensions seem to differentiate between creative and noncreative groups of artists, writers, architects, research scientists, etc., in research at the Institute for Personality Assessment and Research at Berkeley.

When the subjects were asked to take these tests under the triggered-creativity sub-self conditions, the results were highly significant statistically. The triggered conditions were introduced by giving the subjects these instructions: "This time I want you to be William Elephant, or let that part of you that is William Elephant take the test and shut the rest of you off."

The subjects also took these tests without special instructions both before and after the experimental procedure, without any significant change.

Although creativity is difficult to measure directly, there is little doubt that the frame of reference of the subjects taking the test under triggered conditions was quite different from that used under conventional testing conditions. One of the tests measures aesthetic sensitivity. When this test was taken as the creative sub-self, the scores were much higher than could ordinarily be expected. This is of special interest when one notes that anything related to aesthetic sensitivity, its development or description, was avoided in the experimental procedure. And if one can assume that preference for complexity is an indication of creativity, the development of a creative sub-self occurred and could reoccur.

Apparently sub-selves exist. Among these in certain individuals may be found a creative sub-self. And if not there, it can be grown. With the right symbol for a seed crystal and appropriate experiences to go with it, a whole shining, sparkling, exciting, dynamic sub-self, creatively clear, can be synthesized.

But even this is not enough. There may be those who would be content with a button to push for creativity; the creativity symbol seems to perform a kind of push-button function. Then, whenever one felt the need for creativity, he could punch his creativity symbol and tune in his creative sub-self. After the particular problem requiring creativity is resolved, the creative sub-self could fade into ground; and the stuffy, comfortable (perhaps), unimaginative, old, conforming sub-selves could take over again.

Ah, but there's the rub, or more precisely, the two rubs. Remember, we have agreed that any problem that continues to exist is a new problem, which, of course, requires a new solution, one that has not previously existed in the individual's mind. A new solution, in turn, implies the need for creativity. Consequently, whenever the individual is engaged in solving his problems, which may be most of the time, he needs some creativity. To achieve this he would have to keep the button pushed, to continually use the creativity symbol to trigger his creative sub-self, and this might wear out the button.

The second rub occurs in the above phrase, "whenever one felt the need for creativity." Before one can perceive, one must conceive. I'm not sure whether feeling a need falls within the province of perceiving or the state of conceiving, or both. Assuredly, much of the misery that arises within the human condition, including that during which we protest our comfort, occurs when we cannot feel the need for creativity, for change, for altering our lives, when we cannot feel the need to even push the button.

So in both cases the creative sub-self alone is not sufficient over any extended period of life. What must be hoped for is that the characteristics of the creative sub-self can infiltrate other sub-selves. Eventually the entire phenomenal self perhaps might be permeated with these characteristics.

In order to develop your creative sub-self you may wish to use the following as guidelines:

1. Starting with the phenomenal self, the total composite, you must study the aspects of the figure–ground relationship that govern the process of differentiation—the search for personal meaning in the perceived universe.

2. Behavior is determined by perception of the situation—one chooses automatically what he believes to be the most appropriate self for the situation or role.

3. One of these chosen sub-selves would be the creative sub-self. This self is governed by nuances of thought and feeling essential for creative thinking, and lies between the conscious and the preconscious, blending into both. When the conscious level opens itself to new experiences, the creative sub-self can be dominant, governing the differentiating, the perceiving, and the behavior of the person.

4. A symbol for triggering the creative sub-self should be selected. Thus, the symbol could be consciously brought to mind and used to activate the creative sub-self when creativity is desired.

5. When the symbol is used, the creative sub-self should be allowed the deepest and widest perceptual field or personal universe, such that the experiencing could be creative.

6. This symbol should be used to link the external perceptual experiences of the outer world (conscious) and the internal perceptual experience of the body (preconscious).

7. You must be willing to make mistakes. In utilizing the creative sub-self for problem-solving, all aspects of living must be in the context of an open system—be open to finding a new way of doing things.

8. Lastly, it is hoped that the characteristics of the creative sub-self will infiltrate other sub-selves, permeating the entire personality

with creativity and bringing about the development of the full human potential.

The creative sub-self is but a step toward overall creative behavior. The development of a creative sub-self built around a creativity symbol is only a strategy toward total personality change, toward the full realization of human potential.

14

Stephen M. Schoen

LSD and Creative Attention

In the game, "If you could have one wish come true, what would you ask for?" two different realms converge: pure fantasy and realistic intent. The answer might be simple and material—"I would like a million dollars, tax-free." Or it could express complex values requiring a lifetime to work out—"I want to see things as they are." But there are rules. If someone says, "My wish is to have all my future wishes granted," the reply seems like a trick, technically legitimate but somehow out-of-bounds, a connivance that negates the purpose, the very enticement, of the game. For fantasy has not quite got its way enough, it has been temporarily postponed; and conscious will, insuring itself too much, has lost its sharp edge. If the game is played out that way and we muse over its outcome, we may wonder about some eventual retribution, some ironic turn, like the world chaos set loose in H. G. Wells's tale "The Man Who Could Work Miracles," when the hero, spellbound by his own power, commanded the earth to stand still.

Then we may remember that the game has its precedent, after all, in a highly serious moment, the time that God in a dream offered Solomon whatever he chose, and Solomon asked not for power, which is the fullest assertion of willful intent, but for wisdom, or the proper balance of active will and of the given realities, pleasant or harrowing, that life provides. And afterwards, the story goes (the turn of the tale here is toward fruition and abundance), the dream came true; and God gave Solomon not only wisdom, but power, honor, and long life.

Ignoring its possible historicity, we may take the story of Solomon's dream as a creative work about creative work. For in being creative, human beings have perennially rediscovered this balance between the willed act and the involuntary response. Our self-conscious age, so thoughtfully coveting spontaneity, is apt to identify "feeling spontaneous" with "being creative." The point is well taken but incomplete. As, in our being spontaneous, some new feeling or new realization comes to exist in us; thus, as we are uniting our will with the emergence of this feeling or realization, creation of a kind certainly does occur. But another element must enter before we are *creators* in the sense that artists create; it is the work, all the calculation, the conscious discipline, that goes into producing the created thing. And there is still another factor involved, though not the same as spontaneity, which we must leave among the *donnés* of artistic achievement: the presence of talent, that unique combination of skill, facility, and comprehension, that seems entrusted to the artist's safe-keeping rather than to belong to him, of which he is guardian and instrument rather than source.

I emphasize these considerations because they tend to be pushed to one side by persons who find psychedelic experience creative. This neglect is understandable, for the drug effect explores the potential of spontaneous expression itself. I think there is no question that the psychedelic state is on the side of creativity, as tranquilizer drugs, aimed to inhibit emotional tone, are not. It is the audacity of the "consciousness-expanding" effect, its challenge to the ordinary normative standard of awareness, its readiness to pass purposefully beyond the usual boundaries of perception and of feeling, that prompt the current upholders of the *status quo* to suppress psychedelic agents. The unfortunate consequence is that their importance is magnified, in the tradition of all forbidden fruit. But for those who value new discoveries in human experience the drugs remain to be appraised for what they do and what they do not do; and this, in turn, may tell us something of just how they relate to creativity.

I write of my experience with LSD-25, the psychedelic drug of chief interest to date in psychiatry, and the only one I've worked with. I have had LSD one time myself, dosage one hundred micrograms, and I have given it to some forty patients in intensive psychotherapy, dosage one hundred to two hundred micrograms, in most cases one time only.

The growing appeal of LSD to psychiatrists during the last fifteen years lies in the extraordinarily increased self-awareness that it allows. The mode of experience, both of how one feels about oneself and of how one's senses take in things, is so much more fluent, so much more intense, than habitually. One's being is replete and pluralistic. *It is everywhere and yet well defined, for interpenetrations reveal rather than obscure the identity of things; in a grand style the drug speaks not to diffusion of meaning but to one's uniqueness.* And it seems a particularly correct, dramatic discovery for the psychiatric patient, usually oppressed by feeling "different," that the sense of fulfillment and of self-validation be nonpareil. For myself, as for many psychiatrists who believe that the sudden uncovering of repressed attitudes, emotions, and memories need not be feared in well-evaluated therapeutic work, LSD beautifully confirms not only the reality of the "unconscious" *but the soundness of being ready to trust in it.* The drug effect is a confrontation with an imperative; and, as in similar confrontations such as major surgery or a parachute jump, when, no matter what the anxieties, one must go ahead in faith, when faith is the other side of the coin of helplessness and despair, the experience that forces limits may grant new life beyond them.

But all this with reservations. As more conservative analysts would suspect, this extended individuality is not only positive. For example, one patient of mine, a cultivated and esthetically discerning woman of fifty who looked forward eagerly to LSD, had some terrible moments with it of feeling caged in, of suffocating in pure dread. In reality she had never been a patient in a mental hospital, but the shutters on my office windows suddenly became for her asylum bars.

Then, however, only minutes later, outdoors with me and her husband, she was transported with joy at the beauty of a sunlit grove. And in the days that followed she came to feel that she had learned a great deal from the terror and the joy both; that she could connect how she had felt with familiar attitudes and responses, more clearly understood because of the LSD. As she said, "There were real insights, not had in other ways."

For this woman the nightmare horror seemed worth it. Another patient, though he suffered much less, was less compensated. An overly rationalistic young man with no psychotic history, he, too, had periods of joy during the drug experience. Later he explained to me, "Caught up in intellectual pursuits, I fear for the part of me that will die. That part LSD set free and let live." But during his LSD day, he also got vexatiously caught by the number "two." For the next week he was obsessed with "two's" of all sorts: accidentally looking at his watch at two minutes to two; waking in the morning at twenty-two past two; staring by chance at the street sign at Twenty-second Avenue, where the corner building happened to be numbered 222; and so on. While he was very interested in thinking with me about the symbolic meanings involved, which he suggested himself—two sexes, the bilateral symmetry of the body, the philosophical problem of duality, God–Devil, body–mind, and the like, the psychological importance of polar opposites, as in the Yang–Yin dualism—none of this, nor any memories he could recall from his past, brought him relief or clarification. After a week, unclaimed by any insight, the "two's" faded away.

I do not think that there can be a final psychiatric criticism of LSD based on the private anguish or fixations that it discloses. Many workers use the drug repetitively as a matter of course and find that successive experiences help resolve problems raised in earlier sessions. For these people obviously the drug response is not at all "toxic" or "hallucinogenic"; real fish swim in real waters there. My own question about LSD, for all I have found it to provide, concerns the limits of its positive effect, the way it curbs spontaneity, recreating in a new guise the problems of Tantalus without the pain; for in this instance something of one's real hunger and thirst withdraws forgetfully before the fully offered food and drink.

If there is a connection here to spontaneity, how does it show?

First, there is the peculiar leveling of response that LSD induces, whereby everything becomes equally significant; every experience is in capital letters of the same height. There are numerous, often amusing, examples of this. The lover of music plans, just before taking LSD, to hear a favorite Bach cantata or Beethoven quartet during the experience. But if he finds himself listening instead to The Star-Spangled Banner played over the radio by a brass band, nothing is lost: the music is transcendentally beautiful. Or an artist looking at fine reproductions of Chinese landscape paintings during his LSD day finds himself wholly taken up by the ineffable appearance of the white paper around the pictures. One might concede that the interest of the pictures is normally apparent, while that of the plain white paper is especially absorbing for its unexpectedness. Many people with LSD do indeed hear music or see art with a new appreciation of sound, line, and color. But the particular object of the appreciation is always impressively unimportant. The gain in perception is accompanied by a loss in discrimination among the things perceived.

The loss may appear superficial, the loss of a critical faculty, a refinement, an abstraction; while the intensity of the LSD plunges us into the raw flux of experience—the real center of our living, as William James has described it. But the feeling of "otherness" about things different from oneself, to which one can be related in differentiated ways—this too is part of the raw flux. An amoeba has negative as well as positive tropisms to its environment, and the negative tropism is a critical faculty not at all superficial. LSD significantly dissociates the experience of otherness. It is true that the person having the drug usually counts on contact with some authority, whom he recognizes as different from himself, to assure his equilibrium, even his very survival; for, fascinated by the splendor of an oncoming truck, he would probably not step out of its way. But apart from this basic support and whatever symbolic meanings the authoritative person may have to him, he excludes everything but his own new-found variousness. All the mathematician's transfinite numbers gather in his infinity. Tensions between opposing wills cease to mean anything, or disappear in a resolving laughter. The sense of sequence diminishes with the sense of time.

In the course of the drug experience, the only reasonable response is to accept. Those who administer LSD speak of "going with it," "allowing it to take over." The lure of the occasion, its manifest reward, is what it *includes*. But is it the same as spontaneity without a drug? The question is not whether one can evoke the drug condition after a period of using LSD—this may be quite feasible—but whether the two states are not significantly different. The difficulty of transposition from the one to the other follows from the special forfeits the LSD requires. Indeed we see the problem dramatically posed by the very interest in psychedelics. For some enthusiasts who began by proclaiming these phenomena as great illuminating guides to ordinary experience have come, it seems, to live *for* the drug experience itself. And why not? If the experience is that good and its transposition so difficult, why not be engulfed by it? Only then we must admit that we are not speaking of new disclosures about spontaneous living; that the drug response is a special statement of inner life, as trances and visions have been in the history of religion special expressions of mystical life; and that that one directly creative challenge of LSD begins just where the psychedelic effect leaves off: with the discernment of how it does bear on all creative expression.

Total going-with-the-thing, so that the person is at one with his act—that unity is constant throughout creative work. The myriad subtleties of perception, the many-hued world made real by LSD, is a kind of artist's sourcebook in which the boundary between self and nonself is passed beyond, or rather given up. As Frank Barron has pointed out, just this is given up in creative perception. But artistic achievement reveals the greatest difference from the experience of LSD. For it exists in the world of space, time, causality, clear limitation and finitude, in sustained form and stable interrelationship. It exists entirely through having "a local habitation and a name." Like LSD, it contains truths that, although passing, are somehow redeemed from transience. But it exemplifies, as LSD does not, eternity's love for the productions of time.

Fearlessness and naiveté often go together. The proponents of psychedelic experience tend to an ingenuous faith in their readiness to give up a "limited mode" of being. Those passionately in love do not need aphrodisiacs, since aphrodisiacs, though they can induce passion, will never make one fall in love; so we must wonder what kind of equivalence is established by a drug easily called in our day "the chemical equivalent of mysticism." The problem is one of motive. How much does the person really want to give up being limited, being overcontrolled? Even to speak as some men do of the "usefulness" of psychedelic experience is to suggest the resistances to it with which they are dealing. Again, who speaks of the "usefulness" of being in love? Psychiatrists working with LSD are the first to know the strength of these resistances—they and their patients. A few days, or a few weeks, after the transcendent release, the person feels "himself" again: that is, anxious, constrained, overcontrolled. Then the therapist and the patient are back in the ordinary world, standing together in judgment before the fateful question of their work: how much freedom can the person really live with?

I think this is as it should be. We know the anxious man has good reasons for his controls. And it is a kind of nonsense to believe, in the name of unrestrictiveness, that a drug will decisively rid him of restrictions to which at least he has an unrestricted right. He gets rid of them himself, of his own volition, as his psychotherapy succeeds. Further, for a creative state to be maximal, the person's capacity to control himself, to discern the proper limits of expression, is requisite. LSD has a peculiar appeal to the side of us seeking deliberate, direct correction of an impoverished inner life, a too-narrow secularity. And the deepened flow of feeling, the changing, merging, interweaving perceptions that the drug allows, constitute a real criticism of that deficit. But overcontrol is not the same thing as any control. The need for spontaneously operating controls remains, such as inner restrictions that warn us against danger, or the desire to sleep when tired. LSD dissociates these controls. I am reminded of the so-called impulse neuroses, which display not impulse-freedom but a compulsion to impulselike action, sexual and aggressive, when anxiety precludes the person from feeling controls in a free play. For the other big appeal of LSD is to the side of us that, in idleness and often from a high basal level of anxiety, looks for self-realization at a cheap price and does not consider that we are asking for too little.

This one point, that spontaneity depends on good controls, including the control manifested in the ability voluntarily to abandon control, casts particular light on creativeness in mystical experience. Here the single aim of control is decontrol, and the willed decontrol is all. Outward controls do exist for the mystic, in the form of church dicta and institutions, to serve him as guidelines. But even the excellent Jesuit Father D'Arcy, while emphasizing the dangers of a path so lacking in sanctions as "uncovenanted mysticism," feels that many may find the true God in this way.

What, then, of drug mysticism? In his careful and thoughtful article, "Do Drugs Have Religious Import?" Huston Smith writes of some psychedelic response, "Descriptively, the drug experiences cannot be distinguished from their natural religious counterpart." Once more, we are impressed with the scope and authority of their revelations. Dr. Smith allows that there may be "genuine ontological difference between natural and drug-induced religious experience," and later in his paper reminds us that "religion is more than religious experiences." For me, it is these differing contexts of experience that make the ontological difference. Being is defined by its context, as a C-major chord has one "being" in a Czerny exercise and another in a Schubert sonata, having appeared in both pieces in different ways, for different reasons, and to different ends. This is not to deny that one may perform better with the Schubert sonata for having practiced the Czerny exercise. But the more refined the practicing, the more one can be aware of the differences.

Psychedelic experience occurs, I think, at that common border where art, mysticism, and spontaneous self-discovery pause for breath. For them to go on and speak, to fulfill their creative impetus in a way of life or a form of expression, requires the exercise of a further discipline and integration. My image, so far as it suggests a stepwise progression from the one experience to the others, is misleading. For the whole value of LSD, its special quality of absorption, of momentum, of inchoate charms, lies in the fact that it resists translation, that it weaves a logic and a spell of its own. Our chance, it seems to me, is to appreciate all this while yet appreciating something of its irrelevance. "What is laid upon us," Kafka said in one of his aphorisms, "is to accomplish the negative; the positive is already given." But how can LSD bring us to the negative, the doing away with our constraints, when the most that we can expect of ourselves, in taking the drug, is to do away with our constraints against it? And then, led on by its disclosures, we begin to ignore the extraordinary drama of the Christian world view: that God in fact became fully man. Of necessity we forget, since the dissociations of the drug effectively become a denial of just how much of man God can inhabit. Psychedelic mysticism is won by a desertion of the human estate; and the more the mysticism fascinates us, the more the desertion appears intemperate. It is, I think, in Dante's upper hell, among the wasters of life, that the proselytizers of LSD belong.

And yet, on the other hand, creative attention attends to an excess, the excess of Baudelaire's advice: "Be drunk continually! With wine, with poetry, or with virtue, as you please!" Traditionally, artists and religious men have had degrees of interest in drug experience, as Baudelaire himself did; and today they are among the people least afraid of LSD. But their wish to be "drunk" depends on no chance event or extraneous source. It is, rather, of a piece with Solomon's wish, that dream wish proportionate to the visionary dreaming of wholly wakeful man, a wish practical, exacting, and excessive—everything that gave it its power to come true.

[15]

Ruth C. Cohn

Training Intuition

The title of this chapter contains two assertions that are not universally accepted: *intuition is a fact, and it can be trained.*

Although intuition is one of the major tools in all creative endeavors, few references to this phenomenon are evident in professional psychological journals. Intuition, as far as I know, has not been considered a talent that can be trained but rather an equivalent of a magic wand, or an innate, unalterable personality trait. Yet, it is not a mysterious gift that will go away if we touch it, and we are not irrational, mystical fools to be concerned about it.

Experientially, intuition may appear in our awareness as a sudden flash, seemingly coming from nowhere. Or intuition may be there, in our mind, without our noticing its entry. And sometimes it may appear with the strength of a mystic revelation. *The experience we call intuition is characterized by suddenness and certainty, lacking conscious awareness of its source.*

Most intuitions pertain to the field of interpersonal events; but they may also be related to subjects such as music, mathematics, the weather, or the stock market. Solutions to interpersonal artistic, scientific, or practical problems often appear to the searching person after some pause such as sleep or silence.

Intuition must say something valid about reality—the frame of reference we live in. Intuition can be recognition, interpretation, or premonition. When related to something tangible it is called inspiration; inspiration is intrapsychic intuition. *There is no false intuition; there is only intuition or error.*

The author would like to share her conviction, based on professional experience, that *intuition is simply a human talent* like the ability to love, to think, to construct theories, and to create works of art. If this is true, intuition, like all other human talents, can be nurtured and trained, or neglected and destroyed. We train the talent of thinking by carefully exposing children to mathematics and the rules of logic. We train their musical abilities by teaching them to play an instrument and giving them lessons in music appreciation. If we recognize intuition as a talent, we must also consider its training. Until now intuition has been left to grow or perish in an unattended, weedlike fashion.

Let us briefly direct our attention to *three means of insight into reality: perception, deduction, and intuition.* Either of these may lead us to make a statement such as the following: "This man is a painter."

(1) *Perception:* "I observe a man. He has a paint-brush in his hand and paints a picture. I say: 'This man is a painter.' "

In this case we rely on our senses and previous knowledge, into which we integrate the new perception. I perceive the painter as painting, through the use of my senses. I connect what I see (or touch, hear, smell) to my conceptual world: "This man is a painter."

(2) *Deduction:* "I see a man through the window of an art shop. He gives a painting to the owner of the store and gets a receipt. The man has paint on his hands and trousers. He talks to the owner and points to details of the picture. I say: 'This man is a painter.' "

Here we build on perception and previous knowledge. I have accumulated perceptions and memories and connect them step by step to a conclusion. If my premises are correct and I follow orderly, logical procedure, I deduce correctly: "This man is a painter."

(3) *Intuition:* "A man sits opposite me in the bus. I am reading a newspaper. I look up and words come into my mind: 'This man is a painter!' "

Here the steps from the question to the insight are unconscious (and/or in psychoanalytic language: preconscious). *The road from question to answer by intuition is a short cut.* The cues on the road are sensory perceptions, emotions (including drives), memories, and deductions. Yet these cues do not come to awareness. The intuition "This man is a painter" may have travelled on the sensory track (he smells of paint); or on emotional cues (I feel toward him as I do toward painters A and B; I would like to meet painter C); or on memories (his appearance and clothes, his gestures, his facial expressions, resemble painters I have seen); or on deductive tracks (the bus terminal is close to the city's artists' colony, and at this time of the day painters often travel to art galleries in the bus's direction).

It is likely that many elements of sensory, memory, deductive, and emotional origin go into one single intuitive insight; yet intuition appears as a "Gestalt"—a completed pattern or structure. If premises and short cuts are correct, intuition is valid. (Extrasensory perception must be hypothesized as a form of intuition with many missing links in the chain of evidence. If ESP is valid, we must assume that we are unaware of some perceptions and that unconscious unknown receptors exist.)

No recognition or insight is infallible; perception, deduction, and intuition may be correct or may fail us. We must always take the risk of being right or wrong. Each step up the ladder of gaining knowledge, from perception to intuition, rests on all previous steps. The higher the function, the more likely are errors. Our senses may be misled by optical or auditory illusions; we then perceive incorrectly. Our mind may err, using misperceptions of false recall or faulty logical conclusions; then our deductions fail. Our intuitive faculty fails us if any of our pertinent perceptions, memories, intellectual processes, or emotions are faulty or disturbed. The most complicated machines may give us the most valuable service, but the sensitivity and complexity of the parts and combinations provide room for more frequent breakdowns.

We may now tentatively *define intuition as a unique and compli-cated faculty for spontaneous insight resting on:*

clarity of perceptions
adequate storage of pertinent facts
trained thinking
unblocked and alert emotions

Further, emotional alertness, frequently encompassing a passionate desire for response or conclusions, must be unblocked to let in pertinent factors of past and present experiences. Last but not least, our attitude must permit a quiet and silent period until things fall into place.

On a practical level, people are aware of the significance of intuition. A clerical worker states, "I want to recognize my boss's moods before I ask him for a raise. Whether or not I get the raise depends more on his mood than on my performance." A psychotherapist says, "I know my interpretations are often correct, yet my patients cannot accept them because I do not seem to have the intuition of timing them correctly; they often fall flat, or my patients become defensive." A young man complains, "I know people who find their way in strange cities. I can't even find my way in places where I've been before. I have no intuition for distances or directions." A woman laments, "I always trust the wrong person and constantly fall in love with the wrong man. I want to be able to recognize the right man when I meet him."

In order to answer such questions of how improvement of intuition can take place, I would like to describe the development of my interest in the subject of training intuition. *I never asked the question, "Can intuition be trained?" but by chance came to the recognition that such training had occurred as a side effect of a specific method I have used in the training groups for psychotherapists.* I would like to describe some of the content of this method which led to the discovery of training intuition and became the basis for further inquiry.

For many years I conducted a workshop for experienced psychoanalysts, which dealt with the therapist's emotions toward his patients. The specific intent was to differentiate between adequate emotional responses to the patient's needs and progress, and distortions, which inhibit his understanding. If, for instance, the therapist feels toward a patient as if he were his brother, and he endows the patient with his brother's qualities in an illusionary way, he cannot recognize the patient's personality as it really is. He will therefore be handicapped in deciphering the patient's problem. (Technically speaking, this phenomenon is called "countertransference.")

One day I noticed that after a year's participation in this countertransference workshop, a young colleague had acquired sensitivity for people and intuitive skill that he had formerly lacked. This recognition took me by surprise. How had it happened? I felt like a parent who recognizes that his child who had just been a baby "suddenly" was riding a bicycle. A child's growth and intellectual expansion occur through infinitesimal and practically unobservable daily changes and are therefore outside the parents' awareness. Therefore, often the growth of a child is recognized by his parents in a situation that does not obtain every day, such as watching the child at a school performance, playing on the baseball field, or remembering the last birthday party. At such moments the child's growth flashes into the parents' perceptive awareness.

It was with such "parental" suddenness that I became aware of my young colleague's acquired skill of intuiting connections, predicting steps in the sequence of therapy, sensing feelings of other group members, and expressing pertinent associations and imagery about patients under discussion. He had learned to take cues from the environment correctly and rapidly. He had learned to be empathic, to feel for and with other people. His intuition had improved. This man's own torment and our doubts about his professional suitability had vanished. We enjoyed the experience of his emotional acuity and intuitive skill.

I was excited about the evidence that intuition can be trained, and I became observant of the fact that improvement of intuitive skill had not only occurred with this one colleague but was true for many participants of the countertransference workshop, including myself. The next step would be to isolate those factors that might have caused this serendipitous phenomenon. We might then be able to establish a method for the training of intuition not only for psychotherapists but for many people under a variety of conditions.

Basic in the method of the countertransference workshop is the use of intergroup relationships as a tool for learning more about the therapist–patient relationship. If a therapist has certain blind spots toward his colleagues in the group, overlooks or distorts elements of the other person's character, or misses the effect his actions have on others, it is likely that these same difficulties arise in his judgments about and relationships with his patients. The therapist's difficulties and feelings in the treatment situation are discussed openly and linked with events in the immediate relationships with colleagues in the workshop group. The atmosphere is geared toward awareness of expressions, feelings, and thoughts. As members we learn to accept our strengths and frailties, sympathies for and antagonisms against each other. We learn that even negative emotions can be used in the service of ourselves and patients, and that sexual abstinence or restraint with patients does not necessarily imply absence of desire. We learn that we can cope with other people's emotions, including those of patients, if we can understand, condone, and even love our own, regardless of what they may be. We learn that feelings are there to be felt but not necessarily to be acted upon; that intellect and a deeper sense of values and responsibility may guide activities but not extinguish feelings.

I set out to transfer some of the basic elements of the "counter-transference workshop" into an "intuition workshop." Continuing in the same spirit of openness, acceptance, and search, the group now used the experience for an exploration of the concept and fact of intuition. The group members were invited to respond to each other with intuitive observations and communications. The validity of intuitive statements was then checked. Silence was introduced to stimulate sensing, observing, feeling, thinking, and re-evaluating present and past experiences. What was felt and thought during silent periods was later communicated in order to learn more about each other and to check on intuition and errors about silent neighbors. Insight was also gained by experiencing oneself through other participants' perceptions, like looking into one's own house from the other side of the street.

The participants of the five intuition workshops—totalling about seventy people—have in essential ways and with much dedication contributed to the experiences and conceptualizations of this paper. I want to thank all of them for their contributions, especially the one experimental group of lay people and the first pioneering group of psychotherapists. Their enthusiasm has led to a continuous open-end, theme-centered workshop. We use the same searching techniques described in this chapter for other concepts of psychotherapy.

Once the attention of the workshop members was geared to intuiting events in the group, many spontaneous situations arose which were utilized. At the beginning of a second workshop session, for instance, participants brought up the question, "Who of the seventeen group members of the first session would not come back?" Only four names were mentioned. Three people did not return, the three being among the four mentioned. It must be added that none of the three had indicated in any overt way that he would not continue. They had made some negative remarks about the setting, but so had many other people. Conscious cues were taken from manifestations of a member's "surplus aggression," of one's thinly covered anxiety, of someone's denial of feelings of superiority, and from a person's general appearance of being bored and anxious. These reasons were given among others after an intuitive flash that this or that person would not return.

Intuitive recognition of people's emotions through subliminal perception of nonverbal cues is more frequent than we generally realize. It is important to note that the above-mentioned surprisingly accurate intuitive predictions occurred in the beginning of the second session of the lay-group workshop. This seems to indicate that the mere acceptance of the question of "whether intuition can be improved" results in people's attempts to increase awareness of their intuition. (An ability cannot be suggested; it can only be freed from inhibitions and trained for use.)

Early interpersonal intuitions related to questions around areas of vocation of participants, their positive and negative feelings toward each other, the question of whether people would sit on the same or different chairs each time, etc. As trite as some of these examples may appear, their value rests on the amazing frequency of correct predictions and interpretations and on the subsequent study of the cues that led to positive or negative results.

Frequently, errors of "intuitive" statements in early sessions were derived from a need to please or affront the group leader. The wish to submit to or outdo another person, the assumption of certain standards (of right and wrong, pleasing and not pleasing), are likely to disturb correct perceptions and valid intuition. Bias and intuition are incompatible.

Ella thought of herself as being born with a special gift of intuition. She proposed to know not only the moods of her husband and boss but even what they were about to say. This was hard to validate in the group. What could, however, be checked were her statements about people's reactions in the group: "You are silent, Larry, because you are angry at Bill." "I am not," was Larry's answer. "I am silent because I am involved in what Ben said." Ella did not believe it. Of course, she could have been right. Larry might have lied or been unaware of his feelings. Yet after several incidents of a similar nature, Ella started to question her need to be infallible, which appeared to be interfering with her genuine but not omniscient intuitiveness.

In all groups were people who thought of themselves as lacking intuitive skills. This did not always coincide with other people's observations:

Jim, a camp director, was upset about his lack of intuitiveness when hiring counselors for an interracial camp. How could he know, within a short interview, which of the applicants would relate well to the Puerto Rican children? He needed unprejudiced counselors, with warmth and common sense. More often than not his intuitive choices were correct; sometimes he erred. This seemed to occur mainly because he wanted to be liked and found it difficult to say no. A rejected applicant would dislike him, and this was not easy to take. He tended to feel that all people were right until proven wrong. Whenever his rose-colored glasses and his need to be liked prevented him from accepting reality, his intuition failed him.

If our emotional needs, as in Jim's case, interfere with realistic facts, intuition fails. We succumb to wishful fantasies or fearful apprehensions. Apathy as well as overinvolvement blocks intuition. We need a middle road of emotional alertness to allow for intuitive insight.

Interpersonal intuition requires an ability to know and to relate to people as they are. We have to allow ourselves and our children to encounter people with open eyes. Young children's intuition appears to be excellent. They often can sense whether or not strangers are genuinely warm toward them. As long as their spontaneity is not disturbed by social demands "to be nice," they usually have intuitive knowledge of people's feelings and moods. Yet it is erroneous to think that children are more intuitive than adults. Intuition is built on experience, i.e., stored-up knowledge, as well as on spontaneity. Children's experiences are limited; even if their spontaneity is undisturbed, their intuition cannot reach further than their experiences.

If children are pampered and are not taught to consider others, they are likely to lack empathy. If, on the other hand, they have to appear "selfless" and need to fulfill their parents' every wish, they have to give up self-realization and cannot relate to either self or others. Buber has said it well: "If Thou is said, the I of the combination I–Thou is said along with it."

Woman's intuition has frequently been regarded as superior to man's. If this should be correct, and it may be so at least in interpersonal areas, it might partly be based on her social role, which includes maintenance of the emotional patterns of the family. Beyond this, biologically speaking, she must empathically meet the needs of the nonverbal infant. (Empathy is an important part of interpersonal intuition.) Man's intuition will similarly function best in those areas in which he is most involved, which may often be work areas rather than interpersonal relationships. Intuition develops best where we have the greatest backlog of experience and realistic emotional involvement.

To intuit people requires empathy. Empathy is a spontaneous feeling for somebody else, a feeling that puts one into the feeling world of another human being as if "I were he," yet, paradoxically, "leaving me intact as my being me, *feeling within me* how he feels." It is a specific human capacity—to be oneself and yet to cross the feeling border to the other person. A physician can hurt a child with a hypodermic needle and feel that child's pain, fear, and anger without giving up his own secure feeling about doing what is necessary. An empathic parent understands the child's desire to play rather than study but does insist on what he deems to be important at that moment. It is this quality that makes a good educator, friend, and psychotherapist: to feel with the other—yet to remain oneself.

If our own needs are paramount we cannot be empathic; if we are geared to other people to the exclusion of our own needs we cannot be ourselves. *Empathy and intuition function if we can feel with other persons without sacrificing our own integrity.*

Disturbances in empathy that originate in childhood may require psychotherapy. Other disturbances may be due to immediate circumstances and can be remedied by conscious effort or alteration of the disturbing situation. The thirsty traveller in the desert "intuits" mirages because his need for water and coolness impels him; too much deprivation is unacceptable.

If we know the *basic elements of interpersonal intuition, i.e., open experiences with people, empathy, and emotional freedom to let new insight surprise us,* we will find methods of training this skill. The fact that the described workshops were experienced by almost all participants as useful for this purpose was probably due to the groups' interpersonal openness, benevolence, and ability to use silence, take risks, and freely communicate and check intuitions.

In the atmosphere of the workshop the man who felt that his raise depended on the boss's mood could become aware of the fact that his own attitudes were likely to influence the boss's mood. A dependent/helpless attitude on the part of the employee influences the boss's response. If a person takes time out for recognition of his own mood and feelings and trains himself to understand the gestures and fleeting expressions of the next person, he becomes more perceptive of his own feelings and more empathic with other people's moods, including those of the boss.

The psychotherapist who tends to give premature interpretations may become aware of his need to feel more intelligent than his patient. The need to impress may outdo his therapeutic acumen. His emotions are not geared directly to the patient but are caught up with his being the son of a critical father. His empathy and perceptivity to the patient are blocked. Disconnecting the past from the present helps him to become more intuitive in timing his interpretations.

The person who cannot find his way in a strange city may have to make a conscious effort to learn to follow directions, either by maps or compass points. However, he may also need to consider his rebelliousness against having to find his way without the guiding hand of a reliable adult (there is a child in everybody somewhere). It is both the freeing from past bondage and the learning of new cues that lead a step closer to intuitive skill.

The woman who falls in love with men she cannot trust may find out that she is not really unintuitive but that her intuition follows unconscious commands not to dare to love anybody because she is "secretly married to her father." To fall in love with anyone else would be defeat. In such cases emotions are not geared to help the person acquire intuitive knowledge about the real world but to perpetuate a neurotic misconception such as being secretly married to one's father.

Intuition is a silent traveller. It travels from our own conscious questions of today to our inner storage room which contains forgotten or dormant memories and drives. It picks them up, reorders them, and travels silently back to our present consciousness, delivering the answers we have been looking for in a sudden flash. *Valid intuition uses preconscious roads and sensory, logical, and emotional vehicles to connect conscious with unconscious psychological data and organize them.* It then presents us with "obvious" solutions.

We cannot force intuition, but we can invite and train it. It does not grow in empty quarters or barren fields. It thrives on love for ourselves and others. It feeds on the world inside and outside of our body–mind borders. It needs awareness and seeks rest, quiet, and trusting waitfulness. It seeks the company of people and the openness with which to understand them well. It dies with bias, prejudice, and social amenities. It lives in freedom, playfulness, and love of surprises. *It responds best where we work hardest; yet not often does it meet with us unless we are at leisure. We can train and enjoy it.*

[16]

Renee Nell

Guidance
Through Dreams

Dreams had always been an important part of man's life until around the Middle Ages, when the Church took a rather dim view of dreams as a means of revelation. Up to that time dreams had been considered a communication from God. Both the Old and the New Testaments are full of dreams that give guidance or a communication from God, knowledge not available in any other way. In primitive tribes, to this day, the shaman, or medicine man, has the role of interpreting these messages from the gods. If a man has a "great dream," the shaman calls the whole tribe together, and the message of the dream is shared by all. When dreams fell into disrepute, the knowledge of this symbolic communication gradually got lost or distorted. The attraction to the mysterious imagery, nevertheless, remained—as did the desire to glean some communication from it. The result was a regression to a primitive and superstitious kind of soothsaying (mumbo jumbo), which is still alive in "Dream Books" available for a quarter. There we find that a black cat means a letter from abroad, etc.

Around the turn of our century dreams became reputable again. Through Freud and his followers they found entrance into our life. Freud's approach is similar to, but not the same as, Joseph's when he interpreted the dreams of the Pharaoh. Now as then we believe that dreams contain an important message; but, while in the old times we believed that this message came from a source beyond ourselves, we now believe that the source is inside of us, and we call it the unconscious. Now as then we believe that the dream contains a message expressed in symbols that have to be understood and interpreted by a knowledgeable person. While in the past this message was mostly of prophetic character, often meaningful to a whole tribe or of importance as guidance in a heroic task, we now believe that the dream reflects the here and now and is meaningful only to the individual, giving him guidance in the nonheroic tasks of his everyday life.

How does the dream give this guidance? How does one decipher symbols and translate them into meaningful messages? Dreams still give rise to many questions, many speculations: Does everyone dream? Do healthy people have dreams? Do dreams really mean anything? Are they related to what we have eaten? Are they just a repetition of the day's events?

The importance of dreaming to our total physiological and psychological system is proven by the fact that people deprived of dreams will hallucinate. Dream deprivation is brought about by waking the person whenever the machine indicates the beginning of a dream. In this way he is dream-deprived without being sleep-deprived.

Dreams then are part of our natural equipment and a sign neither of health nor of sickness.

Other research has shown that food, heat, cold, and other outer stimuli like street noises, doorbells, and alarm clocks do not influence the dream in any significant way. If these outer stimuli are woven into the dream, they are transformed in a way meaningful to the dreamer; while in one man's dream the overheated room will appear as a smoldering purgatory in which he suffocates, another man might dream that he is sunning himself on the sandy shores of Florida happily resting in his girl friend's arms. Daily events follow the same pattern as sensory stimulations. Dreams do not just repeat daily events, but they select from the hundreds of daily impressions those that convey a meaningful message. The same two men who dreamt so differently about the heat will dream differently about the same event in their workaday life.

What then is the principle by which a dream is put together? What is its process, and what is its pattern? If we can understand the fabric of the dream, we can understand its message to us. This is the prerequisite for an inner conversation with our Self, with the inner voice of warning or encouragement that in the stillness of the night gives answer to the unanswered questions, the doubts, and the anxieties of our daytime life.

We have said that the dream is part of our natural equipment and that our nature reacts when we interfere with this process. Why has nature provided us with this particular faculty? What is its meaning and use? Our whole system functions in terms of tension and relaxation of tension, inhaling and exhaling, ingestion and digestion, and the dream follows that same principle. We "inhale" thoughts, ideas, impressions, during our waking life. The dream is the exhaling, the digestive process, of these experiences. And just as our physiological system in health as well as in sickness strives toward physiological balance, our psychological system with the help of the dream strives towards psychological balance.

An example of this striving is the dream of a Hollywood writer who had gained substantial public acclaim for his work and had become very conceited. Simultaneously he developed dizzy spells for which no physiological cause could be found. He dreamt that he was on a bus that was higher than any other bus, and he was sitting on the top deck. The bus was going at great speed uphill and downhill, swaying dangerously from left to right, endangering his safety and making him experience the same dizziness he felt in his daytime attacks. He thought in the dream, "How can I get out of the bus? It would be so much safer to walk."

The dream here seems to say, "What are you so conceited about—being on top of that shaky vehicle called Hollywood fame? Give up your conceit, walk with the average man, and you will feel better."

Another dream portrayed the same principle. It was dreamt by a person who forces himself toward achievement beyond his natural capacity. He dreamt that he had a strong and good car and was racing it uphill. The car resisted, but he kept forcing it and finally made it to the top. But when he arrived there the tires were bloated, the engine had burned out, and the whole car fell apart and was a wreck. His father stood there and said to the dreamer, who was upset about having ruined the car, "Never mind the car. What about you?" Here the dream sounds the warning to the dreamer not to abuse his physical strength. This principle of balance, of homeostasis, underlies every dream, and it justifies the assumption that the psyche is a self-regulatory system.

We have said that we have to understand the principle, the process, and the pattern of the dream. The process used to make visible the principle of balance is reflection on the events of the day before. It is as if our daytime thoughts presented, "On the one hand"; and the dream echoed, "but on the other hand." Coming back to the man on the bus, the man seems to say, "On the one hand I like to be on top, I like to be carried uphill"; and the dream answers, "but on the other hand it is a dangerous ride that leads downhill too and makes you dizzy to boot." And the same reflection takes place in the next dream. On the one hand, "I'm strong and healthy and can force myself to achieve the impossible"; and the dream answers, "but on the other hand you fall apart at the end."

The pattern of the dream is that of a story, a fairy tale, with a beginning, a middle, an end, and a *moral*. Most of us are removed from the world of symbolism, myth, and fairy tale, and have trouble deciphering the symbol language of the dream and discovering its logical structure. Those who are still close to the unconscious (children, poets, and creative people in general, as well as schizophrenics) often have an easier time understanding dreams than highly intelligent scientists, who are generally removed from this "irrational" area of personality.

But there is nothing mysterious in learning to understand the principle, the process, and the pattern of the dream, once we find the key to decode this long-forgotten language.

Often the dreams of another person seem much clearer, much more obvious to us than our own. With the two dreams mentioned above one might even wonder why such obvious findings do not come to the subjects through logical thinking instead of having to arise from the unconscious. The answer is simple: the conceited writer enjoyed the power feeling of his superior position and did not want to come down from his shaky height. He hoped to cure his dizziness with a pill and his anxiety about his shaky position with a tranquilizer. Logically, then, he would hide the cause of his unpleasant symptoms in the unconscious. Similarly, a man who enjoys the feeling of his physical strength and likes to delude himself as to its limits would rather blame his exhaustion on the weather than admit that even the best machine has its limits.

The outsider who has nothing at stake can often understand the message of the dream much easier than the person who dreamt it. Nevertheless, one can make use of one's own dreams to further insight and to receive inner guidance; one has to become an outsider to oneself. The best way to do this is to write down the dream, put it aside, and forget about it. One should, during the week, note down at least three dreams. Naturally, as the dream reflects on the day before, the date should be included, and a short remark to retain the events of the day preceding the dream. A couple of days after the recording of the last dream, one should look at the accumulated series and find first the main theme that runs through all the three or four dreams like a red thread. After that one should read each dream as if it were a short story, and give it a title.

The next step would be to seek out the feelings displayed by oneself or anyone else in the dream, relating them to similar feelings evoked on the day before. If the red thread running through the short series is one of defeat, one should examine in which way the events of the preceding day touched on a problem of defeat that one did not want to look at.

A young woman who had hastily gone into her marriage discovered after a year that she had never been in love with her husband, but her moral values did not permit her to question the bonds of marriage, let alone consider a divorce. She denied herself and her husband sexual gratification, using the usual rationalizations. She was convinced that she neither missed sex nor was interested in other men, until she dreamt many dreams in which attractive men of her acquaintance or unknown suitors courted her, and in the dreams she was attracted to the point of desiring sexual relations with them. But in each dream attempts to find a place for intimate contact were defeated by the appearance of the husband or the mother, or other unusual circumstances. Consciously, she had suspected herself of being frigid and incapable of love, but the dreams spoke another language and convinced her that she was quite capable of the normal feelings of attraction and desire. Long-forgotten memories of times before her marriage, when she had been attracted to men, came back to her, and she became aware how she had prevented any closeness even then for moral reasons. She began to re-evaluate her overly strict moral standards, as well as the meaning of her marriage. This was a decisive first step toward an important growth experience.

The dream can be of great help in a time of decisions, particularly those decisions that seem hard to make. A man on the verge of success was offered a new position that carried greatly increased income and status. His family and friends were aware that the job offered the great chance he had been waiting for, and they were sure he would seize it eagerly. But the man himself, though aware of all the positive things the job offered, felt that something in him resisted seizing the opportunity. He didn't know what the "something" was, nor if it was justifiable to give in to such a vague feeling. He decided to watch his dreams and see if they could tip the scale one way or the other.

In the first dream he appeared before a judge, who put before him a contract of the firm that had made the offer to him. The firm name as well as the contract were put on paper before his eyes by rubber stamps of different sizes and colors, which the judge pulled out of a desk. He then asked the man to sign the contract; but instead of giving him a pen, he gave him a rubber stamp containing his name. The man refused to use this rubber stamp in great anger, and woke up still feeling the knob of the rubber stamp in his hand. "Rubber stamp" was the phrase that best expressed the spirit that prevailed in that company, and he knew that the "something" that had bothered him and that he had not liked to admit to himself was the fact that he too would have to become a rubber stamp. He decided that he needed more than money and status to be happy, and he declined the offer.

After having turned down the job the man was in demand more than before; each time he received an offer, the material conditions were right, but his feelings still did not go along with his thinking.

So he waited for other dreams, and each one revealed to him the nature of his negative feelings. As he passed up more jobs, his family, his advisors, and he himself wondered if there was anything "wrong" with him. He had by this time become quite conversant with his inner Self, and asked before going to bed, "Should I wait any longer?" That night he dreamt that he was driving toward the plant that had made the last job offer to him, but he couldn't get through the gate because a chorus line of dancing and singing waiters, all clad in white, were blocking him, singing, "We are the waiters, we are the waiters, why don't you join us and wait." The man jumped out of his car, and joined them in a happy mood.

Shortly after that he received another offer, financially the smallest of all, and one that did not carry any status; but it gave him a chance for the kind of creative experimentation that he had longed for in vain. That night he dreamt he was a boy of twelve flying a kite with another boy by the name of John. They were in a good mood, running in the field, coming to a high wall; they climbed it with ease, and behind this wall was a lovely garden with apple trees in bloom, some of which already had fruit on them. There were colorful flowers wherever they looked. John said, "Look at all the apples we'll pick here in the fall." The garden and the prospect of the future harvest gave the man a feeling of peace of mind, joy, and happy anticipation. It was the same feeling he had experienced when discussing the new job possibilities. Coincidentally, the name of the man with whom he had discussed this job was John.

The department he joined was indeed a small garden; he started work hidden away from the public eye. But his feeling had not betrayed him; he had a chance to unfold his creative abilities, the harvest was rich, and in a short time he gained fame for himself and acquired nearly as much money and status as he would have had in any of the other jobs, without having to be a "rubber stamp." The dream, the inner echo to the outer occurrences, had given him the guidance he needed and the courage to listen to his own needs.

A decision-making situation experienced by a woman involved the problem of obligations and guilt. She had undergone a training situation in an institutional setting and felt in many ways close and obliged to the group of which she had become a part. There was a silent understanding that even after she had finished her training she would stay with the group, and she herself had never doubted that this was going to be so. Nevertheless, remarks made by visitors from New York suggesting that she might want to move there increasingly found an echo in her. But she brushed these suggestions aside as not in keeping with the obligation she felt toward the Institute. At that time she started dreaming of trains that were supposedly going toward the Institute. The place in which the Institute was housed appeared in one of her dreams as a railroad station, the "end of the line." The woman dreamt that she boarded the train with conflicting feelings, and it started to move. But instead of going toward the Institute, which was visible in the distance, it pulled away from it and went toward New York.

Several dreams with practically identical content forced her finally to think about the degree of obligation she had toward the Institute compared to the obligation toward herself and her own life. An unsentimental and sober evaluation of the facts revealed to her that the Institute got along without her easily, that she had repaid her debt to her instructors and the group in many ways throughout the years of association, and that there was no reason why she could not follow her own leanings to sever her ties and venture into a new life.

There is a general rule that might serve as a guide for problem solving in a dream: "the other" in the dream is generally more right than *I myself*. In the last example the train knew better than the woman. We have all experienced the dream of not getting to the place where we want to go, not being able to make the telephone connection we so desperately try to make, not being able to keep out the threatening enemy by barricading doors or windows. In general the dream knows best.

A young man dreamt that he had to reach his mother, but it was impossible. He did not have the proper change; the telephone was out of order; a frantic search for another telephone booth just led to another frustration. He woke up anxiously, the dream vividly in his mind. He was at that time trying to convince his mother of his need to change his career. His conversations with her were just as frustrating as the dream. No matter how he tried to convince her, he "could not reach her." He thought what he would have done if the dream had been reality. The solution was very simple: he would have given up trying to reach his mother. And this was exactly the guidance that he needed. There was no reason why he had to have his mother's consent for his change in career. Life became a lot easier when he just went ahead and acted on his plans without having her endorsement.

Here "the other" was the noncooperative telephone and the "moral" of the dream was: don't try to reach people who cannot be reached. Often we dream of a person we want to keep out, and here the same rule should be applied: the person we try to keep out in the dream generally represents a problem that we should let come in, and face. The feeling of anxiety experienced in life as well as in the dream often diminishes immediately when we ask ourselves, "What is it that I do not want to deal with at the moment?"

A very amusing dream was once reported by a woman who, though in her late thirties, was still very much attached to her parents, who had died long before. Their pictures, as well as those of other family members, adorned her mantelpiece. She had never been married, but at the time of the dream had entered into a relationship that seemed to move in the direction of marriage; she was frightened of this prospect. At that time she dreamt several times that somebody tried to force the door open to her room, which she barred with all her strength, waking up perspiring and exhausted from the effort. The dream recurred in different versions practically every night. Finally in one dream she was no longer able to hold off the intruder. To her amazement, he dashed into the room, grabbed the family pictures from the mantelpiece, hid them under his coat, and dashed out of the room again. Upon awakening, the dreamer made sure that her family pictures were still on the mantelpiece, but then started wondering if the intruder had not been right. Was it not perhaps time to replace mummy and daddy by a husband!

A dream that often causes bewilderment and guilt is that of the death of a parental figure or some other person one is close to. Such dreams do not have to cause guilt and confusion, but can be used for guidance once one understands their basic message. It is most important to keep in mind that dreams of death do not necessarily represent a hidden death wish toward the dying person in the dream. On the contrary! Let's assume a grown-up person dreams the death of a parental figure or a protective older sibling. The chances are that the dreamer consciously as well as unconsciously wishes to retain a bond that should have been dissolved long ago. A dream about the death of a parent then means that the person is now ready to relinquish this bond. Parental ties exist whether the parent is still alive or not, and the dissolution of the bond often takes place only many years after the death of the parent.

A woman who at the age of 18 had lost her mother had substituted other mother figures throughout her life and become very dependent on them. When she married, she unquestioningly accepted and even liked her dependency on her mother-in-law. But when her child was born, she increasingly resented the older woman's interference in the household. During a period of trying on the one hand to detach herself from her mother-in-law but on the other hand to retain a friendly relationship, she had sometimes dreamt of her mother-in-law's death. She always felt very guilty about these dreams, assuming that they portrayed a secret wish for this woman's death. It never occurred to her that she should let her die as the mother figure in order to resurrect her as an older friend. With the help of her husband she finally decided to have a decisive clarifying conversation with her mother-in-law. She still was plagued by some doubts as to her own "rights" when she had the following dream.

She and her sister were passing a lovely country cemetery where a funeral was taking place. Rather casually the two decided to join the funeral party; and by the time they reached the grave, the coffin had been put into the ground and covered by earth. The two sisters asked some of the mourners, who all seemed in a quiet and peaceful mood, who the deceased was. One of the mourners answered, "It was Mrs. B. (the mother-in-law), a nice lady, but her time was up." The daughter-in-law felt no shock or sorrow in the dream. She experienced a feeling of quietude inside and remarked to her sister about the lovely sunny day, the singing of the birds, and the smell of the flowers. Upon awakening she felt guilty at not having had feelings of sorrow, but then she understood what her inner Self was saying to her: "You don't need Mrs. B. any more as a mother image. You have a right to let her go." In fact, what she was burying there was her mother complex, and not Mrs. B.

Sometimes we live in a way that is destructive to ourselves, and in order to prevent such destruction the dream will remind us to reconsider our way of life. At such times we might dream a death dream that has quite a different connotation. A businessman who had considerable musical talent had neglected it at the expense of a life completely devoted to business. Though he was successful, he felt unfulfilled; and he had been advised to revive his interest in music. He did so, and found it most gratifying. But after a short time a new business enterprise captivated him completely, and the music was again relegated to the background and was about to be forgotten.

At that time he dreamt that the neighbors' child, a boy of 10, died, and when informed about it in the dream, he cried bitterly in a way in which he had not cried in many years. When he awoke, he rushed over to the neighbor to reassure himself that the child was all right. He found the boy in the best of health, as usual completely absorbed in his study of the violin. The man suddenly grasped the meaning of the dream: the boy, a very musical child, symbolized his own enjoyment in music that he was about to kill. In his busy daytime hours he had not permitted himself the deep sorrow that he had experienced in the dream about this neglect of his creativity. He re-evaluated his life and decided to plan so that there would again be time for music.

A question often asked is whether the healthy person and the neurotic person have different dreams. They may, and they may not. An important difference is the fact that the healthy person can accept the interpretation and act on it a great deal more easily than can the neurotic. The neurotic needs the therapist not so much for the interpretation of his dreams but for the guidance necessary to follow their directions.

But, regardless of whether a dream is dreamt by a healthy or by a neurotic person, in order to get the full value from it, one has to know a great deal more about its symbolism than has been covered in this short outline.

Nevertheless, it is hoped that the few pointers given here will suffice to induce confidence in the fact that the dream is a part of our nature, working towards health and the kind of balance that we refer to as normality. In our outer-directed way of life we have partly lost the gift for introspection. The language of science has deprived us of understanding of the language of myth and of the dream. But we are now rediscovering the use of symbols and dream imagery as a guide to fruitful inner conversation with our Self, and as a means of growth.

Edward W. Maupin

Meditation*

With the collapse of Christianity as a source of individual spiritual experience, prayer has been
largely abandoned. Silent, contemplative prayer appears to have been the West's only widely used, cul-
turally approved form of meditation. Thus with the
loss of prayer the West has lost important benefits
of meditation that have little to do with religious
belief. Meditation is a means for achieving psychological quiet and for developing contact with inner
experience and with deeper resources. This paper
will integrate some of the main themes in a wide
and confusing literature on the subject. Several
techniques of meditation will be presented, which
the reader can explore for himself.

The Westerner is likely to be suspicious of a procedure that suggests to him quietism and retreat
from involvement in the external world. Retreat
seems to have been the outcome in some Oriental,
notably Indian, cultures; but it is evidently not a
characteristic of meditation itself. Zen-trained Japanese samurai and Taoist officials in Chinese gov-
ernment have traditionally been engaged in practi-

* Written in 1964.

cal affairs. The benefits of meditation can easily facilitate life in the external world.

In writing this paper I am torn between wanting to say enough about meditation for readers to be encouraged to try it, yet not to say so much that anyone will be distracted from the main purpose of experiencing it for himself. If you want to know what meditation is about, you must discover it. From what is presented in the literature and from my own observations, I think it is a reasonable way to approach many kinds of personal problems. Calm, greater ability to cope with tense situations, and improved sleep are frequently reported. Improved body functioning has been mentioned (Sato 1958). The pattern of psychosomatic benefits closely follows the well-researched effects of relaxation procedures such as autogenic training (Schultz and Luthe 1959). Meditation often leads to a more solid feeling of oneself, and, with that, more direct awareness of what one is experiencing, and a greater feeling of vitality. One Japanese psychiatrist reports that, when his patients meditate in addition to their sessions with him, they seem to have more energy for constructive work on their problems (Kondo 1958).

Existential psychology offers a useful vocabulary for understanding the importance of meditation. Rollo May (1958) begins his outline of existential psychotherapy with a description of the experience of being. In his vivid example, a patient began her therapeutic growth with a profound experience of "I am," of having an existence quite apart from formulations or labels or social expectations. May notes that this sense of personal being is not, from the standpoint of psychotherapy, itself a solution to deep personal problems; but it is a necessary first step for meaningful work on them.

As we examine the experience of being-in-the-world the relevance of meditation should become more apparent. First of all, I think it would be a mistake to be overawed by reports of this kind of experience—to consider it a rare and very special state to which only mystics can aspire. I have an existence, a presence in the world; and I can watch it as it unfolds. Usually, though, I do not look at it directly, as it *is*, but only conceptually. I have preconceived notions of what my identity *should* be, of where I want it to go, of things I would not want to find there. This first major distraction from experiencing my being directly, then, is my concept of my identity—the whole system of vested interests I maintain in being some picture of myself. Usually this is tied up with how I want other people to experience me, with how they might want me to be. Thus my usual experience of myself is as if seen from the *outside,* through the eyes of other people.

The point is not that thinking about myself in social terms or that conceptualizing in general is wrong; these are useful tools. But I can also learn to experience my being from the *inside,* as only I can know it. Meditation is an excellent method for learning how to observe and experience what *is.* Conceptualizing is temporarily dropped, and I observe the flow of my experience with calm detachment. It is as if I say, "I do not know who I am, so I will watch myself unfold, moment by moment." I stay in the here-and-now, the present, instead of thinking about what is not present. This experience of my living, unlike the identity concepts, can never be complete; it is never a neat little conceptual package. Instead, I watch my spontaneity spring out of a source I cannot completely grasp, and flow past like a river, which is never twice the same.

We can examine this now from the standpoint of some further existential terms. Human beings live simultaneously in three types of "world." In the *Umwelt* I have the world of objects. My identity in this world is as a thing. Being a vital statistic, or presenting myself as a patient with an illness to be treated, or conceiving my experience from the standpoint of neurophysiological events ("My schizophrenia is caused by a constitutional defect") are examples of *Umwelt* identities. In the *Mitwelt* I have the social world, the people I am with. My social identity, much of the conceptualized self I described earlier, belongs to the *Mitwelt.* I am a person who does this, who doesn't do that, who is a father, a lover, a son, who avoids going barefoot to the office and contrives to help a variety of students to gain some knowledge of psychology. These two worlds, or modes of experiencing the world, are essential but incomplete. To experience myself only in these terms is either to be a machine or a cluster of roles and surfaces.

The third world is the *Eigenwelt,* my own world. In May's terms: "*Eigenwelt* presupposes self-awareness, self-relatedness, and is uniquely present in human beings. But it is not merely a subjective, inner experience; it is rather the basis on which we see the real world in its true perspective, the basis on which we relate. It is a grasping of what something in the world—this bouquet of flowers, this other person—means to *me*." (1958, p. 63) Thus my contact with my *Eigenwelt* rescues my thoughts about myself from sterile intellectualizing divorced from feeling. My experience of what is outside myself, too, is enriched by awareness of my own response. Meditation is foremost a procedure for developing contact with this world.

The very profound experience of "I am" such as May's patient reported is probably always one of having force, of being able to cope actively with life, of being capable of choice. But one can also feel helpless, easily overwhelmed, blocked in one's future. There are areas of trauma, helplessness, defeat, in which one can only be defensive or act automatically to minimize the damage. Meditation promotes a sense of deeper personal resources, of solidity and strength, which gradually can encounter and master these areas. The dead, lonely emptiness, the danger, the threat of helplessness, are seen as fantasies to be observed and allowed to pass—like other thoughts that arise in meditation. My experience of being here and now is a solid base, a profound contrast to the fantasies of trauma.

These issues are relevant not only to therapy and neurotic difficulties. The existential value placed on *becoming oneself* is more congenial to meditation than the usual therapeutic goal of fixing something that is broken or wrong. In the here-and-now the self can unfold, grow, develop.

Meditation is first of all a deep passivity, combined with awareness. It is not necessary to have a mystical rationale to practice meditation, but there are marked similarities in the psychological assumptions that underlie most approaches. The ego, or conscious self, is usually felt to be only a portion of the real self. Its conscious, striving, busy attempts to maintain and defend itself are based on a partial and misleading concept of its vulnerability, its needs, and the deeper nature of reality. In meditation one suspends this busy activity and assumes a passive attitude. What one is passive *to* is conceived in many different ways. What is important is that meditation begins with an assumption that the conscious self is partial and that deeper resources are discovered when the activity of the ego is suspended. Instead of diffusing itself in a welter of thoughts and actions, the ego turns back on itself, directs its attention upstream to the outpouring, spontaneous flow of one's being. It is well at this point to distinguish the practice of meditation from experiences of mystical union, *satori*, or the like. Meditation may be worthwhile in itself without these, which the student is unlikely to experience without prolonged practice under skilled supervision.

In surveying the techniques presented in the literature, I find it useful to think of two stages of meditation. In the beginning a person must learn to clear his mind, to become passive. Later, depending on his needs and his orientation, he may use various procedures that utilize the cleared mind.

A relaxed and balanced physical position is required. In Asia the cross-legged lotus positions are ordinarily used. If you want to try, sit on the floor and cross your legs so that your right foot rests on your left thigh and your left foot rests on your right thigh. This is very difficult to do. You might try the slightly easier procedure of getting only one foot on one thigh and crossing the other leg under so that the foot touches the opposite buttock (the half-lotus position), or simply sit American Indian fashion. In all three positions your rump should be raised by means of cushions so that your knees and buttocks form a stable, comfortable, three-cornered base. The back is straight; the hands rest in the lap; the head is erect; the eyes should be open and directed without focusing at a point a few feet ahead of the knees.

The cross-legged positions are not essential. You can meditate effectively in a straight-backed chair with your feet planted firmly on the floor, head erect, and eyes open as before. The most comfortable height should be adjusted with cushions. A less erect posture in an ordinary easy chair can also be used.

Of the initial techniques several will be presented. You may wish to experiment with more than one to find which is most effective for you. Although they are apparently different, they all seem to aim at establishing the same state. This is a clear, relaxed awareness in which the flow of thought is reduced and an attitude of detached observation is maintained. In contrast to the usual thinking activity, which carries one off into abstractions or fantasies, this observing attitude keeps close contact with the here-and-now of experience. Thoughts are not prevented but are allowed to pass without elaboration. This is not a blank state or trance, and it is different from sleep. It involves a deep physical relaxation as well as a letting go of the usual thinking activity. Actually, one discovers very early how closely psychological and physical relaxation are related.

How can the mind be cleared? One method focuses directly on detached observation of mental activity until it quiets down. For example, Chaudhuri, drawing on yoga practice, writes:

> The radical approach begins with the resolve to do nothing, to think nothing, to make no effort of one's own, to relax completely and let go one's mind and body . . . stepping out of the stream of ever-changing ideas and feelings which your mind is, watch the on-rush of the stream. Refuse to be submerged in the current. Changing the metaphor, it may be said, watch your ideas, feelings and wishes fly across the mental firmament like a flock of birds. Let them fly freely. Just keep a watch. Don't allow the birds to carry you off into the clouds. (1965, pp. 30–31)

Another method is to focus attention, not on the thought activity, but on the state of mind that lies behind the thoughts. Benoit suggests that attention be kept on the feeling of physical and personal existence from moment to moment. "This effort of relaxation consists in a certain glance within. This inward glance . . . is that which I make towards the center of my whole being when I reply to the question: 'How are you feeling at this moment from every point of view at the same time?' " (1959, p. 85)

A variant of this is to ask who is doing this thinking, feeling, acting. Brunton writes:

> First watch your own intellect in its working. Note how thoughts follow one another in endless sequence. Then try to realize that there is someone who thinks. Now ask: "Who is this thinker?" (1935, p. 56)

Writing about a similar exercise used in Chinese Ch'an (Zen) Buddhism, Luk adds, "As mind is intangible, one is not clear about it. Consequently some slight feeling of doubt arises about 'who' " (1960, p. 38). He recommends that this feeling of doubt be cultivated and maintained.

Some methods use concentration on the body or on breathing to promote the clear state. Rousselle, describing Taoist meditation, suggests that attention be directed to the center of the torso at about the level of the navel. Thoughts, when they arise, should be "placed" in this center of the body, as if they arose there. "Consciousness, by an act of the imagination, is shifted to the solar plexus" (1960, p. 87). This procedure especially helps to promote a feeling of vitality and "strength from the belly."

Wienpahl gives excellent instructions for breath concentration as used in Japanese Zen training:

> Breathe through the nose. Inhale as much as you require, letting the air come in by distending the diaphragm. Do not draw it in, rather let it come to you. Then exhale slowly. Exhale completely, getting all of the air out of your lungs. As you exhale slowly count "one." Now inhale again. Then exhale slowly to the count of "two." And so on up to "ten." Then repeat. . . .
>
> You will find this counting difficult as your mind will wander from it. However, keep at it, striving to bring your mind back to the process of counting. As you become able to do this with reasonable success, start playing the following game with the counting. As you count "one" and are slowly exhaling, pretend that the "one" is going down, down, down into your stomach. Then think of its being down there as you inhale and begin to count "two." Bring the "two" down and place it (in your imagination, one might say) in your stomach beside the "one." . . . Eventually you will find that your mind itself, so to speak, will descend into your stomach.
>
> You will find yourself carried away on trains of thought, but you will have increasing success in bringing your mind back to the counting. Get rid of thoughts, as it were, not by pushing them out of your mind, but by concentrating on the counting. Eventually you will be able to be quiet in both body and mind, and you will have learned how busy your mind ordinarily is. (1964, pp. 8–9)

If you select one of these methods and practice it daily for half-hour or forty-five-minute periods, you will eventually be able to clear your mind fairly readily. Falling asleep may be a problem at times, and then it is useful to interrupt the practice for a minute or two of brisk walking. Or you might briefly direct attention to the process of falling asleep itself. You may feel bored and restless with the task. If this becomes a problem, observe the feeling. Is there something about letting go that is frightening and that causes you to resist? Observe your resistance. Another comment: most writers suggest that you don't think of good and bad. This means, partly, that both what is comfortable and uncomfortable, pleasant and unpleasant, be accepted as they emerge. It also means a generally accepting attitude toward yourself.

If you find yourself taking a negative attitude, beating yourself over the head, as it were, to do a good job of meditating, try to observe this self-critical, hostile attitude in yourself. As the ego activity is reduced, inner material, some of it formerly outside awareness, begins to emerge. This is one reason why practicing more than an hour at a time is usually inadvisable without supervision. At any rate, these contents will disturb the clear state and should be observed with detachment. Herrigel writes:

> This exquisite state of unconcerned immersion in oneself is not, unfortunately, of long duration. It is likely to be disturbed from inside. As though sprung from nowhere, moods, feelings, desires, worries and even thoughts incontinently rise up, in a meaningless jumble. . . . The only successful way of rendering this disturbance inoperative is to . . . enter into friendly relations with whatever appears on the scene, to accustom oneself to it, to look at it equably and at last grow weary of looking. (1953, pp. 57–58)

Visions and images are also to be treated as illusory distractions. It should be noted that, while the breath concentration is limited to a motionless, sitting posture, the mind-observing techniques can be practiced in the midst of any activity.

I carried out a psychological research study in which college students were trained to meditate (Maupin 1965). These subjects sat on backless stools, the height of which was adjusted with cushions so that, when they sat erect, with their legs apart and feet firmly on the floor, a comfortable, balanced position could be maintained. They were instructed to let their breathing become relaxed and to count exhalations. They practiced daily for forty-five minutes for about three weeks. At the end of that time, six students of the thirty had experienced a very detached, clear state at least once. A less responsive group had managed to become quite immersed in the breathing but had not reached the clear state. The least responsive group usually felt relaxed after the sessions, but the flow of active thinking had not slowed down as much as with the other two groups. All subjects had uncomfortable or distressing episodes, too, which they had to learn to accept and observe.

The subjects had been given psychological tests before beginning to practice. Measures of attention and concentration were not clearly related to their later response to the exercise. But measures of tolerance for ambiguous situations and comfort in the face of unusual or unconventional inner experience predicted rather well how they would react to the practice. The most responsive subjects were the most comfortable with ambiguity. They gave responses to the Rorschach ink blots that departed from tightly logical modes of thought yet had a comfortable, creative, and well-controlled tone. They were also most likely to report spontaneous visual imagery during free association and to report more autokinetic movement. In general, then, it appears that a person's attention or concentration skills are likely to be sufficient for meditation provided he is relatively unafraid of ambiguous or unconventional experience.

This study, of course, deals only with people in the very early stages of learning how to meditate. Some of the most responsive subjects were experiencing episodes of clear detachment as early as the first week. Less responsive subjects may simply have needed more weeks of practice than they were given. It also appears that the deeply relaxed, clear state comes and goes as new experience emerges which must be encountered and observed with detachment. Gradually, over a longer period of time, the bulk of this material may be dealt with, and the clear state should become more constant. Some of these subjects might also have responded more extensively if they had used a technique other than breath concentration. Finally, while comfort with unusual inner experience may have determined how rapidly these subjects responded to the practice, it seems likely that meditation itself increases the ability to deal with this experience.

Earlier it was mentioned that production of the clear state might be considered the first of two stages of meditation. There are various techniques that use the clear state once it is established. Actually, it is quite worthwhile simply to continue the original procedures, and more advanced techniques will not be reviewed in detail. Tantric yoga begins here to introduce various visualizations, contemplation of symbols, and concentration on parts of the body. Comprehensive surveys are given by Govinda (1959) and Zimmer (1960). The aim seems to be a systematic exploration of deeply unconscious, prelogical, and archetypal experience. Such techniques obviously require a skilled guide.

It is at this point, too, that the *koans* used in some sects of Zen Buddhism are introduced. (Ogata 1959) These are paradoxical statements that cannot be understood with ordinary logic. When they are contemplated in meditation, the idea is not to run through the words, but to penetrate to their meaning, the state of mind that they express. A graded series of *koans* focuses the student's experience toward *satori* and enables the Zen teacher to judge where the student is in his development. As a formal technique the *koan* system probably requires guidance, but no review of meditation could close with anything more expressive than the following *koans:*

> The Sixth Patriarch said to the monk Emyo, "Think neither of the good nor the evil; but tell me what are your original features before your parents gave birth to you?"
>
> Daibai once asked Baso, "What is Buddha?" and Baso said, "Your very being is Buddha."

[18]

Willis W. Harman

The Psychedelic Experience

I

After fifteen years of research on the uses of LSD in therapy, and five times as many years of sporadic work on the effects of mescaline, a number of conclusions can confidently be drawn regarding these and the other psychedelic agents. One is that the experiences occasioned by these chemical psychic catalysts sometimes result in observable changes, and on occasion in dramatic changes, in personality and behavior patterns. Another is that when these changes take place, they are functions of a whole constellation of factors—expectations of subject and therapist, the subject's trust in the therapist and in himself, the context within which the drug is taken, the general cultural milieu, the idiosyncratic nature of the subject—and not a specific drug reaction. Yet another conclusion is that there appear to be no types of experience reported as following the taking of psychedelic drugs that do not occur spontaneously or as a result of performing deliberate experiments or following certain

199]

practices or disciplines. Thus in considering the psychedelics we are directing our attention to but one of many keys to the exploration of the self—one, however, that may be peculiarly adapted to our times. (As a passing thought, it seems somehow appropriate that our technological culture, which has presented us with problems never before faced by man, should have also produced the refined tools that enable us to transcend some of its effects.)

The rampant confusion and controversy that surround the subject of the psychedelic agents is due to a multiplicity of causes, of which two are particularly relevant to the subject of this volume. One is a failure to realize the vastness of the continuum of types of experience that may be prompted by the psychedelics. As a result, one oversimplifies by assuming that the particular part of this spectrum that one may have encountered represents "what LSD does." The second important factor is the collision between belief changes that often accompany the LSD experience and the predominant metaphysic of the culture. We shall deal with these in turn.

Let us, then, sample the spectrum of psychedelic experience and the multiplicity of ways in which change seems to take place. In an attempt to impose some order on this we shall specifically describe three ways in which the enhanced awareness of the psychedelic experience occurs and is put to use. (Needless to say, no such ordering system does justice to the richness and variety of this or any other aspect of human experience.) First we shall give some examples of ways in which a problem-solving activity is facilitated through increased ability to examine, nondefensively, one's habitual actions and responses, to reinterpret experiences of the past, and to speak to oneself, as it were, symbolically regarding such matters. Second, we shall look at the phenomenon of communications from the self by integrative symbols. And third, we shall attempt to discuss a more direct apprehension of the self—not mediated through symbols but apparently perceived as a consequence of temporary removal of perceptual blocks usually present. This last discussion will lead us into the metaphysical conflict mentioned above.

II

A good deal of the research on the psychedelic experience has been in a therapeutic context. That is to say, the subjects have brought to the experience problem areas in which they want solutions or at least lessened discomfort. This relief has often come about in ways familiar in more conventional psychotherapy—through ventilation of feelings, lessened ego defensiveness, loosened intellectual controls, increased emergence of unconscious material, and reappraisal of the self with resulting increased self-acceptance. But sometimes it occurs in unexpected ways.

Having the subject view himself in a mirror is a favorite device among psychedelic therapists. The woman who sees in the mirror not her own image, but—with incredible realism—her mother, may receive a message regarding the extent to which she has internalized her mother's standards and desires, and substituted them for her own, to the extent that her own identity is sacrificed. Such an insight comes with forceful impact, since it is so obviously one's own awareness coming through. One patient reported, "I looked in the mirror and was shocked when I saw my face was made of stone. This evidently was an expression of the façade that I hide behind." It is not uncommon for a person to see his reflected image as horribly repulsive, which gives him a clue as to his self-image. With experimentation, he may discover that he can equally well view himself as completely acceptable or even extraordinarily beautiful. He may thus conclude that the way he views himself in life is possibly disadvantageous, and in the end under his control. One subject repeatedly became violently nauseated each time he looked in the mirror— eventually the point got across with force. From another subject's report we read:

> I was handed a mirror and told to look at myself. It is hard to describe the feeling of revulsion that this produced. The face I saw was unsymmetrical and ugly. The eyes were ugly, the mouth was ugly—I hated myself and hated to look at myself. Worst of all, I was completely false. Nothing I say, it seemed, or pretend to be, is the real me. I tried other things, and kept coming back to the mirror. But I couldn't accept what I saw—couldn't even look the image in the eye. This went on for about half an hour, and I began to see the part my father had played in this. He was always too busy to give the family any time, and I never had his companionship to the extent that I wanted it. It seemed that he rejected me, and as a result I was rejecting myself. It was a remarkable and strange experience, to really feel myself hating myself, and to see the origins of

this reaction. I didn't feel blame for my father, but rather felt sorrow over what he had missed in life through not having warm personal relations with my mother or his children.

Photographs of family members often are a rich source of personal insight. They seem to come to life, often with the appearance they had at some significant past point in time, and relationships may be seen with extraordinary clarity as in the following examples:

> I looked at several pictures and then at one of my father—a stern steely looking one. The feeling immediately overwhelmed me. A heavy hand fell on my neck and a pain pierced my left eye. I said, "That's what it is—those eyes. I'm dead when he looks at me. He's killed all the feeling in me . . . I feel it, the shutting down, the dullness . . . He never liked me . . . I can see him trying to swallow. You've still got your hand on my neck, haven't you? . . . I did it for years. You wanted me to bow my head so badly. I just want to be free. His hand is still on my neck after 30 years . . ." Then I began to feel compassion for him—how he had wanted to force me to love him and how proud and yet fearful he was. I told him that I understood his pain, and I would try and help him, but that you cannot demand love from your children, but must let them be free. I felt how alike we were, so proud and so afraid we won't be loved; I cried for him. Then I realized that it was my expectations of myself that caused that feeling of deadness to come. I myself condemn myself—I carry him with me, inside.

A father reported:

> I was given a photograph of my oldest daughter, which brought me to tears instantly. "What I've done to her!" I cried, referring to the sudden insight that I had deprived her of love all her life. Between sobs I remarked, "I usually see everything in her but the beauty." I had never observed her as beautiful before, I suddenly realized, but instead had been critical of the ways in which she failed to be exactly what I wanted her to be. "The love I show to her is false, and the real love I can't show."

A middle-aged woman subject had brought to the session two photographs, of herself and of her father, both at age twenty. She looked at them side by side:

> What did I think about the girl in the picture? It was a pretty face, but kind of hard. It's not a woman's face at all. Frozen into an

image of Daddy. Neither of us grew up. And in the same way. Poor Daddy, he'll never even know it . . . Now her face was frozen into a block of ice. Daddy's image. Carrying some of his psychological burdens around, too. All these years. Surely now I can let them all go. They have been unproductive for us both.

Early traumatic experiences are sometimes recalled, relived, and reinterpreted. These seem (in spite of theoretical considerations that would appear to preclude this) to include memories of the physical birth experience. (This is different from a symbolic rebirth, which also occurs, sometimes accompanied by somatic sensations of pressure and emergence.) The following example is from a subject whose birth had been difficult, behind schedule, and employing obstetricians' instruments:

I suddenly felt myself grasped, squeezed down, and in the womb. The back of my neck and upper vertebrae were crushed in pain. Then I was moving out and felt the wonderful feeling of freedom. Faintly I saw a hospital scene with nurse and doctor, distinctly smelled the ether. Instantly I knew and blurted out, "I wasn't born on time. They couldn't wait for me to be born." And from this intense feeling of not living up to expectations, of not coming into the world on time, hinged my insatiable need of approval and my driving compulsion with time. I could see all the patterns of my life tying into this main root—my need for approval, my feeling that there is never enough time and we must never waste time but get things done as fast as possible. Always driving, driving for the goal.

External objects may become the vehicle for symbolic projections. A rose seems to be a particularly potent and open-ended symbol. For example:

As I thought of the word jealousy the rose curled at the edges and died. "How jealousy cripples," I remarked.

The inside of the rose became black and the outside of the petals were a bright red. Suddenly in the center of the rose . . . was a tiny bleeding baby and I knew exactly what it was. It was a baby I had lost when I was five months pregnant. I had lost the baby in the toilet and had picked it up—the center of the rose was just like a picture of it . . . It was such a shock that your past can come back and slap you in the face like that, especially something you hadn't thought of in years . . . All the time I was looking at the rose it was trying to open its petals and couldn't seem to quite make it. Like the rose, a baby was trying to be born and didn't quite make it either.

I looked into the rose and as it opened the space between the petals seemed to be the bad black again . . . The rose would seem to be wilting a little bit . . . I said I didn't like the rose. T—— asked me what the rose stood for and I said female or love. He said, didn't I want to be that, and I said I didn't know.

T—— shows me the rose. Rose breathes, opens and closes, appears to be composed of endless layers all unfolding. Suddenly resembles uncircumcised penis, my husband's. Push it back gingerly. An effort to touch it. Feel vaguely fearful. Then fear passes and I am able to hold it without shrinking . . . Some basic fear of male genitalia as well as resentment.

I was still feeling afraid, and T—— handed me a rose. "Look at this rose. What would happen to it if it became afraid of life?" It would wilt, I answered, "It wilted as you said that." And it did, indeed. It just seemed to become limp and lifeless as he spoke.

III

Symbolic content projected on external objects can have a more universal, as contrasted with a strictly personal, meaning. For example:

The rose was dying on the outside (outside petals burning) while growing at the inside. I thought of life and death, new life replacing the old.

I looked at the rose for a long time. The beauty was exquisite, far prettier than any flower I had ever seen. As I kept looking at it I suddenly said, "I see me!" I was quite shocked at this unexpected comment but it seemed very real for me to make it. I didn't understand the comment at the time but afterwards the significance came to me that I am really "at one" with the rose and with nature. We are both part of a much larger being or power (God) just like two leaves are part of a tree.

I looked deeply into my eyes (in the mirror) and tried to remember back to a time before I was. The feeling I had was that there had never been a time when my spirit had not existed . . . My face changed to that of a German youth and then to that of an Oriental.

It seemed I must have been hundreds or thousands of persons before I was my present self. I thought at the time that my spiritual self dipped down from reality and entered my spiritual body for a few years and then returned to the sea of love, beauty, knowledge and power when I died. It seemed like my spirit as a human being had always existed as an individual entity rather than as a portion of the great sea in which everyone shared.

The center of the rose changed into a bucket of red hot glowing coals which symbolized the power that I had inside me—controlled power/energy. This power is the power inside everyone that is available for all of us to use . . . I was completely awed by the effect.

All around me was a universe of vibrant, pulsating life; the life-dance of the universe was ecstatically beautiful. I looked through the window, and saw with a feeling of reverence the hedge separating our house from the adjacent one. I saw the yellow autumn leaves, moved by the wind . . . Everything was colorful, meaningful, beautiful . . . Each thing, mobile and immobile, sentient and insentient, was alive with life and purpose. My mood was one of divine detachment . . . born out of an awareness of the profound meaningfulness of the world; it was the result of a joyous, carefree understanding of all life.

Similarly, the symbolism seen while looking within, with eyes closed, may present more universal meanings:

For the next hour I experienced hundreds of different scenes, intensely beautiful and meaningful . . . I saw the reason behind art. I saw sculpture, dance, painting, music, and architecture, all merged and blending. Everything seemed to be an expression of the total unity, the life force . . . I saw great spirals of man merged with concept, merging in dance and sculpture, all rising from this single source and up into a single objective, the expression of this source . . . At times I was in a great cathedral with a multitude of people, their voices singing and echoing in it. This cathedral was most immense and magnificent, full of color and light which was pouring down from above. I was taken from this cathedral into a dark-colored field for a moment, and suddenly, as the music rose, millions of jewels exploded in front of my eyes like fireworks . . . The all-pervading message that I sensed during this hour was the interrelationship of everything to everything else, it all being an expression of the same thing.

After sitting for a while staring into the fire, I remember being moved along with something that kept picking up speed, then all of a sudden being part of a waterfall, going over the top, becoming part of the spray, which in turn became a bird, then several birds flying over the waterfall. There was an extreme feeling of freedom, release, ecstasy. From this point on I do not remember thinking of myself as being a body, or any thing. I seemed completely unaware of the body. I had a tremendous feeling of being; not being something, but just *being*. There was a feeling of oneness with everything. I felt also that I had come to a place where I had been before, and the word "home" kept repeating itself. I thought, "It's wonderful to be home!"

The nature of life and death is a theme that presents itself in a myriad of ways:

I felt that we were all one being. The image was similar to that conveyed by the picture of a pool of viscous fluid which has been splashed. Individual droplets rise out of the parent mass and eventually fall back and merge. While they are away from the liquid, each blob is a unique individual and has a unique destiny.

The music suddenly changed to a Russian requiem sung by a very low basso. This touched off a whole series of feelings and moods which followed one another in fairly rapid succession. I laughed at the profundo tones of the singer; I was serious; I experienced sadness, grief, horror, detached whimsy over the theme suggested by the music, death. I could experience one after the other, and somehow they seemed different sides of one and the same thing. The horror of death seemed something unpleasant which appears when one tries to evade reality; the unpleasantness disappears when one recognizes the horror as part of himself and "embraces" it. (This was the word which came to me.) Pleasantness or unpleasantness seemed an unreal distinction; there is only living and feeling, or not responding and not feeling. Sadness or joy, pleasure or pain seemed more the same than opposites; the alternative is non-responding. At one point, I lying on the couch, appeared as on a funeral bier, and the persons around me as mourners; it seemed faintly humorous, and I wanted to tell them there was nothing to be sad about.

I found myself lying on the couch and I was asking myself the question, "What is the purpose of existence?" and the answer was, "It is to become aware." And in order to become aware, I realized that there was an infinity of worlds or rather dimensions each overlapping and contiguous in space and time, so that if I opened my eyes and looked at the walls I saw not a single image, but multiple images, as if I were looking into mirrors back to back with an infinite number of images all stretching out into the distance, except that these images were all overlapping and side by side as if I could see dozens and dozens of pictures and dozens of walls all in the same place but infinitely many. And that it was necessary to essentially inhabit and live in each of these worlds one by one and come through them all because in each one as you rose from the lower to the next, your height of awareness would increase. And there would be more and more awareness as one rose and went around and around this spiral from level to level to level. I was aware that I was in a very low level, quite far down in this chain, and that there was a very long way to go before reaching the top.

I stood in front of what appeared to be . . . like a set of record albums. I saw that I was able to pull thin slices of this from the group, and as I would pull one out, it expanded into three-dimensional form and I could enter. It was like a life, or a world all its own, and I went down the line trying one, then another. I had the feeling that possibly this is how the soul decides what to do next, but I didn't really find out why one would be chosen over another . . . In one of these slices I was taken up some stairs, and I found a long balcony with several doors. I went from one to another, opening them. On the other side of each door was a world, but they were dead worlds with nothing moving. Almost by accident I exerted my will a little bit and life began to stir. I found that as I practiced this I grew more and more powerful until I could simply look at a scene and it would spring into life. I had a feeling of immense power and yet I knew that I was not the source of that power. I could create, but it was by letting the power flow through me. At that moment then I knew both strength and gratitude; I was given a new concept of humility.

Symbolic material of this sort is particularly impressive to the individual since it is so apparent to him that he is generating these messages and presenting them, so to speak, to himself. The changing of self-image, and consequently of personality characteristics and life pattern, through such integrative symbols, is a powerful technique which is central to the "constructive technique" of C. G. Jung and to the psychosynthesis approach of Assagioli.

IV

The varied types of experience of which we have spoken up to now appear to be only preparation for a kind of perception that is not hallucination, not symbol, but immediate apprehension of what is. This comes not all at once, but bit by bit, as the individual, before the tribunal of himself, judges himself ready to receive it. Because it so transcends human experience of the ordinary sort, such perception when translated back in terms of verbal description appears paradoxical or incomprehensible.

Thus descriptions such as the following must be interpreted as the veriest hints, as the most unsatisfactory metaphors. They deal with realms of human experience where the tools of the poet are of more help than those of the exact scientist. They can be reduced to nonsense by scrutinizing them as one would critically examine a new scientific hypothesis. And yet as hints or pointers toward what one may ultimately discover for himself, they are not nonsense.

> This *knowing* . . . goes beyond the body, the mind, the reason, the intellect, to an area of *pure knowing* . . . There is no sensation of time. God is no longer only "out there" somewhere, but He is within you, and you are one with Him. No doubt of it even crosses one's awareness at this stage. You are beyond the knower and the known, where there is no duality, but only oneness and unity, and great love. You not only see Truth, but you *are* Truth. You *are* Love. You *are* all things. The consciousness or awareness is expanded far beyond that of the normal state. And this level of consciousness, which actually is available to us at all times, is found to be that part of us which, for want of a better way to express it, might be called the "God-ness" of us. And we find that this God-ness is unchangeable and indestructible, and that its foundation is Love in its purest form . . . You realize fully that nothing can ever hurt you or bother you, not even death.

> I was immediately aware that I exist (not just at that moment, but always) in a transphysical universe, perceived spatially although it seemed clear that the usual space concepts don't necessarily apply . . . As when one turns his attention outward he finds the vast physical universe stretching out an infinite distance in all directions, so on turning inward I had come to a vast realm of inner space . . . All of this vast realm is somehow me. Even as I perceive

it, I am only becoming aware of myself . . . This newly discovered "I," outside of physical time and space, is responsible for the creation in space and time of the physical universe . . . Following this intense and brief period of realization, I became aware that this totally strange state of being had been, somehow, familiar as well. It was as though somehow, in some previous state of existence, I had known well what was now coming to consciousness as a "new" experience.

In a classic study of man's higher awareness the Canadian psychiatrist R. M. Bucke described the state he termed "cosmic consciousness":

> The prime characteristic of cosmic consciousness is, as its name implies, a consciousness of the cosmos, that is, of the life and order of the universe . . . Along with this there occurs an intellectual enlightenment or illumination which alone would place the individual on a new plane of existence—would make him almost a member of a new species. To this is added a state of moral exaltation, an indescribable feeling of elevation, elation, and joyousness, and a quickening of the moral sense, which is fully striking and more important both to the individual and to the race than is the enhanced intellectual power. With these comes what may be called a sense of immortality, a consciousness of eternal life, not conviction that he shall have this, but the consciousness that he has it already.

Speaking of the consequences of this enlightenment the English poet–scientist Edward Carpenter remarked,

> So great, so splendid is this experience, that it may be said that all minor questions and doubts fall away in face of it; and certain it is that in thousands and thousands of cases the fact of its having come even once to a man has completely revolutionized his subsequent life and outlook on the world.

V

Research results in the field of psychedelic therapy substantiate the conclusions implied by Bucke and Carpenter, namely that the states of consciousness to which the psychedelic drugs are one means of access tend to result in generally wholesome alterations in personality and behavior pattern. In one recent study a specific attempt was made "to test the hypothesis that the LSD experience tends to be followed by a major reconstruction of one's value/belief system, which in turn is followed by less rapid changes in personality and overt behavior in major life areas." Personality and behavior change were assessed by psychological tests, independent behavior-change interviews, and staff clinical ratings. An indication of changes in beliefs and values was provided by a hundred-item Q-sort made up of belief- and value-statements. It was found that certain of these hundred statements were, on the average, espoused more fully following the psychedelic experience than previously. Furthermore, the increased preference for these statements was highly correlated with therapeutic gains and generally desirable personality changes as observed at two-month and six-month post-LSD retestings.

The belief-statements that were thus found to be in some sense an indication of healthy-mindedness are given below, placed end to end to form a sort of capsule cosmology:

> When one turns his attention inward, he discovers a world of "inner space" which is as vast and as "real" as the external, physical world. Through exploring this inner world, each of us potentially has access to vast realms of knowledge through his own mind, including secrets of the universe so far known only to a very few. And the deepest desire of man is to know himself and to experience his relationship to the universe about him.
>
> As a result of my experiences, I believe that I exist not only in the familiar world of space and time, but also in a realm having a timeless, eternal quality. Behind the apparent multiplicity of things in the world of science and common sense, there is a single reality in which all things are united. (For example, it seems quite possible for people to communicate telepathically, without any use of sight or hearing, since deep down our minds are all connected anyway.) Man is, in essence, eternal and infinite. Somehow, I feel I have always existed and always will. I feel that the mountains and the sea and the stars are all part of me, and my soul is in touch with the souls of all creatures. Although this may sound absurd, I have the feeling that somehow I have participated in the creation of everything around me. I feel a deep sense of meaning and purpose in life.
>
> I have the deep conviction that there are, at the core of one's being, no forces or impulses of a destructive nature. Rather, there is a wisdom in the unconscious mind which knows far better what is

good for us than does our conscious mind with all its reasoning power. Thus the surest guide in life is not the intellect but intuition.

Seeing who I really am, it is silly to ever feel basically inadequate, because anything I really need to do, I have the necessary resources for. There is no need to be fearful of the future; I now see that death, trouble and pain are not evils which one must be resigned to, but, rather, experiences which contribute to human growth. Whereas I may have once thought that people could hurt my feelings, or make me angry, resentful or bitter, or cause me embarrassment, I now see that in a very real sense no one can hurt me unless I let him. Once it might have seemed natural and inevitable that a person should have a basic anxiety concerning his own death. Yet I now have a deep conviction that of course the real self exists on after the death of the body. Thus it seems completely possible to walk with serenity through life even though the world may at times seem to be falling to pieces about one.

Here is strikingly displayed the second of the two causes for confusion mentioned in the beginning—the discrepancy between on the one hand belief changes such as those described above, apparently wholesome in that they lead to desirable behavior changes, and on the other, the generally accepted scientific world view. By commonly applied standards, the fact that the LSD subject accepts his experience as valid and verbalizes such beliefs as those represented above, would be taken as definite evidence that he had fallen into a delusional or psychotic state. They appear to be completely incongruous with contemporary scientific thought. And yet they seem to be pragmatically more beneficial and therapeutic than those, more in line with orthodox thinking, for which they were substituted.

VI

We have attempted, in the preceding paragraphs, to clarify the place of the psychedelics among "ways of growth," first by noting that there seem to be three distinct, though merging, ways of using the psychedelic experience in self-revelation, and secondly by pointing out how the implicit metaphysical outlook in modern technological culture can seem to be in conflict with, and to work against, the kind of insight obtained through the psychedelics. In so doing, we have by no means exhausted the issues in the psychedelic-drug controversy. Such questions as "just how safe are they?" and "what has and has not been demonstrated?" we leave to other articles to explore. What kinds of legitimate access to these chemical tools will be available to the ordinary person, and under what conditions, the future alone can reveal.

While it is true that adequate controlled clinical studies of psychedelic therapy are not yet accomplished, still *it is abundantly clear that the psychedelic agents can, under certain conditions, provide one of the most direct and effective ways to self-discovery and growth.* It is equally clear that they will not automatically or necessarily do this. They can be simply a way of adding an occasional thrill to an otherwise drab existence, or a way of escaping from the anxieties of a complicated life into a kind of psychedelic tranquility. The deep intention of the individual who uses them, and the skill of his guide, are determinative.

It remains to be seen how society will solve the problem of making these tools available to those who can use them with profit to themselves and mankind, while yet controlling them adequately to prevent flagrant misuse. Stringent control against misuse was tried with regard to alcohol several decades ago, and given up as impracticable. Controlling black-market suppliers of LSD is potentially a much more difficult task than stopping rumrunners and moonshiners. If a satisfactory solution to this perplexing problem is to be found, it will require the active assumption of responsibility by those who see the potential values to be derived from the best use of the psychedelic chemicals.

Gayle Privette

Transcendent Functioning: The Full Use of Potentialities

I

"If I only had the key to unlock the door to abilities and powers that I know are inside me. . . ." At one time or another most people have probably expressed such frustration at not being able to use abilities they "know" they possess. There is a growing body of scientific evidence that supports this hunch, indicating that indeed people do have powers that ordinarily are not used.

Research not only confirms the existence of tremendous powers within people but is uncovering clues to some conditions that free ordinarily latent abilities. The act of releasing powers to perform at levels superior to normal behavior is an entity that has been examined and studied. This entity, transcendent functioning, is behavior that goes beyond, or transcends, average behavior. It is more creative, more efficient, more productive—in some way better—than habitual behavior. Transcendent functioning is a level of behavior rather than a type of behavior.

In recent research, experiences of transcendent functioning were studied. The incidents involved many types of activities and abilities, such as physical strength in a crisis, prowess in an athletic event, creative expression through an art form, and intellectual mastery of a problem. Although the incidents were diverse, requiring different types of abilities in many types of situations, there was one obvious factor in common. Each person performed—in whatever activity he was engaged in—at a level that was superior to his normal behavior. His accomplishment exceeded what could have been predicted for him in that particular situation. The following descriptions illustrate high-level use of potentialities, the experience of transcendent functioning.

II

A young musician described a saxophone recital:

> . . . All of a sudden nothing seemed to matter except the music. . . . The things I practiced seemed to just come out; I never thought about which fingering I would use or when I would breathe; it just came out naturally. All I thought about was expressing myself in the way that I thought the piece should sound. I never noticed there was an audience after the first eight bars of music. Not until I was finished did I even remember their applause but only my feeling of satisfaction in playing the piece the way I actually felt it should be played.

A woman wrote of surprising physical strength in a very different situation:

> . . . Three months after my baby was born, my mother phoned and told me that some FBI men were coming out to pick up some things we had that were missing from the base. I didn't think we had them, but I didn't know if my husband might have gone ape and took them. Well, my luck! He wasn't there, and all I could find was his tool box, and it was really heavy. . . . I knew if they found it on the

place, they'd take him to jail. So I picked it up and ran down in the woods behind the house, climbed two fences, and hid it a half mile from the house.

After all this . . . my mother called again to tell me she was only joking. When my husband came home I showed him his tool box. He brought it to the house and weighed it. It topped the scales at seventy pounds. I couldn't even take it off from the scales after I found out he didn't have anything that didn't belong to him.

A law-enforcement officer described a time when he was called to a double-fatality traffic accident:

. . . Blood and death, *per se,* I had been exposed to in war and other accidents, but I did not know how I would react in an intimate situation. . . . I didn't know the victims . . . but one bloody mess that hardly looked human called to me, and out of what was once a face, appealed for help. He did not want physical assistance, but some close personal contact, some love and affection. He knew he was going to die, he said, but he was lonely.

For an instant I felt repulsed, then I knelt down and placed his head in my lap and held his hand. This grip was the answer. I had given him what he needed. The episode was short, but I remember the compassion I felt for him, and then the anger at this needless waste of life and potentiality of living that had occurred.

Shortly thereafter he died; the ambulance came and took him away. . . . Up to that time I did not think it possible for me to become personally involved in this manner or situation. I don't know if I could again. It is hard to say.

The last excerpt described a bowling score of two hundred thirteen for a person whose average was around one hundred thirty:

. . . For some reason, everything was working beautifully—me, the ball, and the pins. . . . At the time it all seemed very unreal. . . . There was no push or force to urge me on—it all began as part of a very relaxed situation. . . . As long as I was relaxed, everything seemed to click, and I could make no mistakes or do nothing wrong. It was an elating experience.

These descriptions represent different types of behavior: a musical performance, a physical performance under stress, an incident of human relationship, and a physical performance in a relaxed situation. From study of a large number of incidents that involve different types of behavior, different kinds of environmental settings, but a similar level of performance, it is possible to identify some conditions that are likely to facilitate full use of potentialities. The uncovering of certain obstacles that frequently prohibit transcendent functioning suggests reasons why usual behavior is far below the limits of possibility. These findings indicate a number of ways of promoting transcendent functioning and lay a foundation for further investigation of the potentialities of man.

III

Examination of experiences of transcendent functioning reveals that an important factor is full, clear focus upon an object, such as a task, a problem, or a need of his own or of another person. Focus is undivided, and a single object stands in bold contrast to its surroundings. Full focus may be conceived as having one hundred pairs of eyes; as fewer eyes look at other things, they can focus upon the principal object being viewed. Usually a person does not focus sharply upon any one object, and no one thing is clearly differentiated from all others. Focus is fuzzy, with results much like a photograph snapped with the lens not quite adjusted.

At any given moment a person responds to everything in his awareness. Ordinarily, focus may be divided among a nagging headache, a nearby conversation, the reactions of other persons, planning for some future event, and a task that needs to be done. Response is made to each of these awarenesses. Such diffuse response is usually ineffective, but it seems to constitute much of ordinary activity.

Bringing an object into clear focus calls forth, or even demands, full response. In defining his concept of inclusion, Martin Buber suggests that an encounter with another person demands full response. Illustrating this, Buber has said that if a man in caressing a woman ever once feels what she feels, from beneath her skin, while also feeling with his own hand, he has to—he must—love her.

When a person focuses fully and clearly upon an object, his chance of responding fully and effectively is greatly increased. This is illustrated in the familiar sand-lot expression: "He can't hit it if he can't see it!" A person cannot respond effectively to anything that is not in focus; yet he may respond fully to *anything* that is in full, sharp focus.

With sharp focus upon an object, the unexpected or improbable may be declared possible in a language understood by the person. The symbols of possibility are not universal but are very personal. Perhaps the person who transcends the expected interprets "possibility" where others see "improbability." Commonplace events have been the triggers for many great moments of scientific discovery. An object that is unimportant for most people may be a significant symbol for one person who views it clearly and fully from his unique perspective.

Only when self and object are left in sharp focus are they free to come together in meaningful relationship. The difference between meaningful and ineffective relationship is illustrated in the difference between community and mob (which is a magnified view of a conforming society). In community an individual has the sense of being separate and also a part of the whole. He performs a unique function that is meaningful to the group: he is the village smith, unique, the only one; and the village needs a smith to be complete. He has a strong sense of identity, yet a strong feeling of being a part of the larger identity—of being related meaningfully to the others. In a mob there is no sense of personal identity aside from feeling a part of the group. There is no differentiation; neither self nor group is in focus; the person does not act—he is carried. In ordinary behavior, as in a mob, one seldom has a strong sense of identity but seems to blur into the situation. In an incident of transcendent functioning, self and object are separate yet meaningfully related to one another.

IV

Several types of obstacles are frequently barriers to full focus and full response and consequently to transcendent functioning. Any internal need that is unfulfilled and demands some amount of attention blocks full focus upon a single object. Research suggests that the most common psychological need that obstructs transcendent functioning is the need for approval from other persons. In times characterized by average behavior, approval is important, and the need for approval diffuses focus and seems to prohibit full and clear awareness of one object. Ordinarily, even while a person is overtly engaged in an activity, he focuses in part upon the wishes and demands of other persons, and he responds in part to these. In events of transcendent functioning a person focuses fully upon one object, relatively unaware of how other people see him and evaluate him.

Abraham Maslow has postulated a hierarchy of needs, whereby a person moves to concentrate on less pressing needs as he fulfills ones that are more basic. Ordinarily most people are to some degree preoccupied with their need for approval from other persons. In rare times this need is either momentarily fulfilled or is subordinated to something more valuable. In either case, the person focuses on some object, with little attention diverted to his need for approval.

Other obstructions to full focus are found in psychological involvement with associated or irrelevant matter. Such mental processes as the memory of the pleasant or unpleasant event during the previous hour, anticipation, planning, and problem-solving all share in a person's psychological field at any given time. Evaluating an object as worthless, improbable, wrong, or likely to produce bad results prevents its selection as an object for full focus. This immediately can be seen as valuable for the individual and society—even at the level of survival. The preformed evaluation that it is unwise to touch a hot stove is of obvious value. Such evaluations, however, are inaccurate in many instances and block the accomplishment of desirable tasks.

Our society is full of traps that promote an opacity and practically guarantee that usual vision will be blurred vision. For instance, we become accustomed to contradictions that are never reconciled but are compromised. Churchgoers and humanists profess allegiance to love as an ethical imperative; but in practice it seems more respectable to ignore one's neighbor. One talks with him about TV or barbecue pits but seldom discovers what he fears, what he needs, what is important to him, what makes him happy, what makes him cry. The trap that dulls the senses is not the fact that people endorse love yet fail to make it real in their lives, but the fact that this contradiction is never acknowledged. Love comes to be defined as something less than real caring, personal interactions are seen as having more meaning than they actually have—so there is no contradiction.

It seems that the saints of history were usually humble people who confessed to many sins. Perhaps the reason they grew to sainthood is that they did not close their eyes to the contradiction between their ethical beliefs and their actions. Because they retained their ability to see possibility, they were able to perform deeds of noble human greatness that so transcend the actions of normal human behavior that they belong in the realm of saints.

Schools make a sizeable contribution to the impairment of vision. Not only is little done to foster curiosity or the pursuit of fascination, but measures are taken to put a stop to wondering about unexplored possibilities by indoctrinating the student with belief in the infallibility of the printed word. The unacknowledged ambiguities and contradictions in our educational institutions speed the growth of psychological cataracts, causing blurred vision. Students come to expect not to understand things that are well within the realm of understanding. The assumption that answers can be graded as right or wrong is treated as a certainty by many teachers, and students come to define "improbable" as meaning "impossible," and thereby dull their sensitivity to superficially covered possibility.

Parents counsel their children to be honest, not to lie, steal, or cheat; yet children hear their "excuses," see the masks presented to guests, and deceitful flattery offered a person who was labeled a bore before he arrived. The father says, "Son, have the courage to stand on your own two feet; don't follow the crowd." But Pop is observed as one more of the conformists.

The point that is relevant here is not that parents cheat on income tax, but that parents, schools, churches, and other social institutions, by glossing over contradictions, initiate the young into a society that believes that peering through psychological cataracts is 20/20 vision. Children often call attention to contradictions and accurately interpret simple but badly mangled statements that are patently obscured by adults. It does seem a childlike quality to give a straightforward interpretation to a simple event or statement. Sophisticates can hardly know if they enjoyed a movie until they have read the reviews. The obstructions to clear, sharp focus do not seem to be merely the product of individual neuroses, concurrent mental processes, or unfulfilled needs, but are in part cultural phenomena that are transmitted from generation to generation.

V

Full focusing seems to happen in two ways: obstacles or the psychological significance of obstacles first may be removed, allowing full focus upon a single object; or the object may have so much intrinsic worth for a person that ordinary obstacles are diminished in comparison, as stars are unseen in the sunlit sky. Promoting transcendent functioning has two facets: the removal of obstacles; and discovering, clarifying, and developing objects of genuine worth.

A number of unorthodox methods effectively minimize the power of obstacles in order to allow a high level of functioning. Hypnosis, faith healing, and the placebo effect, each eliciting change without the use of an observable agent, demonstrate the diminishing of obstacles in order to let full focus occur. A hypnotist lulls away obstacles, calling for attention to his voice, his words, his suggestions. Faith healers and evangelists who bring about genuine change in some people demand attention. The answer, "Yes, I believe!" is far different from the usual, "I believe in God the Father, Son, and Holy Ghost," which is mumbled in unison on a Sunday morning. The placebo, a sugar pill, has a more complex organization for diminishing obstacles. Twentieth-century sophistication demands faith in science, not witch doctors' voodoo, stage magic, or other less modern mysteries. With them one is wary of a hoax. Our society adds a background of faith in science for the laying on of the curing placebo.

Because psychological needs frequently obstruct full focus, living in a way that supplies fulfillment and satisfaction of needs maximizes the chance for transcendent functioning to occur. Self-knowledge followed by planned efforts intended to provide gratification for one's particular needs is important. Counseling or psychotherapy, education, and nursing offer opportunities for discovery and gratification of important needs. Devoting time to any method that facilitates sensitivity to one's own needs is an investment in full use of potentialities as well as in mental health.

A frequent barrier to full focus and transcendent functioning is the need for approval from other persons. The most effective and lasting way to remove this barrier is to earn the respect and approval of others. It is possible to design experiences for oneself or for another person wherein success is likely to occur. Knowingly or obliviously, most people at some time retreat to situations that in the past have elicited applause from other persons. It is common to be concerned knowingly with success experiences for children, but somewhat rare for an adult to plot success for himself. Why not systematically and intentionally place oneself in situations that are likely to earn respect from others? In such planned experiences, a by-product is frequently the knowledge that failures are not as shattering as they had appeared.

Full focus occurs not only after obstacles have been removed but also when the object is of such worth that it overpowers obstacles. A crisis may catapult an object of great worth into a perspective that reveals its value for the observer. A goal previously evaluated as improbable suddenly may be seen as possible. A teacher's words, "You can do it," or a woman's flash of knowledge that her husband might go to jail, can put the task so clearly into focus that previous obstacles lose their psychological significance. Honest and spontaneous praise that is effective seems to cause the recipient to respond, "Who, me? Well, why not?" and then proceed to accomplish the "unheard of."

Sometimes a strong expression of disbelief operates as a challenge and forces the actually improbable task into clear focus, and thus into the realm of possibility. Often getting mad is the forerunner of accomplishment. Perhaps anger furnishes the "click" by sharply cutting out extraneous feelings, thoughts, and sensory experiences that serve as obstacles between the person and his goal. Then he is prodded to forge his way over other barriers.

Transcendent functioning is more likely to occur alone than in a joint endeavor involving other persons. The values of aloneness—not loneliness—are important to experience and are probably most effectively learned in childhood. Being alone, and liking it, gives a child a chance to know himself, to experience his thoughts as his own, to crystallize his own questions, to try for his own solutions. Helping a child to formulate a question that he can value enough to address himself to seriously, and then allowing independent work for the solution, can help him to experience full use of his potentialities. It seems likely that concentration upon a few, rather than scattered focus on many, topics would be fruitful. When one is face to face with a task, the problem seems to tease until it fits into the right words and announces itself, resplendent with fascination, obscuring all other thoughts and commanding attention.

Eastern disciplines that incorporate exercises in concentration and meditation are fruitful areas for investigation for learning to control focus better. Western religious training has also used extreme mental discipline in orienting monks and nuns. Skinner's teaching machines offer useful exercises in concentration, but the end result, mastery of skills rather than creative response on the part of the user, is discouraging. Instructional devices attract and even fascinate students. The device in many cases commands more attention than the material it presents; the frame may be more appealing than the picture.

Frank Shaw has suggested for industrial organizations that work situations be planned to allow persons the opportunity of functioning outside the narrow limits set by job definitions. Individuals who can follow their own fascinations consequently function more joyously and more effectively. By discovering what has worth or interest for himself, a person can place himself in the most likely situation that is available for coming into contact with objects on which he can more readily and fully focus. Methods are needed to discern evidences of talent and interest or values. An interesting and sometimes enlightening view of one's values comes from examination of thoughtful and honest answers to such questions as, "What sort of thing most often fascinates me?" "What gets my attention when my mind is free, in the nonrestricted moments of daily life when concentration on a task is not needed—showering, shaving, riding to work?"

It is probable that capacity for fascination is a learned, or imitated, ability. Tom Sawyer's whitewash job demonstrates the contagious nature of fascination—even feigned fascination. A teacher who is intrigued with a subject may kindle a blazing interest within his students. It is probable that a good teacher serves as a precisely ground and powerful lens through whom students see objects that come to have value for them. Only by pointing to the substance—not the decoration—does the teacher help the student encounter objects of worth to which he may seriously relate himself. When he can focus clearly and respond fully, the gratification of feeling the full use of potentialities frequently may lead a child toward new trials at transcendent functioning.

One can identify and overcome obstacles that frequently interfere with productive processes. It is also possible to discover and to create values that have enough worth to elicit strong commitment and active involvement. In removing obstacles and crystallizing values, a person learns to focus sharply and to respond more fully to other persons and to situations he encounters. Then transcendent functioning may occur frequently, and normal behavior characteristically utilizes talents that once were rarely seen potentialities. Somehow, life is more alive; a person comes to be more of whatever he may become. In fullness one reaches out, openly and generously, to the world and to his fellow men.

Notes on Contributors

Paul Bindrim is a licensed clinical psychologist who has had a private practice in Hollywood for over twenty years. He has been a prime innovator in the scientific development of nude group therapy and nude sensitivity training.

George I. Brown, an associate professor in the Graduate School of Education, University of California, teaches courses in group leadership and interaction, awareness training and the creative process. He is director of an Esalen-Ford project exploring ways to integrate emotional, sensory and intuitive experience with the conventional intellectual dimensions of learning.

Ruth C. Cohn is a practicing psychoanalyst and psychotherapist in New York City. She is director of the Workshop Institute for Living-Learning, and teaches at the National Psychological Association for Psychoanalysis as well as Postgraduate Center for Mental Health.

Jack R. Gibb is an organizational consultant in La Jolla, California, and a fellow and member of the National Board, National Training Laboratories, Washington, D.C. He is also president of the American Association for Humanistic Psychology, and recently was a resident fellow at Western Behavioral Sciences Institute.

Harold Greenwald of New York City has a private practice in individual and group psychotherapy. In addition, he is a faculty member of the Metropolitan Institute for Psychoanalysis and consultant to the Pride of Judea Treatment Center. He is president of the National Psychological Association for Psychoanalysis and author of *The Call Girl: A Social and Psychoanalytic Study*.

Bernard Gunther is a teacher of body awareness at Esalen Institute,

Big Sur, California. He has developed his own approach to body awareness, sensory encounter and relaxation which is called sensory awakening.

Gerard V. Haigh was awarded a two-year postdoctoral fellowship at the Menninger Clinic, and has been on the psychology faculties of the University of Chicago, Springfield College and Arizona State University. He is a partner of Psychological Service Associates, and has done extensive human relations training with college groups, the Peace Corps and various community agencies.

Willis W. Harman is director of the Educational Policy Research Center. As professor in the division of Engineering-Economic Systems at Stanford University, he conducts a graduate seminar to assist individuals in identifying and realizing their full potentialities.

Sidney M. Jourard is professor of psychology at the University of Florida. He is a past president of the American Association for Humanistic Psychology, and has conducted seminars and workshops at Esalen Institute. Professor Jourard is the author of *Personal Adjustment, The Transparent Self,* and *Disclosing Man to Himself.*

John Mann is professor and chairman of the department of sociology at the State University College, Geneseo, New York. He is co-director of the National Center for the Exploration of Human Potential, and author of *Changing Human Behavior*. He has also been a principal investigator for various mental health and rehabilitation projects.

Edward W. Maupin is co-director with William Schutz of the Residential Program at Esalen Institute. Prior to that, he was on the staff of the Neuropsychiatric Institute at UCLA. His Ph.D. dissertation on psychology from the University of Michigan was probably the only one in American history on the subject of meditation.

Claudio Benjamin Naranjo was a research psychiatrist at the Medical School of the University of Chile from 1962 to 1967. Currently on leave from there, he holds the post of research associate at the Institute of Personality Assessment and Research, University of California.

Renée Nell has been a practicing psychologist for twenty years. In 1966 she founded The Country Place, a treatment center for emotionally disturbed adults where operation by the residents, its Jungian orientation, and free attitude regarding sex have created innovations in milieu therapy.

Gerhard Neubeck is a member of the department of psychology at the University of Minnesota where he is also director of the Post-doctoral Marriage Counseling Training Program and assistant director of the Family Study Center. In addition, he is president-elect of the American Association of Marriage Counselors.

Herbert A. Otto is director of research at Achievement Motivation Systems in Chicago. He is also director of the Human Potentialities Research Project and co-director of the National Center for the Exploration of Human Potential. He is the author of *Guide to the Release of Human Potential, Guide to Exploring Your Potential,* and editor of *Explorations in Human Potentialities.* His articles have appeared in many professional publications.

Patricia Gayle Privette is an assistant professor of psychology at the University of West Florida in Pensacola. She was co-author with Charles H. Merrill of "A Humanistic and Experiential Approach to Personal Development" which appeared in the *Personnel and Guidance Journal,* November, 1965.

Magda Proskauer practices physiotherapy in San Francisco specializing in body awareness and breathing therapy. Prior to that, she was on the staff of the Columbia Presbyterian Medical Center where she dealt mainly in the treatment of polio and cerebral paralysis.

Stephen Schoen has a private psychiatric practice in San Francisco. His main areas of concern are intensive ego-strengthening psychotherapy, conjoint family therapy and group therapy.

Minor White is a professor at MIT where he inaugurated a creative photography program. His works are in the permanent collections of the George Eastman House, Museum of Modern Art, Art Museum of Chicago and several colleges. He has been editor of *Aperture* since its inception in 1952.